WITH GREAT
POWER
COMES GREAT
PEDAGOGY

WITH GREAT POWER COMES GREAT PEDAGOGY

TEACHING, LEARNING, AND COMICS

EDITED BY
SUSAN E. KIRTLEY,
ANTERO GARCIA,
AND PETER E. CARLSON

UNIVERSITY PRESS OF MISSISSIPPI / JACKSON

The University Press of Mississippi is the scholarly publishing agency of the Mississippi Institutions of Higher Learning: Alcorn State University, Delta State University, Jackson State University, Mississippi State University, Mississippi University for Women, Mississippi Valley State University, University of Mississippi, and University of Southern Mississippi.

www.upress.state.ms.us

The University Press of Mississippi is a member of the Association of University Presses.

Copyright © 2020 by University Press of Mississippi
All rights reserved
Manufactured in the United States of America

First printing 2020

∞

Library of Congress Cataloging-in-Publication Data

Names: Kirtley, Susan E., 1972– editor. | Garcia, Antero, editor. | Carlson, Peter E., 1977– editor.
Title: With great power comes great pedagogy : teaching, learning, and comics / edited by Susan E. Kirtley, Antero Garcia, and Peter E. Carlson.
Description: Jackson : University Press of Mississippi, 2020. | Includes bibliographical references and index.
Identifiers: LCCN 2019049770 (print) | LCCN 2019049771 (ebook) | ISBN 9781496826046 (hardcover) | ISBN 9781496826053 (paperback) | ISBN 9781496826060 (epub) | ISBN 9781496826077 (epub) | ISBN 9781496826084 (pdf) | ISBN 9781496826039 (pdf)
Subjects: LCSH: Comic books, strips, etc., in education.
Classification: LCC LB1044.9.C59 W58 2020 (print) | LCC LB1044.9.C59 (ebook) | DDC 371.33—dc23
LC record available at https://lccn.loc.gov/2019049770
LC ebook record available at https://lccn.loc.gov/2019049771

British Library Cataloging-in-Publication Data available

CONTENTS

Preface: New Directions for Comics Pedagogy...vii
Acknowledgments..ix
Introduction: A Once and Future Pedagogy..3
    —SUSAN E. KIRTLEY, ANTERO GARCIA, AND PETER E. CARLSON

PART I: FOUNDATIONS OF COMICS PEDAGOGY 21

Text, Object, Transaction: Reconciling Approaches to the Teaching of Comics............... 23
    —DALE JACOBS
Wonder Women and the Web: How Female Comics Creators Leap from Private to
    Public in a Single Bound 38
    —AIMEE VALENTINE
Teaching Typical Comics: Overcoming the Biases of Comics Pedagogy with Online Tools..... 53
    —BART BEATY
Put Some Light into the World: An Interview with Brian Michael Bendis and David Walker 68
    —JOHNNY PARKER II

PART II: COMICS PEDAGOGY IN PRACTICE 83

On Copying.. 85
    —EBONY FLOWERS KALIR
Thinking in Comics: All Hands-On in the Classroom 92
    —NICK SOUSANIS
Transmedia Superheroes, Multimodal Composition, and Digital Literacy.....................117
    —BEN BOLLING
Truth, Justice, and the Victorian Way: How Comics and Superheroes Might Subvert
    Student Reading of Classic Literature 135
    —BENJAMIN J. VILLARREAL
The Uncanny Power of Comic Books: Achieving Interdisciplinary Learning through
    Superhero Comic Books 149
    —JAMES KELLEY
Teaching the Unthinkable Image: An Interview with Lynda Barry........................... 168
    —LEAH MISEMER

PART III: FUTURE DIRECTIONS IN COMICS PEDAGOGY ... 185

Comic Art Research: Achievements, Shortcomings, and Remedies ... 187
   —JOHN A. LENT

Misunderstanding Comics ... 207
   —JOHNATHAN FLOWERS

In the Cards: Collaboration and Comics-Making in the Traditional English Classroom ... 226
   — FREDERIK BYRN KØHLERT AND NICK SOUSANIS

Educated Bitches: An Interview with Kelly Sue DeConnick ... 239
   —JENNY BLENK

Conclusion: The Great Responsibility of a Comics Pedagogy ... 245
Contributors ... 249
Index ... 253

PREFACE: NEW DIRECTIONS FOR COMICS PEDAGOGY

This is a book, quite obviously, about comics and education, and it began, appropriately enough and as so many wonderful things do, at a comic con. Peter and Antero had been friends for many years when Peter and Susan met after participating in the Comic Arts Conference at WonderCon. And though the three of us come from different backgrounds and areas of expertise, we shared a love of comics and of teaching, and more specifically, teaching with comics. We worked together to present workshops for teachers interested in incorporating comics into classrooms at Comic-Con International: San Diego, and it was through these workshops that we met a great many teachers, students, and creators who all shared a firm belief in the power and potential of graphic narratives as a means of instruction and expression.

Through these presentations we realized a need for a more concerted conversation about comics pedagogy—a dialogue that included K-12 teachers as well as university professors, devoted readers, and creative professionals, in addition to scholars across the disciplines, from the sciences along with English departments. We see this volume as an act of entering the "Burkean parlor" of discourse surrounding comics in education, adding voices from creators and scholars from a variety of areas, and doing so in a way that we hope offers insight into the state of our field and points to directions for future research and invitation. Certainly this book isn't the last word on the subject, but rather a collection of ideas that we hope will inspire others to embrace comics in classrooms across ages and subject areas *and* continue this conversation, hopefully at a comic con very soon.

ACKNOWLEDGMENTS

This project originated in conversations during the Comic Arts Conference at WonderCon and continued through our Teaching with Comics workshops at San Diego Comic-Con, and we are indebted to the organizers and participants in those spaces who encouraged us to bring together our enthusiasm for pedagogy and comics into this volume. We are also grateful to Vijay Shah and the terrific folks at the University Press of Mississippi and to Ebony Kalir Flowers for allowing us to use her amazing art for our cover. Our contributors have offered their insightful words and wisdom and we are incredibly honored and inspired by them.

Peter: I want to thank my parents, Dave and Cindy, for promoting the power of reading; my family, Anni and Nola, for inspiring my every action; and my former students and colleagues at Animo South Los Angeles High School for daring to build a community of superheroes, transforming me in the process.

Antero would like to acknowledge Travis Miller, who donated his comic-book collection to a shared classroom library and demonstrated the transformative possibilities of comics pedagogy. At their best, comic books have the power of bringing people together; I am grateful for the opportunity to learn alongside my two coeditors I call friends. Finally, thank you Ally, as always, for your support in this and many other nerdy, intellectual pursuits in the name of equity and justice.

Susan Kirtley wishes to thank her co-conspirators Peter and Antero for their friendship, good humor, and brilliant ideas throughout the project. Those who contributed to the volume offered their insights and intellect, and I'm so happy to share their enthusiasm for comics pedagogy. Thanks also to the fantastic students and colleagues at Portland State University and to the PSU Faculty Development Fund for support. I am eternally grateful to Kathy, Peter, Mom, and Dad for their encouragement. And finally, I send special love and appreciation to my inspiration, my joy, *mea lux*: Sone, Leone, and Evelyn.

WITH GREAT POWER COMES GREAT PEDAGOGY

Introduction: A Once and Future Pedagogy

—SUSAN E. KIRTLEY, Portland State University
—ANTERO GARCIA, Stanford University
—PETER E. CARLSON, Green Dot Public Schools

The field of comics studies has exploded in recent years, bringing a wide range of participants into this ever-growing scholarly space. In looking across the *kinds* of disciplinary scholars engaged in this work, teaching and learning have been centered in the efforts of those who are writing about and studying comics. As such, this edited collection sets out the stakes, definitions, and exemplars of contemporary *comics pedagogy*. From K-12 contexts to higher-ed instruction to ongoing communities of scholars working outside of the academy, comics pedagogy is at the heart of the work in which today's "aca-fans" engage; most of us are educators, and the role of comics in our teaching is often substantial. Building off the interdisciplinary interests and approaches to teaching comics and teaching *with* comics, this volume brings together diverse voices to share key theories and scholarship on comics pedagogy. By bringing scholars, creators, and educators across various fields and settings into conversation, this volume significantly expands scholarship on comics pedagogy.

Minds in the Gutter: A Brief Introduction to Comics Studies

Comics studies is a relatively new field with, according to Gregory Steirer, "a general start-date of the early 2000s" (265), and given its neophyte status, it is still formulating its foundational narratives. In 2011, contributor Bart Beaty argued that "the current state of the scholarly study of comics is strikingly akin to that of film in the 1960s. . . . Despite the fact that comics are significantly older than cinema, consecration as a legitimate art form has not come easily, and the academic study of the form is still marginal" (106–7). Comics studies has indeed struggled for legitimacy within the academy, and as many scholars and educators have witnessed first-hand, it is often maligned for the popular nature of its subject matter. Philip Troutman noted that the field "sits somewhat uneasily within the academy, both because of the medium's image/text composition, which sets it outside traditional disciplinary purviews, and because of its popular nature, which has engendered both an ivory-tower skepticism on the one hand and an 'anti-academic' response by some popular culture scholars on the other" (120). Troutman continues, arguing that comics studies "is always coming but never quite arriving" (120). However, despite resistance from academe and on occasion from comics fans and practitioners, tangible evidence demonstrates that comics studies, may, in fact, be arriving imminently. Scholarly books on comics are regularly published by university presses. Peer-reviewed academic journals devoted to comics studies are flourishing. Courses on comics are now being offered on numerous college campuses, and some universities boast comics studies programs and courses of study. The Modern Language Association established a Forum for Comics and Graphic Narratives, and the Comics Studies Society and International Comic Arts Forum represent two of the growing number of scholarly societies devoted to the study of comics. Despite any challenges, the field is growing, and growing rapidly.

One of the hallmarks of comics studies is its interdisciplinary nature, which makes the field extremely exciting, innovative, and difficult to locate within institutions. This interdisciplinary focus has, at times, caused consternation amongst scholars. Gregory Steirer posits, "Though scholars from different disciplines make up the field's participants, the failure of these scholars to establish for their work a collective goal (even if the goal remains essentially in question or dispute) beyond that of researching comics means that the field is interdisciplinary only in the shallowest descriptive sense" (278). Charles Hatfield echoed this sentiment in his article on "Indiscipline, or, the Condition of Comics Studies," suggesting,

> in other words, comics studies might become the very opposite of a critical backwater; it might take part in the ongoing and essential reexamination of how, by whom, and under what auspices knowledge is produced in academe. In any case, comics studies, to thrive, must find a stable conceptual basis that is in no way interchangeable with conventional disciplinarity. In order to address seriously the lack of institutional footing for comics studies, and in order to raise standards in the field (which need not mean imposing one rigid set of standards on scholars from multiple disciplines), comics scholars need to develop and make explicit their commitment not simply to multi- but to interdisciplinarity. We need to articulate a rigorous pluralism—self-aware, synthetic, and questioning—if the field is to flourish.

Comics studies must, then, embrace more than a surface or fleeting interest in interdisciplinary scholarship, a crossing of disciplines in name only, and challenge ourselves to truly engage with other fields of knowledge to create compelling and worthy scholarship that does justice to the form.

Thus far the conversation around comics generally falls into three discourse communities or "modes of address," as outlined by Craig Fischer, who states, "I'd identify at least three different modes of address—fan appreciation, essayistic criticism and academic criticism—and at least two of these modes use jargon to create a sense of connection between writer and audience." Academic criticism has, as suggested by Fischer, a tendency to be dense and sometimes difficult to parse. Furthermore, this criticism has become codified around a particular canon of texts, leaving much of the landscape of comic art unexamined. Thus, even though comics scholarship is on the rise, it currently stands as a narrowly circumscribed domain, with academic studies of comics focusing, according to scholars such as Bart Beaty and Benjamin Woo, almost completely on a selection of highly lauded creators, such as "Art Spiegelman, Alan Moore, Neil Gaiman, and, to a lesser extent, Chris Ware" (6). In fact, the majority of what Hillary Chute has called "today's contemporary canon" (14) is composed of auteurs creating "literary" or "art house" comics, largely ignoring the more mainstream publications, a myopic vision we hope to see expanded in the future.

While the sphere of comics scholarship is slowly expanding to include more titles and creators, criticism generally relies on one of several strategies, as Gregory Steirer articulates, citing the "factual," "reiterative," "sociocultural," "ideological," "auteur," "industrial," and "formalist" approaches. Steirer argues for a wider perspective and an opening of the field beyond these few methodologies, suggesting, "What comics studies requires from its practitioners if it is to achieve a coherent (or even productively incoherent) disciplinarity is that we spend slightly less time focusing on comics as our research object and slightly more time focusing on comics research itself—its history, its methods, and the intellectual and institutional goals that will determine its future" (278). And while Steirer's criticism is certainly still valid, since his critique was published in 2011 the field truly has blossomed, exploring additional approaches, with sub-specialties developing even within comics studies itself, such as comics pedagogy.

Comics pedagogy examines ways in which comics can be used in various learning contexts, and the area is thriving as educators, scholars, and creators work together to understand how comics can encourage visual literacy and multimodal thinking for students. Comics are worthy of study in classrooms in and of themselves, for, as Michael Uslan argues, "Comic books are a manifestation of popular culture, and as such deserve study in their own terms. But comics can also be studied as a reflection of our society, and their study can be part of our attempts to understand ourselves and our society" (191). In addition to studying comics as the subject matter, graphic narratives can also teach students about various disciplines, including history, political science, anthropology, environmental studies, philosophy, and so on. Furthermore, comics can be used in classrooms as tools for communication and a way of thinking through ideas in any discipline and at any age range.

Why would one want to bring comic art into a classroom? For one thing, in order to fully participate in society, our students must be able to name and speak to that society. As Paulo Freire articulates in *Pedagogy of the Oppressed*,

> human existence cannot be Silent, nor can it be nourished by false words, but only by true words, with which men and women transform the world. To exist, humanly, is to name the world, to change it. Once named, the world in its turn reappears to the namers as a problem and requires of them a new naming. Human beings are not built in silence, but in word, in work, in action-reflection. (76)

In order to fully participate and, ultimately, to transform the world, our students must be able to name it, and today, to name our culture is to acknowledge the importance of the image. When outlining dual coding theory, Mark Sadoski and Allan Paivo explain,

> Through our sensorimotor experiences in the world, we develop a remarkable ability to understand and use language, based on a specialized linguistic code, as well as a remarkable ability to retain, manipulate, and transform the world around us mentally using a nonverbal code of mental images. (28)

It is clear that our students are increasingly immersed in an image-based culture, and visual literacy is key to communicating in contemporary society. In fact, in *The Image and the Eye*, Ernst Gombrich asserts that "we are entering a historical epoch in which the image will take over from the written word" (37), echoing numerous scholars who lament the demise of literacy, literature, and the book itself. In fact, the 2001 census shows that literary reading has fallen 10 percent from the 1982 census, which equates to the loss of twenty million potential readers. Even more striking are the numbers reported for young adults. In 1982, 60 percent of young adults engaged in literary reading, while in 2002, only 43 percent do so.

While it seems doubtful that we will ever abandon text entirely, it certainly seems naïve to neglect the importance of the interaction of text and image in communication. David Byrne, the Talking Heads frontman turned media scholar, explained in an interview with D. K. Row:

> I think we communicate graphically, through icons and imagery much more than we realize. And I think, for the most part, we are communicated to graphically.... And because it's not primarily text, and we don't have a grammar and understanding of it, we've never learned to talk about images and icons.... So it becomes one-way communication: We're being talked at but we can't talk back. We can talk back verbally but that's in a different language and it pushes different buttons. That's part of what draws me to this and the other things I do: I want to learn the language that is being spoken to me.

In order to prepare our students for writing beyond the classroom (and increasingly within it), we must begin to discuss not just alphabetic based literacy, but also address the importance of images.

Moreover, studying comics promotes multimodal literacy. As contributor Dale Jacobs points out in *Graphic Encounters: Comics and the Sponsorship of Multimodal Literacy*, "Reading comics involves a complex, multimodal literacy and . . . that by thinking about the complex ways comics are used to sponsor multimodal literacy, we can engage more deeply with the ways people encounter, process, and use these and other multimodal texts" (3). Comics can encourage a more deliberate reading and writing process and might also invite new kinds of expression. Sean Howe contends that in comics, the "juxtaposed words and images invite readers to dwell, to reflect, and to meditate inside a compositional space where the pace and tone of reading as well as the interaction with the medium are pliant and controlled by the reader/interactor" (ix–x). This flexibility encourages a different sort of interaction with the text and asks students to slow down and ruminate on the process of making meaning. Furthermore, well-established educational research describes how students make meaning drawing upon multiple intelligences and strengths. Marek Bennett notes in his comic on "Multiple Intelligences," that comics "provide ample opportunities to exercise all the intelligences." Including comics in classrooms allows students to exercise various intelligences and to integrate them through text and image. In her article "Multigenre, Multiple Intelligences, and Transcendentalism," Colleen Ruggieri argues, "By reading the comic books, my students were able to use this different genre to interpret social commentaries, make connections with works they'd studied in class, and develop their own views on the subjects of individualism, nature, and passive resistance" (61).

Clearly, scholars have begun to answer the call for research and writing on comics pedagogy, and there are some wonderful, practical guides for bringing comics into K-12 classrooms. Books like *The Graphic Novel Classroom: POWerful Teaching and Learning with Images* by Maureen Bakis (Corwin: Thousand Oaks, 2014), *Teaching Graphic Novels: Building Literacy and Comprehension* (Waco: Prufrock Press, 2014) by Ryan J. Novak, *Using Graphic Novels in the Classroom Grade 4–8* (2010) by Melissa Hart, and *Teaching Graphic Novels: Practical Strategies for the Secondary ELA Classroom* by Katie Moninall (Gainesville: Maupin House, 2010) all provide detailed lesson plans and units that K-12 teachers can be easily adopted and replicated in classrooms. The anthology *Teaching the Graphic Novel*, edited by Stephen E. Tabachnick (New York: MLA, 2009), gives a more critical perspective, focusing on university instructors, and providing introductory chapters on understanding the form before delving into social issues, individual creators, and different courses. This very useful text offers a number of short, useful essays for college teachers using comics for the first time. *A Comics Studies Reader*, edited by Jeet Heer and Kent Worcester (Jackson: Univ. Press of Mississippi, 2009), however, works as a textbook for introductory comics studies courses at the university level, collecting landmark essays from important authors such as Charles Hatfield, Thierry Groensteen, Bart Beaty, and Hillary Chute. *The Power of Comics: History, Form, and Culture*, edited by Randy Duncan and Matthew J. Smith (New York: Bloomsbury, 2014), also works as a textbook and would be particularly useful for a comics history course at the university level. And of course, Scott McCloud's *Understanding Comics* (New York: Harper Collins, 1994) is a classic introduction to theory and form. While building on and recognizing previous scholarship, this anthology works differently, reaching out to educators at all levels as well as fans, bringing the voices of creators, scholars, and educators into conversation, exploring theory in practice in dialogue with industry professionals.

The Big Tent of Comics Pedagogy

Comics pedagogy continues the tradition of interdisciplinarity within comics studies, bridging various fields and discourse communities, both within academic spaces and beyond. Below we demonstrate the primary roles that comprise the burgeoning field of comics pedagogy (see figure 1.) While we see substantial benefit in the overlapping fields and identities of our community, we want to highlight the ways these different groups accentuate different aspects of student-driven, comics-centered pedagogy today. However, while we see these differences as important, we also recognize that, for the most part, those studying, writing, and proselytizing the power of graphic narratives in classrooms share a common passion for comics. Of course it isn't necessary

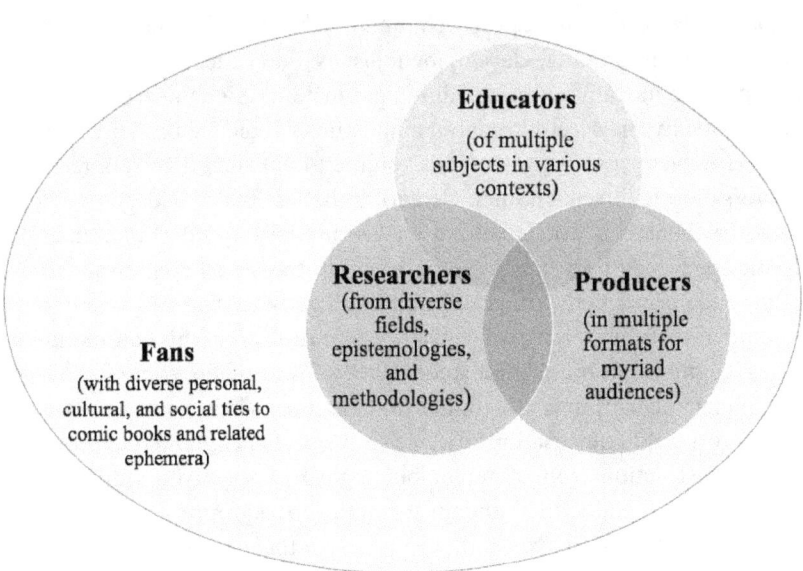

Figure 1: The converging participants of a field of comics pedagogy

for an instructor using comics in the classroom to self-identify as a comics fan any more than an instructor incorporating Chaucer would have to name themselves a "Chaucer fan." However, for educators who are serious about mindfully integrating comics into their curriculum, it certainly helps to have an appreciation or, hopefully, an enthusiasm for the medium, an excitement often associated with fandom in the case of comics. This comics fandom underscores nearly every aspect of how and why comics are leveraged for and designed into pedagogical approaches. This affiliation as a comics *fan* or enthusiast is one that bleeds into other aspects of the careers we take up, the topics we teach, the ways we treat our work. Fandom—as both a separate topic of rich study and as a broader point that links otherwise disparate audiences—functions as a key lynchpin for connecting the members of a comics pedagogy field both literally and figuratively. In cities across the globe, comic conventions continue to grow in popularity.

In addition to identifying as comics fans, a majority of those engaged in the field of comics pedagogy are, understandably, educators. Perhaps obvious is the fact that those interested in teaching with and through comics are often educators who actively read and participate in the culture surrounding the comics as a medium. Overlooked in this recognition is the fact that comics fans teach in myriad academic settings and for learners of various ages, identities, and linguistic practices. The interdisciplinarity of educators means that comics pedagogy addresses early childhood educators that may use sequential art for early cognitive development just as it may mean developing complex graphic narratives for explaining graduate-level engineering concepts. Such diversity may feel like only tenuous links could be drawn across the field. However, we've organized this volume to put such diverse interests in conversation with one another. Centering the fact that a pedagogy emphasizes the theoretical tenets behind an instructional approach, an emerging comics pedagogy provides a rationale behind the use of comics and comic production principles within classrooms of diverse contexts.

Similar to the wide range of educators that are a part of this community, we also recognize that the comics studies field of researchers come from many disciplinary backgrounds. As comics studies scholars have come to recognize, these cross-field conversations mean that researchers are often approaching comics instruction from different ontological perspectives, with different methodologies, and with abundant theoretical backgrounds. This can mean shedding new light on texts and our understanding of how comics function within learning environments, but it can also mean that seeking to translate and communicate comics research effectively can be a challenge. Further, simply by the nature of academic labor, we recognize that the vast majority of comics studies researchers often spend a large portion of their career as educators—from large setting lectures to intimate doctoral seminars. The intersection of research with, about, and through comics and the teaching of such is a fundamental component of how a large portion of our academic community engages in their work.

Finally, we recognize that producers within and about the comics industry are also an important foundation within the comics pedagogy community. This includes writers, artists, editors, and other individuals involved in the day-to-day creation of comics that are consumed by audiences globally. It also recognizes that—within today's participatory culture—production is much more fluid than in the past; bloggers, cosplayers, convention organizers, and a bevy of other creators also emphasize that comics-related production is not tied solely to the pages that are read by an audience. Not surprisingly, there is a substantial diversity within this space as well—from genres to audiences to formats, comics producers speak to and develop work for various audiences and for various purposes. Likewise, this volume highlights that comics producers are often purposefully involved in critically teaching and supporting comics pedagogy, as evidenced by our numerous contributors involved in the industry as producers of comics, including Lynda Barry, Jenny Blenk, Brian Michael Bendis, Kelly Sue DeConnick, Ebony Flowers, Nick Sousanis, and David Walker. Though the figure above suggests discrete kinds of audiences participating within this growing field, we want to emphasize that there is substantial and productive overlap. Every contributor to this volume falls across multiple categories in their professional and personal commitments to comics and to instruction. From creators that occasionally teach such as Brian Bendis, David Walker, and Kelly Sue DeConnick, to educators that also produce or study comics like Nick Sousanis and Ben Bolling, to researchers that often spend much of their professional time engaged in teaching about and through comic books. Understandably, these categories bleed across and inform one another.

These overlapping categories mark the field as an emerging discipline. Comics studies is still formulating its foundational narratives, and, for that matter, its vocabulary, borrowing liberally from film studies, literary theory, communications, art, art history, and the publishing industry, just to name a few of the many fields from which scholars draw inspiration and language. For example, while a comics publishing professional might refer to the point of view or perspective of a comics page, a scholar trained in literary theory (and in particular narrative theory) might reference internal and external "focalization" and "ocularization." An academic trained in film studies might prefer to discuss the "camera angle." Clearly, while interdisciplinarity strengthens the field, the varying traditions and discourse communities can make discussion complicated and, at time, confusing.

In this volume we seek to communicate as lucidly as possible, identifying any insular language and developing connections across traditions. However, this does mean that the style, writing conventions, and epistemological grounding of research shifts from chapter to chapter. Our various fields use a lot of different vocabulary and adheres to genre-specific demands; intentionality toward sharing knowledge about comics pedagogy requires interpreting and listening across these divides. Likewise, the kinds of intellectual questions, teaching approaches, and interpretations of comics will vary throughout this volume based on how authors are situated within different configurations across figure 1. We see this diversity as a strength of this volume that moves away from a field mired in theory taken for granted. For instance, contributor Johnathan Flowers presents a critical examination of the Scott McCloud's pervasively influential *Understanding Comics: The Invisible Art* in order to expand the field of Comic Studies towards "an understanding of comics from multiple perspectives" beyond "McCloud's 'blank slate' as *the* prototypical reader."

What Do We Mean By Pedagogy and Comics?

By definition, a pedagogy centers both the theories that shape one's approach to teaching and the methods of instruction and facilitation. This mixture of theory and practice—*praxis*—is an ever-evolving dialectic. Similarly, the relationship between pedagogy and comics is one that remains in flux, and this volume captures preliminary thought from a wide variety of scholars in order to seed the field for a pedagogy-driven conversation across academic disciplines. Making clear the diverging pathways for classroom instruction, we want to ground a few approaches to comics-related instruction and several key commitments that underlie a growing interpretation of comics pedagogy.

Along with Samuel Delany, we believe that "you could do things in comics that could be done in no other medium; that as an aesthetic form, comics were irreplaceable," and comics can be studied as texts worthy of scholarly examination in and of themselves, as Ben Bolling does in his chapter. Like Delany and Bolling, we believe that graphic narratives merit attention in educational settings alongside more traditional texts. Comics can also provide a window into other disciplines, a way of approaching a variety of subjects—from literature classes to history, art, math, graphic medicine (see Squier), and so on. Furthermore, comics can be used as ways of communicating and thinking, utilizing text and image to study and render the world, relying on visual and verbal modalities of expression. Going into more detail below, we see the four types of comics pedagogy most frequently enacted in classrooms today as:

- Teaching *with* comics;
- Teaching *about* comics;
- Teaching *through producing* comics; and
- Teaching comics *production* as a means of processing thinking and learning.

The first two types of teaching on this list are likely the most common upon which comics scholars focus. Whether teaching a concept through connecting to a parallel comic book or analyzing key ideas as represented within comic books, teaching *with* comics is one of the most frequent ways that educators can pull comics into other fields for learning and scaffolding. Likewise, a deeper analysis of particular titles, genres, eras, writers, and artists as specific topics to teaching *about* comics is an approach that can often align with English courses, art, and the growing comic studies field.

The second two types of teaching listed involve the production of comics for specific purposes. Teaching through producing comics introduces the form and mechanics of the medium in order to offer a communicative outlet for students alternative to text structures more traditionally used in classroom settings. Student narratives, be they fiction or nonfiction, are the most common examples, although using comics to sequentially display instructions are also representative of this project-based learning intent on production.

While the essential focus of teaching through producing comics is the culminating product, this approach focuses on empowering students with the elements of comics construction as problem-solving tools for carrying the cognitive load while learning any topic or approaching any task. For instance, in *Classroom Instruction That Works: Research-Based Strategies for Increasing Student Achievement*, authors Mazano, Pickering, and Pollock assert that "drawing pictures to represent knowledge is a powerful way to generate nonlinguistic representations in the mind" (82). The authors of *Reading for Understanding: How Reading Apprenticeship Improves Disciplinary Learning in Secondary and College Classrooms* expect teachers "to help students become self-directed, strategic readers"; therefore, "Teachers must find a way for them to feel safe voicing confusion about what they are reading" (67). Comics production as a cognitive processing tool meets this expectation. In *Text Mapping Plus: Improving Comprehension through Supported Retellings*, Lapp, Fisher, and Johnson document that "students who create their own graphics improve their understanding of what they read, remember the salient features of texts, and are more confident in their retellings" (424).

Alongside the rise of classes on making comics, there is also a classroom-focused movement to incorporate comic art as a way of thinking. This approach, too, struggles with vocabulary. Mike Rohde argues for using what he calls "sketchnotes," notes that incorporate text and image in *The Sketchnote Handbook*, while Sunni Brown prefers the term "doodle," a process of "making spontaneous marks (with your mind and body) to help yourself think" (*The Doodle Revolution* 11). Ivan Brunetti sticks to "cartooning" in his book *Cartooning: Philosophy and Practice*, while Lynda Barry focuses on "finding the image" in *Picture This* and *What It Is*. And though these practitioners vary in their vocabulary, they share a belief that combining the visual and verbal engages multiple intelligences and provides another way of thinking through ideas, resulting in a powerful and useful skill. This flexibility encourages a different sort of interaction with the text and asks students to slow down and ruminate on the process of making meaning. Ivan Brunetti argues that "cartooning ... is a translation of how we experience, structure, and remember the world" (8), and we have a great opportunity to harness that visual literacy in classrooms and encourage multimodal thinking.

Pedagogical Comics Knowledge

Foundational to how classroom teachers are trained today is Schulman's description of *pedagogical content knowledge*. Recognizing that simply knowing the content one may be teaching (e.g., science, literature, algebra) is not enough, Shulman notes that this kind of knowledge "goes beyond knowledge of subject matter per se to the dimension of subject matter knowledge for teaching" (9). Pedagogical content knowledge includes knowing the best approaches for conveying a particular topic, the best ways to tailor such information for a particular class or set of students, and "an understanding of what makes the learning of specific topics easy or difficult: the conceptions and preconceptions that students of different ages and backgrounds bring with them to the learning of those most frequently taught topics and lessons" (9).

Though Shulman's work has expanded since it was first articulated, it continues to function as a key means for understanding a relationship between content and effective means for classroom instruction. In this way, comics can be seen on the one hand as a means of delivery for some other content areas' pedagogical domain. Several of the chapters in this book allude to scaffolding comics-based instruction for conveying complex ideas and intellectual histories within other fields. At the same time, the teaching *of* comics requires centering the content knowledge of (at least a portion of) the vast, growing fields of comics history and comics studies for pedagogical planning. Likewise, the introduction of comics—regardless of whether they are at the center of a course's topic or not—requires considering the kinds of literacy-driven and culturally bounded challenges that may be faced in classrooms. For example, the use of speech balloons, the order of reading panels, and sound effects are all conveyed within comics in ways that typically adhere to conventions that are understood and historically developed over time; new readers of these conventions may not interpret them the same, and we recognize that such conventions shift over time and within different cultural contexts. A comics pedagogical content knowledge is both a foundational component of developing a comics pedagogy and an important area for future research.

Book Overview

The histories and initial tenets of comics pedagogy outlined here are a single snapshot of a field only now stepping into its adolescence. The approaches, practices, and tensions that will likely arise in coming years will be revealed across myriad "lines of practice" (Azevedo). That is, as Azevedo writes in describing the learning practices of model rocket enthusiasts, teaching instruction falters when based on single theories and interests. In contrast— and as prevalent in our organization of this volume—intertwined interests and practices allow for a robust set of learning principles to emerge over time. Likewise, the role of comics as a source of interest and passion is also intrinsically a part of the motivation in moving forward this pedagogical enterprise. As Azevedo notes, "Tapping into people's long-term interests holds the promise to keep them engaged and productive" (179).

In considering that our relationships to comics are evolving and often come from sources of personal identity, nostalgia, and history, each of us finds ourselves immersed within a comics-driven classroom with different interpretations of what comics *mean* and different assumptions about the promises that they hold. Acknowledging these pathways, one of the strengths of this particular project is the diversity of voices represented within; the collection boasts a particularly wide range of outstanding comics scholars and creators, and includes both critical pieces and interviews with notable comics professionals. We have organized this volume around three key areas: "Foundations of Comics Pedagogy," "Comics Pedagogy in Practice," and "New Directions for Comics Pedagogy." In doing so, we acknowledge that these categories overlap substantially, yet we feel these permeable boundaries accurately reflect the field and our approach to it.

We open the book with "Foundations of Comics Pedagogy," a section devoted to offering key theoretical and methodological approaches that have driven comics pedagogy thus far. In the opening piece, "Text, Object, Transaction: Reconciling Approaches to the Teaching of Comics," Dale Jacobs examines the vexed relationships educators have had with comics, with some suggesting that comics are distractions antithetical to both literacy and morality, while others posit graphic narratives as a site on which alphabetic literacy might be scaffolded. These parallel developments of comics pedagogy have left us with two distinct ways of thinking about teaching with comics that seldom overlap, and this chapter reconciles these approaches within a larger framework that advocates for a diverse set of methodologies in the teaching of comics. In the section following, Aimee Valentine provides an introduction to the patriarchal history of comics, while highlighting female creators who have found a new role in classrooms and in public consciousness, in "Wonder Women and the Web: How Female Comics Creators Leap from Private to Public in a Single Bound." In "Teaching Typical Comics: Overcoming the Biases of Comics Pedagogy with Online Tools," Bart Beaty surveys the state of current comics scholarship, focusing on what is lost when the field focuses on teaching and studying "typical" comics at the expense of the larger comics world, and speculating about how scholars can overcome this bias by embracing online tools. The section concludes with an interview by high school English teacher and comics author Johnny Parker II with acclaimed comics writers David Walker and Brian Michael Bendis in a rousing conversation discussing their intentions and goals as writers and educators.

The second section, "Comics Pedagogy in Practice," details comics pedagogy in action, offering specific, practical approaches to teaching using various texts, multiple themes, and differing subject matter. The first piece in the section highlights the possibilities of the comics form in scholarship, exploring Ebony Flowers Kalir's approach to teaching comics, which examines the importance of duplication in creative practice, and graphically illustrating how copying incites a physical response that is related to working with images and necessary for making comics in the essay "On Copying." In the following chapter, "Thinking in Comics: All Hands-On in the Classroom," Nick Sousanis provides an introduction to his own comics course, providing specific strategies and examples of his pedagogy, creating a window into his classroom. In "Transmedia Superheroes, Multimodal Composition, and Digital Literacy," Ben Bolling describes his approach to "Networked and Multimodal Communication: The Transmedia Batman," a class in which students engage the Batman mythos in print, radio, television, film, music, and other media, and invites students to build proficiency in multimedia composition. Benjamin J. Villarreal takes a different approach in "Truth, Justice, and the Victorian Way: How Comics and Superheroes Might Subvert Student Reading of Classic Literature," exploring his attempts at using comics and their themes to help freshman-composition students make sense of Victorian literature's influence on contemporary popular culture and the challenges it offers. Next, James Kelley champions comics in STEAM classrooms, reporting on his study that examines the extent to which a contemporary superhero comic-book curriculum can be used as a cultural tool to help middle-school students master science literacies. Finally, Leah Misemer interviews infamous comics creator Lynda Barry in a dialogue that speaks to a pedagogy marked by innovation and inclusion.

The final section, "New Directions for Comics Pedagogy," looks to where the fields of comics studies and comics pedagogy are headed, turning our focus to new areas and questions for scholarship. We open with John A. Lent's proposal for "Comic Art Research: Achievements, Shortcomings, and Remedies," in which Lent, one of the originators of the field, argues that the future study of comics and cartoons must examine the political economy of comics and the legal studies of copyright, censorship, and intellectual property. Johnathan Flowers then offers a critique of McCloud's foundational text, *Understanding Comics*, in "Misunderstanding Comics," and argues that a critical reading of the text will encourage students to engage in a dialogue that invites transformative action. "In the Cards: Collaboration and Comics-Making in the Traditional

English Classroom," a piece by Frederik Byrn Køhlert and Nick Sousanis, posits a more collaborative approach to comics pedagogy. This essay invites collaboration, and we see this as the cornerstone of our approach, working together, for and with our students, to promote comics as subjects worthy of study, to engage in explorations of various disciplines and subject matter, and to produce graphic narratives as a way of thinking, innovating new ways of seeing and thinking, and taking seriously the great responsibilities of a contemporary comics pedagogy. Finally, the section closes with Jenny Blenk's interview with trailblazing comics writer Kelly Sue Deconnick.

Similar to an initial issue of a comic series, we intend that this volume grows a community and propels its conversations further. Particularly considering the diverse discursive practices found in this volume—from casual conversations with some of the biggest names in the comics industry to academic analyses of comics epistemology to empirical scholarship within classrooms—we embrace the variety of how comics pedagogy is forged.

WORKS CITED

Azevedo, Flávio S. "Lines of Practice: A Practice-Centered Theory of Interest Relationships." *Cognition and Instruction* 29, no. 2 (2011): 147–84.

Bakis, Maureen. *The Graphic Novel Classroom: POWerful Teaching and Learning with Images*. Thousand Oaks: Corwin, 2014.

Bennett, Marek. "Multiple Intelligences & Comics." https://www.nd.gov/cte/crn/elementary/docs/multiple_intelligences_comic.pdf. Accessed 10 August 2018.

Beaty, Bart. "Comics Studies: Fifty Years after Film Studies." *Cinema Journal* 50, no. 3 (2017): 106–10.

Brown, Sunni. *The Doodle Revolution*. New York: Penguin, 2015.

Duncan, Randy, and Matthew J. Smith, eds. *The Power of Comics: History, Form, and Culture*. New York: Bloomsbury, 2014.

Chute, Hillary. "Comics as Literature? Reading Graphic Narrative." *Pmla* 123, no. 2 (2008): 452–65.

Chute, Hillary. *Graphic Women*. New York: Columbia, 2010.

Delany, Samuel. "Introduction." In Neil Gaiman and Mark Buckingham, *Miracleman: The Golden Age*. New York: Eclipse, 1992.

Fischer, Craig. "Worlds Within Worlds: Audiences, Jargon, and North American Comics Discourse," *Transatlantica* 1 (2010). https://journals.openedition.org/transatlantica/4919

Freire, Paulo. *Pedagogy of the Oppressed*. New York: Continuum, 2000.

Gombrich, E. H. *The Image and the Eye: Further Studies in the Psychology of the Pectoral Representation*. Ithaca, NY: Cornell University Press, 1982.

Groensteen, Thierry. *The System of Comics*. Translated by Bart Beaty and Nick Nguyen. Jackson: University Press of Mississippi, 2007.

Hart, Melissa. *Using Graphic Novels in the Classroom Grade 4–8*. 2010.
Hatfield, Charles. *Alternative Comics: An Emerging Literature*. Jackson: University Press of Mississippi, 2005.
Hatfield, Charles. "Indiscipline, or, The Condition of Comics Studies." *Transatlantica* 1 (4 November 2010). http://transatlantica.revues.org/4933
Heer, Jeet, and Kent Worcester, eds. *Arguing Comics: Literary Masters on a Popular Medium*. Jackson: University Press of Mississippi, 2004.
Heer, Jeet, and Kent Worcester, eds. *A Comics Studies Reader*. Jackson: University Press of Mississippi, 2009.
Hendrix, John. *Drawing Is Magic*. New York: Stewart, Tabari, and Chang, 2015.
Jenkins, Henry, et al. *Spreadable Media: Creating Value and Meaning in a Networked Culture*. New York University Press, 2013.
Krashen, Steven. "The 'Decline' of Reading in America, Poverty and Access to Books, and the Use of Comics in Encouraging Reading." December 28, 2006. http://www.sdkrashen.com/content/articles/decline_of_reading.pdf
Lapp, Diane, et al. "Text Mapping Plus: Improving Comprehension Through Supported Retellings." *Journal of Adolescent & Adult Literacy* 53, no. 5 (2010): 423–26.
Marzano, R., D. Pickering, and J. Pollock. *Classroom Instruction That Works: Research-based Strategies for Increasing Student Achievement*. Alexandria, VA: Association for Supervision and Curriculum Development, 2001.
McCloud, Scott. *Reinventing Comics: How Imagination and Technology Are Revolutionizing an Art Form*. New York: Perennial, 2000.
McCloud, Scott. *Understanding Comics*. New York: Kitchen Sink Press, 1994.
Moninall, Katie. *Teaching Graphic Novels: Practical Strategies for the Secondary ELA Classroom*. Maupin House, 2013.
Novak, Ryan. *Teaching Graphic Novels: Building Literacy and Comprehension*. Waco: Prufrock Press, 2014.
Rohde, Mike. *The Sketchnote Handbook*. Atlanta: Peachpit Press, 2012.
Row, D. K. "Interview with David Byrne." *Portland Oregonian*. March 2, 2005.
Ruggieri, Colleen. "Multigenre, Multiple Intelligences, and Transcendentalism." *English Journal* 92, no. 2 (2002): 60–68.
Sadoski, M., and A. Paivo. *Imagery and Text: A Dual Coding Theory of Reading and Writing*. New York: Routledge, 2013.
Schoenbach, Ruth, Cynthia Greenleaf, and Lynn Murphy. *Reading for Understanding: How Reading Apprenticeship Improves Disciplinary Learning in Secondary and College Classrooms*. San Francisco: Jossey-Bass, 2012.
Shulman, Lee S. "Those Who Understand: Knowledge Growth in Teaching." *Educational Researcher* 15, no. 2 (1986): 4–14.
Squier, Susan M. "Literature and Medicine, Future Tense: Making It Graphic." *Literature and Medicine* 27, no. 2 (2009): 124–52.
Steirer, Gregory. "The State of Comics Scholarship." *IJOCA*, Fall 2011: 263–85.
Tabachnick, Stephen, ed. *Teaching the Graphic Novel*. New York: MLA, 2009.

Troutman, Philip. "Interdisciplinary Teaching: Comics Studies and Research Writing Pedagogy." In *Graphic Novels and Comics in the Classroom: Essays on the Educational Power of Sequential Art*. Edited by Carrye Kay Syma and Robert G. Weiner. Jefferson, NC: Macfarland and Co., 2013. 120–32.

Uslan, Michael. *The Comic Book in America*. Indianapolis: Indiana UP, 1973.

PART I

FOUNDATIONS OF COMICS PEDAGOGY

As we come together to cultivate and delineate the field of comics pedagogy, scholars currently continue to struggle with issues of identity and definition. Yet despite any differences, those we've met at conferences and in classrooms all share a similar desire to serve our students in the best possible way and a belief that comics function as useful teaching tools that engage multiple intelligences and diverse student populations. Furthermore, we as instructors (and editors) recognize that our students often enter the classroom, even at an early age, with advanced skills in translating the signs, symbols, and images that bombard them every day, a keen and finely tuned visual literacy rarely recognized in the academy. As scholar Gail Hawisher and her colleagues note, "People often acquire and develop the literacies they need in places other than the classroom where, often, instructors tend to limit literacy activities to the narrow bandwidth of conventional written English" (670). The reading of graphic texts, of the images, icons, and symbols of the everyday, is a fundamental literacy, one that can help bridge divides, between home and school, between people, and between disciplines.

However, despite the potential identified by so many educators, comics have long been considered lighthearted entertainment for children at best, and immoral and corrupting tales of crime and horror at worst, and the image of the mischievous student hiding a thoroughly noneducational comic book inside a much more edifying textbook has become a frequent trope in popular culture. Thus, even though comics are now enjoying an increased profile, particularly in educational journals and university circles, teachers may still encounter resistance when incorporating comics into classrooms. Therefore, in this section on "Foundations of Comics Pedagogy," we present four different pieces that address the fraught development of a theory of comics pedagogy with all its fits and starts. These chapters represent a variety of perspectives on this developing field—K-12 instructors, theorists, university instructors, and creators. In the first piece, Dale Jacobs acknowledges the decidedly conflicted history between educators and comics, setting out some of the central concerns of teachers. He argues for an approach that moves beyond current comics pedagogy, which seems to primarily focus on using comics as a means to teach other subjects. Instead, he urges instructors to embrace the study of comics for *what they are and what they do*, not forgetting the unique affordances of the form, but rather emphasizing the distinct vocabulary and interdisciplinary nature of comics. Aimee Walker maintains that female creators have long been marginalized in comics history and comics classrooms, and educators and scholars have a responsibility to incorporate and recognize female comics creators, a project now much more accessible to students and creators through the web. Bart Beaty also looks both to the past, noting the narrow scope of foundational work in comics pedagogy, and to the future, contending that educators have an opportunity to move beyond the comics canon and encourage students to study new texts through online tools. A vision of this new kind of comics classroom is very much in evidence in high school teacher Johnny Walker's interview with comics writers and now educators Brian Michael Bendis and David Walker, who offer insight into their teaching styles, as well as their own literacy narratives as students. As Walker explains, "I'm a published writer, I'm an educator, but I still want to learn stuff." These practitioners of the craft argue for the importance of acknowledging representation, in classes and comics, an imperative point that must be considered in any comics pedagogy. While these pieces all represent different aspects of the past and future of comics pedagogy, they share an understanding of the value of comics in classrooms, believing, as we do, that exploring the relationship between word and picture allows students to draw on their own "insider" knowledge as they negotiate the challenges of entering the academic community.

Text, Object, Transaction: Reconciling Approaches to the Teaching of Comics

—DALE JACOBS, University of Windsor

At the beginning of "The Practice of Book and Print Culture: Sources, Methods, Readings," Leslie Howsam poses several important questions related to practice. She asks, "How do scholars actually 'do' studies in the history and culture of the book when it comes down to working with sources, adopting methodologies and constructing arguments? How do our chosen source materials and methods shape our (mostly unspoken) definitions of 'book culture' or 'print culture?'" (17). Substitute comics studies for book/print culture here, and the questions, as well as the necessity of asking them, still function in ways that emphasize the similarities of concerns between the two fields. As Blair Davis and Benjamin Woo note in their introduction to "Roundtable: Comics and Methodology" in the inaugural issue of *Inks: The Journal of the Comics Studies Society*, "Comics scholars come from departments of literary studies, film and media studies, history, and so on, bringing with them different research traditions and assumptions" (57). Questions of methodology are, consequently, central to our pedagogical approaches and to the ways we, as comics scholars, teach comics studies in our home departments.

Over the long history of comics, educators have had a vexed relationship with the medium. In the terms of literacy education, comics have moved from distractions seen as antithetical to both literacy and morality, to a site on which alphabetic literacy might be scaffolded, to a set of multimodal texts that use a combination of sequential art and text in order to create narrative meaning for the audience. Currently, judging from the number of journal articles and conference presentations on comics and composition in the past few years, it is clear that comics have become an accepted part of and tool for teaching multimodal composition. In a quotation that sums up much current thinking about comics within the field of composition studies,

Gabriel Sealey-Morris writes in "The Rhetoric of the Paneled Page: Comics and Composition Pedagogy" that "comics complicate notions of authorship, make sophisticated demands on readers, and create a grammar and rhetoric as sophisticated as written prose, while also opening up new methods of communication" (31). The attitudes towards comics among literacy educators have changed drastically over the years.

Similarly, when viewed through the lens of literature pedagogy, comics have moved from disposable, dangerous entertainment, unwelcome in schools in any form, to pop culture supplements to the alphabetic literature it was assumed students needed to study, to "graphic novels"—literary works worthy of study in their own right. Now comics such as *Maus*, *Fun Home*, and *Persepolis* are regularly included in literature classes, whether the main focus is on comics or not. These parallel developments of comics pedagogy within English departments, in both high schools and universities, present us with two distinct ways of thinking about teaching with comics that seldom overlap or take into account ways of teaching comics that predominate in other disciplines.

As an interdisciplinary field, however, those of us who teach in comics studies in universities need to not only acknowledge these disparate disciplinary approaches, but attempt to capitalize on their various strengths as we engage with students in the classroom. Rather than focus on the multiple ways that comics can be used for specific pedagogical purposes (as in the recent collections *Graphic Novels and Comics in the Classroom* and *Teaching Comics Through Multiple Lenses*) or on using comics as a means of teaching specific subjects (as seen in another recent collection, *Teaching Comics and Graphic Narratives*), we need to "move beyond instances of comics integration as a means of teaching other ideas—of teaching *through* or *with* comics—and make space for studying comic *as* comics," as James B. Carter asserts in his short "Pioneer's Perspective" contribution to *The Secret Origins of Comics Studies* (30). Further, as Charles Hatfield argues in "Comics Studies, the Anti-Discipline," the foreword to that same volume, "Comics Studies forcefully reminds us that the disciplines cannot be discrete and self-contained; in effect, our field defies or at least seriously questions the compartmentalization of knowledge that occurs within academia" (xix). This vision for the field can, however, only come to fruition if we make a concerted effort to bring it about. This chapter focuses on what it would mean to teach comics *as* comics and comics studies *as* a fully interdisciplinary endeavor. As I pursue this notion of interdisciplinarity, I want to begin by examining the ways in which questions of definition influence our teaching and research methodologies before turning to the field of book history, not only for the kinds of practical questions seen above, but also for the utility of its own hybrid methodologies to the current state of comics studies.

Within interdisciplinary fields such as comics studies and book history, terminology is often the locus of anxieties that carry over into discussions of how we teach and research. In discussing the very term "book history," Howsam notes how "'book' itself is beset with multiple meanings and shifting form—even while casual use of the word appears to refer to something that was fixed by the technology of printing with movable type" ("Practice" 18). Defining comics is, if anything, an even thornier proposition; as Charles Hatfield has written, "Definitions [of comics] are not merely analytic but also tactical" ("Defining" 19). That is, the very act of defining is a way to make an argument about the field, a way to stake out one's methodological position. Consider Scott McCloud's famous definition of comics as "juxtaposed pictorial and other images in deliberate sequence, intended to convey information and/or to produce an aesthetic response in the viewer" (*Understanding Comics* 9). The emphasis here and in *Understanding Comics* as a whole is on the way that this definition emphasizes that comics is a medium with its own particular set of affordances. Henry Jenkins, in his response during the aforementioned roundtable to a question about how he teaches comics, is typical of many teachers of comics studies: "My approach in the classroom was inspired by Scott McCloud's insistence that comics are a medium and not a genre" (59). Even if one disagrees with elements of McCloud's definition, his overall approach is accessible to students and works well as a starting point from which to discuss how comics work. So ubiquitous is *Understanding Comics* in undergraduate comics-studies classes that it is impossible to overestimate its pedagogical influence.

This emphasis on form can also be seen in the Comics and Methodology roundtable when Scott Bukatman states that "being in an art department has freed me from emphasizing narrative in the way that comics scholars in English departments would be encouraged to do" (59). Within Bukatman's disciplinary context, form and art are more important than narrative in the study and teaching of comics. Such an emphasis opens up a productive theoretical and pedagogical conversation about how comics operate as a medium and how they convey information through their unique affordances. However, if we look again at McCloud's definition and Bukatman's statement, and the way they privilege image, we can see how this emphasis reveals their methodological biases as artist and art historian, and constricts how we might view even the workings of the medium itself.

Consider another definition: Robert C. Harvey's argument that comics are "a blending of visual and verbal content" (76). It is a statement on which I tried to build in *Graphic Encounters: Comics and the Sponsorship of Multimodal Literacy*, writing,

> comics—comic books, comic strips, and graphic novels—are media that use a combination of sequential art and text in order to create narrative meaning for the audience. This combination of words and images—multimodality—works to create meaning in very particular and distinctive ways; in a multimodal text, meaning is created through words, visuals, and the combination of the two in order to achieve effects and meanings that would not be possible in either a strictly alphabetic or strictly visual text.... As cultural artifacts, sites of literacy, means of communication, discursive events and practices, sites of imaginative interplay, and tools for literacy sponsorship, comics are far more than simply "sequential art." (5)

While I also focus on form and on comics as a medium (or, to be more exact, multiple media), you can certainly see my disciplinary biases as someone trained in composition and rhetoric and housed in a department dominated by literature scholars. Unlike Bukatman, I cannot divorce myself from narrative, both because it figures too prominently in my departmental context and because it is a productive avenue of inquiry. Moreover, the filter of multimodality is one that for me comes from developments in the last fifteen years within composition and literacy studies, which in turn came from Gunther Kress's work on visual literacy and social semiotics and the subsequent multidisciplinary work of the New London Group in the area of multimodal literacies. In developing this definition, I saw that McCloud's emphasis on comics as a medium focuses our attention on form in very useful, but at the same time potentially limiting, ways. Though I do mention comics as "cultural artifacts" and "discursive events," my research and pedagogical practices were then mainly limited to formal considerations and the ways in which comics could be seen as a medium of communication and individual comics as sites of literacy. The multiple locations that informed how I thought about comics and comics pedagogy at the time both opened up and occluded possibilities for teaching and research methodologies.

In this definitional exploration in *Graphic Encounters*, I also cited Dylan Horrocks and his long response to McCloud's work, in which he proposes that comics can be seen as a cultural idiom; a publishing genre; a set of narrative conventions; a kind of writing that uses words and pictures; a literary genre; and texts (34). As I have continued to teach and research in comics studies, I realize that while I incorporated some of these ideas, simply acknowledging the existence of the others is not enough. What would it mean to take these definitions, and the disciplinary methodologies they imply, seriously? Teaching students, for example, to view comics as a common cultural or subcultural experience—that is, adopting some methodologies from sociologists or cultural historians—broadens the possibilities of the classroom. Similarly, approaching comics from the standpoint of narrative conventions or genre can give a much fuller picture than simply looking at considerations of form, just as looking at comics form adds immensely to literary discussions of comics. My colleagues in literature sometimes do not have the formal vocabulary to discuss comics, just as those of us in composition or art history or communication are sometimes without the means to adequately address narrative or genre concerns. Further, in thinking through the variety of approaches that Horrocks briefly lists, what happens when we consider comics as a publishing genre? What could the field of book history add to comics studies and to the ways in which we teach our students to think about comics? In order to explore this question further, let me begin by returning to Howsam's initial question: "How do scholars actually 'do' studies in the history and culture of the book, when it comes down to working with sources, adopting methodologies and constructing arguments?" ("Practice" 17). The answers to this question will, I think, help us to be more productively self-reflective about what it is that we "do" in comics studies, while at the same time providing us with another set of pedagogical and research lenses that can inform those practices.

In addressing scholarly practices in book history, Howsam focuses on scholars' home disciplines, much as I have been doing to this point (and to which members of the Comics and Methodology roundtable allude). She writes,

> literary scholars look at a book primarily in terms of text, while bibliographers are focused mostly upon the material object. Those two sides of the biblio-coin cannot, of course, be separated; but one can face up while the other remains down. Historians, while conscious of text and object, tend to see the book more in terms of a transaction: the biblio-coin is used for exchange. The transaction occurs in a communicative relationship between and among individuals, groups and generations of human beings—readers, writers, editors, printers and so forth. The transaction is both commercial and cultural. ("Practice" 18–19)

While one of these ways of knowing and its attendant methodologies may come to the fore while the others momentarily recede, book history, like other truly interdisciplinary endeavors, succeeds when all of these strands inform the work of practitioners. That is, text, object, and process all need to be taken into account as one researches and teaches. Attending only to one's own disciplinary notions of what is central and ignoring the questions and concerns of the other constituent disciplines results in something that may be akin to book history, but is, in the final analysis, not book history.

However, as Howsam points out in *Old Books and New Histories: An Orientation to Studies in Book and Print Cultures*, such an interdisciplinary approach can also lead to a kind of disorientation, "Because all these disciplines assert their own theoretical assumptions and methodological practices, and each one changes as new generations of scholars challenge their predecessors" (4). Such is clearly the case within comics studies as well, though with one sub-discipline clearly predominant. Of the constituent fields that comprise comics studies—including (at a start) art history, cartooning, librarianship, cultural studies, political science, linguistics, literacy studies, rhetoric, communications, composition, and English education—it is clear that the majority of practitioners were trained or are housed in literature departments. That is, despite the reliance on McCloud's work in so many undergraduate comics-studies classes, the predominant methodologies in the field, both in terms of research and teaching, derive from the study of literature. As Bart Beaty and Benjamin Woo argue in *The Greatest Comic Book of All Time: Symbolic Capital and the Field of American Comic Books*, literature scholars (mainly in English, but also from other departments of language and literature) "have contributed immensely to the development of comics studies, but the pull toward the problematics and methods of a single discipline has had significant repercussions on the development of this putatively interdisciplinary research area," and their influence "has profoundly shaped the way that comics are understood" (28, 29). The predominance of the methodologies of literary study and teaching has led not only to an emphasis on the narrative in the text (to which both Bukatman and Howsam allude), but also to questions of which texts are worthy of attention. That is, with literature in the ascendant position within the interdiscipline of comics studies, questions of canonicity remain at the forefront in terms of both research and teaching.

In *How Professors Think: Inside the Curious World of Academic Judgment*, a fascinating study of the process of peer review across disciplines in the humanities and social sciences, Michèle Lamont addresses how the canon has remained at the core of what English literature scholars value. She writes that since the late 1970s, English has "[broadened] its mission—to the tasks of producing, teaching, and celebrating literary canons, the profession has added the job of reflecting on the canonization process itself" (70). Even through the so-called theory wars of the 1990s and even to today, literature has still concerned itself with texts and with debates about which texts deserve attention, including within the classroom. Woo and Beaty recognize the way in which these imperatives of canon formation have been imported into the burgeoning field of comics studies, writing, "Despite the form's dubious and marginal origins, notions of quality, greatness and exemplarity have become so entrenched in the standard operating procedure of comics scholarship that they—and the biases they introduce—disappear into the background" (15–16). What follows in *The Greatest Comic Book of All Time* is a kind of What-If narrative in scholarly form, a speculation about what comics might be studied and taught if different paradigms were emphasized rather than the literary one that has promoted texts such as *Maus* and *Fun Home*. While I find such questioning of the premises, biases, and methodologies of the field invigorating and see them as wholly necessary, it should be pointed out that such discussions of "the canonization process itself" fit squarely within what has been happening in English departments for the past forty years. That is, if we move beyond an assumption that English departments are only concerned with a specific kind of aesthetic sensibility, we can instead productively draw on literature's concern with texts, canon, and narrative *in conjunction with* methodologies of the home disciplines of other scholars within comics studies. The question then becomes how can we move beyond such critique of the methodological assumptions that inform research and teaching in comics studies and towards an interdisciplinary stance that productively draws on the multiple constituents of the field?

Let me here return to book history as it is instructive both as a model of interdisciplinarity and as a recombinant methodology that can be usefully incorporated within comics studies. As we have seen, book history that is truly interdisciplinary treats books—as well as periodicals—as texts, objects, and transactions (both commercial and cultural). A practitioner of book history needs to keep all of these ways of knowing in mind rather than defaulting to his or her home discipline and its attendant biases. While there have been a number of models of what this triple vision might entail, I find Sydney Shep's model of production, distribution, and consumption to be the most useful, focusing as it does on "the complex dynamic intercrossings between people (prosopography), places (placeography) and objects (bibliography)" (66). Here Shep provides an exemplar of interdisciplinary method, a way of thinking that goes beyond what is possible in any of the separate disciplines that make up book history. While she acknowledges that one's research (or, I might add, teaching) activity might tend towards one part of this model at a given time, she maintains that "the pull of the other elements balances the possibility of the researcher [or teacher] being captured by the potential black hole of a single domain" (67). However, if we consider such a tripartite approach in terms of comics studies, it also offers scaffolding on which a truly interdisciplinary model might be constructed. That is, what if we begin by thinking about comics as texts we might interpret (as literature scholars, art historians, linguists, or theorists of the comics form might), material objects that we hold in our hands (as librarians, archivists, or scholars of material culture might), and as cultural transactions (as literacy scholars, communication scholars, political scientists, rhetoricians, sociologists, or historians might). Borrowing an approach that emphasizes text, object, and transaction allows us to utilize interlocking methodologies that, especially when expanded in ways that are directed specifically towards comics, can provide us with a working interdisciplinary method to guide both our research and teaching.

When we approach a comic as a text, it is necessary to think not only about narrative and themes (as one might in a literature class), but also about how meaning is created through the comics form, how artistic tools such as line, color, and shading operate (in terms of aesthetics, narrative, theme, and so on), and the relationship between all of these considerations at the textual level. In much of my previous work on multimodality, my focus was on how meaning is created at the level of the text and in my teaching, the idea of how comics work as a form has been of paramount importance. Even at this basic level of the text, though, it very quickly became apparent that I needed to teach notions of multimodal literacy (as derived from my own discipline of composition and rhetoric) in conjunction with insights from art history about line, color, and shading, and formal comics theory (starting with McCloud and Eisner, but branching out to thinkers such as Groensteen, Kannenberg, Postema, Hatfield, and Kukkonen). This combination of methodologies for examining comics as texts seems to parallel what Carter calls "PIM pedagogy": "panel and page analysis, imagetext, and multimodal notions of image study." Carter sees such attention to the comics text as the necessary scaffold on which further study can be built. I concur. Since I teach English majors, narrative and thematic questions are never far from their minds, and the links I make to those ideas are mainly reminders of what they are learning in their other classes. However, when students understand how the comics form works and the affordances of the medium, they can complicate their thinking about how narrative and theme play out in individual comics texts. At the basic level of comics as texts—without even moving on to material object or cultural transaction—a fully interdisciplinary model necessarily complicates the approaches we use to teach comics studies.

When we add to our teaching the idea that comics are also material objects, we incorporate ways of thinking from librarians, archivists, and scholars of material culture that turn our attention to comics as physical objects. We begin to ask questions such as how does the material form of the comic affect the way in which we read? How is our reading different if we encounter a comics narrative as single issues, in collected print form, or as a digital version? How, as Ian Hague asks in *Comics and the Senses: A Multisensory Approach to Comics and Graphic Novels*, are all of our senses engaged as we read comics? As Hague insists, "Comics are not simply static objects that can be considered from an atemporal perspective. They change and are changed over time, modifying the space they occupy as they are being read" (5). How, for example, does touch affect the way we engage with a comic and the way we ultimately make meaning from it? What happens if we consider with our students "the materials of its composition, their textures, hardness, flexibility, weight, and temperature" (6)? How do these aspects of the comic affect our reading? What about our other senses as we interact with the material object of the comic? Moreover, what happens if we consider the various kinds of paratexts that accompany different forms of comics? How would Gerard Genette's work help us and our students to consider how paratexts like advertisements and covers in single-issue comics provide a very different frame for the narrative than paratexts like back-cover blurbs and bonus material (such as scripts and thumbnails) in collected editions? And what if we consider the difference in these formats in the context of comics publishing? By treating comics as material objects in our teaching, we add a productive series of questions and set of avenues for exploration that are not available when we examine comics only in a textual sense.

Finally, we need to consider the ways in which we can think about comics as sites of commercial and cultural transaction. How do commercial considerations affect artistic choices? How do various players in the production of comics (publishers, editors, distributors, artists, colorists, letterers) interact with each other to produce and distribute comics? What kind of cultural transactions occur with the reader at the locus of the comic? If we address these specific questions, we might for example examine the ways in which one company, such as Archie Comics, has responded to changing demographics of comics readers, especially within the last twenty years. We might explore with students the founding of Image Comics and the ways in which commerce and art are entwined in that specific example. We might consider fanzines and letters columns in the history of comics and the ways in which readers interacted with both creators and publishers through these outlets. Asking such questions about commercial and cultural transactions through these kinds of specific examples helps students to understand comics more fully, in ways that move beyond form or narrative alone.

As someone trained in composition and rhetoric, I have often thought about the study of comics through the lens of literacy studies and about comics as a site of literacy sponsorship, a concept introduced by Deborah Brandt.

She writes, "Sponsors, as I have come to think of them, are any agents, local or distant, concrete or abstract, who enable, support, teach, model, as well as recruit, regulate, suppress, or withhold literacy—and gain some advantage by it in some way" (166). What happens, then, when we ask students to consider publishing companies, artists, writers, censors, teachers, and other people or groups associated with the production and distribution of comics as sponsors of literacy? Or what happens if we engage students about questions of comics and symbolic capital, following the example of Beaty and Woo in *The Greatest Comic Book of All Time*? That is, how might we examine what is valued by different groups of readers in the cultural transactions around different types of comics? How might we think about the ways in which comics are imbricated in contemporary political or social cultures, as does Matthew J. Costello in his book *Secret Identity Crisis: Comic Books and The Unmasking of Cold War America*; about comics and youth culture, as does Bradford W. Wright in *Comic Book Nation: The Transformation of Youth Culture in America*; or about comics history, as does Amy Kiste Nyberg in *Seal of Approval: The History of the Comics Code*? These examples serve to provide a very small sample of the possible approaches to comics within the umbrella of commercial and cultural transactions. When we bring such ways of thinking about comics into the classroom, in conjunction with an emphasis on comics as both texts and material objects, we are introducing students to comics studies *in toto*. Teaching at this intersection means sometimes moving beyond our comfort zones, beyond the methodological approaches of our subdisciplines, and embracing a more fully interdisciplinary approach.

When I first had the opportunity to teach comics, my courses were rooted in my training in rhetoric and composition and my position in a department of English. The first class I developed in 2007 was a class for third- and fourth-year students called "The Rhetoric of Comics" and focused on the form and how it had been and could be used rhetorically. On the syllabus for that course, I created a framework and posed a number of questions that would form the bases of inquiry for the semester.

> In this course we will examine the rhetorical uses of comics and the rhetoric surrounding comics in order to think through important questions of multimodality, rhetorical genre theory, intertextuality, and rhetorical theory. In particular, we will explore the following questions: To what rhetorical purposes are comics used? In what rhetorical situations? With what audiences? How are roles for both writer and reader created/negotiated in multimodal texts? How do writers create multimodal meaning—through the interaction of words and images—within specific rhetorical environments? How is "truth" represented/constructed through

visual, textual, and multimodal rhetorics? What is the relationship in these texts between the writer and his or her social context, and how is that represented by the visual codes and multimodal rhetorics of these texts? In what ways do multimodal texts participate in multiple genres? In what ways does the multimodal form change the genres and vice versa? How do multimodality and the material form of comic books and graphic novels intersect? How does the production and consumption of these texts represent a distinct form of multimodal literacy? How can thinking about these literate practices complicate our ideas of literacy? How can thinking about these texts complicate our ideas of rhetoric?

Though there is a nod to comics as material objects and cultural transactions at the end of this list of questions, it is clear that this class was designed from a particular disciplinary standpoint. This disciplinary approach can also be seen in the second comics class I taught, a fourth-year seminar entitled "Comics and Literacy," an outgrowth of the research I was doing at the time for *Graphic Encounters*. Finally, I taught another fourth-year seminar simply titled "The Contemporary Graphic Novel," which I framed through many of the same questions about form and multimodal literacies as the previous iterations of my comics classes. However, I also asked, "Why should we take comics seriously?"—a question that reflected both my departmental home and the implicit argument I was making to my colleagues about the value of comics.

Throughout these classes, my focus was mainly on comics as texts, with occasional forays into comics as cultural transactions, filtered mainly through the particular subdisciplinary lens of literacy. Questions of comics as material objects were acknowledged but seldom given much room for discussion, while questions of comics as texts or cultural transactions were confined for the most part to those that would arise from the methodologies for composition and rhetoric or literature. Certainly teaching through such disciplinary biases was helping students to think about the disciplinary concerns of rhetoric, literacy, and literature; to some extent, comics were being used in the service of the particular disciplines in which I was enmeshed. In teaching this way, my focus was still on the development of students as English majors and the attendant benefits of those ways of thinking. However, I was missing the opportunity to introduce students to notions of interdisciplinarity and to approaches that might expand their ways of knowing. These courses did not allow me to help students see what it might mean to approach a subject from multiple positions and through multiple lenses. I was teaching students about particular aspects of comics in what I still consider to be productive ways, but I was not teaching *comics studies*.

It was not until a couple of years ago, when I was asked to teach a class geared towards second-year students, that I began to try to address some of my methodological biases. In retrospect, I had been teaching the kinds of upper-year classes about comics that should presuppose a grounding in the interdisciplinary nature of the field, but the introductory course that could provide that grounding was simply not there. In many ways, I had the opposite problem that Beaty describes as common in the Comics and Methodology roundtable: universities with "Introduction to Comics" classes with no upper-year classes to follow (59). As I began to conceive the new second-year course, I realized that I needed to move beyond teaching mainly about form and about the limited cultural transactions involved in examining comics and literacy. That is, the course needed to be an introduction to comics studies that could serve as a scaffold for the upper-year courses that students might take in subsequent years. It was a conscious effort to create a methodologically diverse course not because everything needed to be crammed into one semester (as Beaty laments in the roundtable discussion), but because I could do so with the expectation that students would have the opportunity to go on to more specialized courses (such as the course I often now teach in "Comics Theory") that would draw on this interdisciplinary introduction (59).

What I decided to teach was a class called "The History of the Comic Book in North America" as an attempt to introduce students to the field of comics studies in all its diverse methodologies and ways of thinking about comics. The important component here is not the scope of material covered in the class—the focus could have been productively altered in any number of useful ways—but the questions asked and the methodologies invoked. To illustrate this point, let me quote at length from the course description section of the syllabus for "The History of the Comic Book in North America."

> Over the last several years, comics and graphic novels have been an ever more visible and well-regarded part of mainstream culture, reviewed in major newspapers and featured on the shelves of both independent and chain bookstores. Major publishing houses now publish work in the comics medium, while both school and public libraries are building graphic novels collections in order to try to get adolescents into the library. How did we get here? How can the present state of the comics medium be traced through the history of the comic book in North America? How do word and image work together to create narrative within the comics medium? How does the sequential nature of comics work to create meaning and structure narrative? Have the answers to these questions changed over the history of the comic book in North America? How do stories function within comics and how have they functioned over the history of the

comic book? To what purposes have comic books been used? In what situations? With what audiences? What is the place of genre in the history of the comic book? In what ways does the multimodal form change the genres and vice versa? How do multimodality and the material form of comic books intersect? Why should we take comic books seriously? In looking at the practical, theoretical, and commercial aspects of history of comic book publishing in North America, we will examine issues such as remediation, genre, seriality, artistic influences, materiality, distribution, political activism, literacy sponsorship, and censorship, as well as theories about how to read comics. By looking at this history, not only will we be able to see how the medium got to where it is now, but also be able to use these concepts to think about publishing in general.

While it is clear that I teach this class from a particular standpoint and that my bias towards comics as a medium is still in effect, what I think is important here is the focus on questions, issues, and methodologies that bring together approaches from the constituent disciplines of comics studies.

In order to illustrate this idea, let me return very briefly to book history and Shep's framework of production, distribution, and consumption, and specifically her focus on "the complex dynamic intercrossings between people (prosopography), places (placeography) and objects (bibliography)" within that model. In examining the history of the comics book in North America, we study not only creative teams—writers, artists, and letterers—but also editors, publishers, distributors, and retailers, as well as readers, all of whom interacted with comics in a variety of ways throughout the process of production, distribution, and consumption. Place is built into the course by virtue of the geographical limitation of North American comics, allowing us, for example, to think about particular instances of comics censorship in the late 1940s and early 1950s. In addition, we discuss New York as the commercial center of the comics publishing industry and home of many creators, but also as the site of many of the stories within the comics texts. Finally, we consider comics as objects, discussing issues such as what it means to switch between reading different formats (floppy, collected, digital), the process of collecting, and the ways in which the material object fits as part of both the artistic and commercial sides of comics.

The approaches used in addressing these and other questions and issues in the course are certainly not exhaustive of the subdisciplines that comprise the field (after all, how could they be?). What the class does, however, is attempt to examine comics as texts, material objects, and commercial and cultural transactions in a multiplicity of ways that begin to offer a complex picture of the field of comics studies and to introduce students to questions of interdisciplinarity. As Hatfield writes in "Comics Studies, the Anti-Discipline," as members of the field, we must be able "to step back far enough to see where our individual disciplines can work together, and what they can contribute to a truly interdisciplinary project of knowledge-making" (xix). In suggesting these general ways of approaching interdisciplinary teaching in comics studies, I seek to push the field towards the future that Hatfield envisions.

WORKS CITED

Beaty, Bart, and Benjamin Woo. *The Greatest Comic Book of All Time: Symbolic Capital and the Field of American Comic Books*. London: Palgrave Macmillan, 2016.

Bechdel, Alison. *Fun Home*. New York: Houghton Mifflin, 2006.

Brandt, Deborah. "Sponsors of Literacy." *College Composition and Communication* 49, no. 2 (1998): 165–85.

Carter, James B. "PIM Pedagogy: Toward a Loosely Unified Model for Teaching and Studying Comics and Graphic Novels." *SANE Journal* 2, no. 1 (2015).

Carter, James B. "A Pioneer's Perspective: James 'Bucky' Carter." *The Secret Origins of Comics Studies*. Edited by Matthew J. Smith and Randy Duncan. New York: Routledge, 2017. 28–30.

Costello, Matthew J. *Secret Identity Crisis: Comic Books and the Unmasking of Cold War America*. New York: Continuum, 2009.

Davis, Blair, Bart Beaty, Scott Bukatman, Henry Jenkins, and Benjamin Woo. "Roundtable: Comics and Methodology." *Inks: The Journal of the Comics Studies Society* 1, no.1 (Spring 2017): 56–74.

Dong, Lan, ed. *Teaching Comics and Graphic Narratives*. Jefferson, NC: McFarland, 2012.

Genette, Gerard. *Paratexts: Thresholds of Interpretation*. Translated by Jane E. Lewin. Cambridge: Cambridge University Press, 1987.

Hague, Ian. *Comics and the Senses: A Multisensory Approach to Comics and Graphic Novels*. London: Routledge, 2013.

Harvey, Robert C. "Comedy at the Juncture of Word and Image." *The Language of Comics: Word and Image*. Edited by Robin Varnum and Christine T. Gibbons. Jackson: University of Mississippi Press, 2002. 75–96.

Hatfield, Charles. "Comics Studies, the Anti-Discipline." *The Secret Origins of Comics Studies*. Edited by Matthew J. Smith and Randy Duncan. New York: Routledge, 2017. xi–xxii.

Hatfield, Charles. "Defining Comics in the Classroom." *Teaching the Graphic Novel*. Edited by Stephen Tabachnik. New York: Modern Language Association, 2009. 19–27.

Hill, Crag, ed. *Teaching Comics through Multiple Lenses*. New York: Routledge, 2017.

Horrocks, Dylan. "Inventing Comics: Scott McCloud Defines the Form in *Understanding Comics*." *Comics Journal* 234 (2001): 29–52.

Howsam, Leslie. *Old Books and New Histories: An Orientation to Studies in Book and Print Cultures*. Toronto: University of Toronto Press, 2006.

Howsam, Leslie. "The Practice of Book and Print Culture: Sources, Methods, Readings." *The Perils of Print Culture: Book, Print and Publishing History in Theory and Practice*. Edited by Jason McElligott and Eve Patten. London: Palgrave Macmillan, 2014. 17–34.

Jacobs, Dale. *Graphic Encounters: Comics and the Sponsorship of Multimodal Literacy*. New York: Bloomsbury Academic, 2013.

Lamont, Michèle. *How Professors Think: Inside the Curious World of Academic Judgment*. Cambridge, MA: Harvard University Press, 2009.

McCloud, Scott. *Understanding Comics*. New York: Harper Perennial, 1994.

New London Group. "A Pedagogy of Multiliteracies: Designing Social Futures." *Multiliteracies: Literacy Learning and the Design of Social Futures*. Edited by Bill Cope and Mary Kalantzis. New York: Routledge, 2000. 9–37.

Nyberg, Amy Kiste. *Seal of Approval: The History of the Comics Code*. Jackson: University of Mississippi Press 1998.

Satrapi, Marjane. *Persepolis*. New York: Pantheon, 2003.

Sealey-Morris, Gabriel. "The Rhetoric of the Paneled Page: Comics and Composition Pedagogy." *Composition Studies* 43, no.1 (Spring 2015): 31–50.

Shep, Sydney. "Books in Global Perspectives." *The Cambridge Companion to the History of the Book*. Edited by Leslie Howsam. Cambridge: Cambridge University Press, 2015.

Spiegelman, Art. *The Complete Maus*. New York: Pantheon, 1996.

Syma, Carrye Kay, and Robert G. Weiner, eds. *Graphic Novels and Comics in the Classroom: Essays on the Educational Power of Sequential Art*. Jefferson, NC: McFarland, 2013.

Wright, Bradford K. *Comic Book Nation: The Transformation of Youth Culture in America*. Baltimore: The Johns Hopkins University Press, 2001.

Wonder Women and the Web: How Female Comics Creators Leap from Private to Public in a Single Bound

—AIMEE VALENTINE

Formal and customary restrictions within print publications have shaped the evolution of comics for centuries. Comics creators working in print media are long accustomed to developing comic strips, comic books, and other graphic narratives with certain constraints in mind, perhaps most obviously those print-based parameters concerning color, format, and length. Within the sphere of commercial print media, comics content has also been constrained, particularly since the formation of the Comics Code Authority in 1954. Another limitation that mainstream comics content has suffered is one of perception, particularly as it relates to gender. Historically, mainstream print publications have limited their support to those creators and narratives considered by editors and advertisers to be most commercially viable—that is, in their projected appeal to subscription holders, general audiences, and established fanbases. Throughout the decades, comics by or about women have been commonly perceived by publishers as less commercially viable. This intrinsic bias has posed a further constraint on female comics creators wishing to publish narratives about women. Without support from mainstream publications, for many decades these creators were limited to self-publishing or publishing through small, independent print outlets. Rather than appearing alongside their male counterparts, the work of female comics creators and female-centric narratives thus appeared most often in little-publicized, underground zines. These zines generally had severely limited budgets and often relied on cheap copy machines, resulting in comic art that was poorly reproduced. Distribution of the work, too, was often limited to small print runs serving indie mailing lists, or to local comics shops that placed those comics in the back section. In short, comics created by women or about women were essentially barred from a truly public eye and relegated to a virtually subterranean private sphere, as documented in the many archival research projects of celebrated comics "herstorian" Trina Robbins.

With the internet expanding to become part of mass culture about twenty years ago, comics creators as a whole quickly realized the benefits from access to unlimited and less regulated spaces. But an open publishing platform is perhaps most transformational for marginalized artists in the medium. In the open space of social media, for instance, there is little room for the argument that legitimizing women's narratives means they must be commercially viable. The freedom to publish work that reflects their unique experiences and perspectives, and offers dramatically improved image quality with access to a global audience, has finally drawn female comics creators from out of the shadows. One might say this digital revolution in technology and communication flings open the doors from which female comics creators can now leap into view. Rather than evolutionary or incremental development, we look toward the promise of a publishing revolution. I call this the "single-bound theory" and apply it here to the field of comics. Just as many revolutions in publishing have in the past, this change in the status quo rests on new technologies and modes of communication. In the case of women in comics, it is the World Wide Web.

I. The Issue

But are female creators truly unfettered? It wouldn't seem so. Comics publications, especially in print media, have indeed demonstrated greater inclusivity in the last decade. Nevertheless, comics narratives continue to be male-centric and authored by male creators. Recent predictions by some comics scholars and cultural critics might mollify us to some degree by suggesting that the work of women will gain greater prominence. We can consider, for example, the gender gap in DC and Marvel comics as followed by cultural critic Tim Hanley. In his "gendercrunching" articles, he closely monitors statistics in those mainstream outlets and finds that while the proportion of female creators has slightly increased over the past few years, they remain underrepresented. At the same time, according to Christine Ro, those female creators are still primarily limited to crafting stories about women, whereas their male counterparts maintain creative control over male, female, and nonbinary characters. One might wonder what will need to change now. Wasn't the web itself adequate springboard? In this exploratory essay, I first address two hypotheses for the projected increase in the number of published female comics creators. Next, I share my experiences as founder and editor of an online comics journal for women who make or write about comics. Interviews with Nicole Hollander and Noel Franklin, two female comics creators, further serve as anecdotal but integral accounts of different trajectories taken in publication as the artists explore questions relating to form, content, and gender issues, thus providing a more nuanced and personal understanding of their perspectives as women working in both print and online venues. Finally, I conclude with a reflection on the important role that graphic narratives by women might play in our classrooms.

II. Why Might We Expect a Boom in the Publication of Female Comics Authors?

One hypothesis points to an evolution in societal attitudes and values concerning gender and comics. As guest editor for the 2014 edition of *The Best American Comics*, noted comics scholar Scott McCloud refers to a prediction he made a decade prior—that the comics industry would reach a female majority within twenty years. He writes, "Such a prediction was pure fantasy in 2004. Ten years later, in 2014 . . . okay maybe it still sounds like pure fantasy to a lot of you, but I know some in art education and parts of the publishing industry who are quietly nodding along with me right now. Girls read. And guess what? They also write and draw" (McCloud 75). Both McCloud and *New York Magazine*-affiliate Vulture.com claim that females now make up 50 percent of comics readership. At first glance, this appears to support McCloud's suggestion that more girls will also begin to make comics. Indeed, he points out that some schools boast a 50 percent female population amongst comics majors. The correlation is not clear, however. Does reading and studying comics necessarily mean that female students will produce and publish them in the near or even distant future? Our concern that there is a dearth in the publication of women cartoonists prompts a further question: how many women are currently making comics?

It is impossible to glean such numbers when the products of those efforts are still nearly invisible in the current mainstream print market. However, we do know from early all-female publications such as *Twisted Sister, Wimmin's Comix*, and *It Ain't Me, Babe Comix*, which began in the 1970s and ran for several decades, that there exist a number of women who persisted in this medium though their efforts may be largely unsung today. The work of a few well-known female creators, such as Alison Bechdel and Lynda Barry, serve as exceptions to the rule. What is called for, we might argue, is wider representation of women's graphic narratives. Perhaps, as McCloud hopes, the next ten years is all that is needed for such an evolution to take place.

Other critics are also quick to seize victory for women in the current comics climate. Journalist Abraham Riesman proclaimed that 2014 was the year that "feminism conquered comics culture."

> Every month brought more comics series starring women, be they superpower-possessing, broadsword-wielding, mystery-solving, or merely life-living. We learned that comics readership is now roughly 50 percent female. The Big Two, Marvel and DC, made some glaring missteps in their depictions of gender—but more memorable than the missteps were the backlashes, led by intelligent and progressive voices in an ever-stronger online and real-life community. We're still a long way from gender parity in industry hiring, and other marginalized communities have yet to experience the same kind of boom in representation, but the trend toward inclusivity is unmistakable. (Riesman n.p.)

Take note, however. This "trend toward inclusivity" as proof of a firmly established feminism within the genre is based on an evaluation of the number of women depicted in comics combined with the assertion that female readership has also increased. The proclamation of victory does not include women as comics creators, nor does it do anything to address fair representation of their work in public venues alongside male counterparts. After all, Riesman reminds us that gender parity is still elusive in commerce. The conquering heroines, it would seem, exist primarily as the fictional female figures that are produced and disseminated by men.

That males continue to monopolize the US comics industry is evidenced by the annual selections for *The Best American Comics*. The anthology series touts an open submission policy for reviewing any comics published in the prior year, whether the work is mainstream or self-published. Keeping observations that year from McCloud and Riesman in mind, we find that among the individual writers and artists selected for *The Best American Comics 2014*, twenty-three are male and seven are female. That is over three times as many men as women. The ratio is only slightly improved among the five mixed writer-artist teams, which comprise six men and four women. All told, the anthology features work by twenty-nine men and eleven women and so reflects nearly three times as many male contributors.

We can anticipate two explanations for this discrepancy: First, the 2014 edition features work published in print or online in the previous year because of the anthology's publishing deadline. And since 2013 wasn't the "year that feminism conquered comics," we mustn't expect that the 2014 edition would accurately reflect the victory for women that Riesman claims. Second, the publication partially relies on comics creators and magazine editors to submit work for review, and so some control over which comics are chosen for the anthology rests with those who take that initiative. Could it be that perhaps female creators or their editors are simply not submitting work for review? Series editor of *The Best American Comics,* Bill Kartalopoulos, stated that he actively seeks out new work at conventions, and that he includes independent minicomics as well as more supported work. Therefore, the paucity of female artists represented in the series could also be attributed to the lack of visibility at male-dominated comics conventions. With these caveats in mind, we might conclude that the 2014 edition is not representative of the conquering feminist.

To be fair, we might also consider *The Best American Comics* of 2015, edited by Jonathan Lethem, a novelist with a background in art. This edition features thirty-seven contributors, all of whom are the single artist-writer of their included comics work. Of those, there are only thirteen female creators—about a third of creators altogether. Further, one of the thirteen women featured is Roz Chast, a cartoonist for the *New Yorker* who has been publishing comics and monographs since the 1970s. This is not in any way to slight her selection in the anthology since her graphic memoir *Can't We Talk About Something More Pleasant?* is certainly more than worthy of inclusion. I would merely point out that of the thirteen female creators whose work was selected as among the "best," at least one other was well-acclaimed by mainstream publishing standards. Published in 2014, Chast's graphic memoir was already a *New York Times* bestseller and had won several awards and been a finalist for the National Book Award. If we fast-forward to the most recent edition of the anthology, we find that there were works included by eleven female and twenty-two male comics creators. Thus as recently as 2018, the gender gap between contributors does not suggest there is significant improvement in female representation among the "best" of American comics creators.

An evolution towards more representative comics work is perhaps still in the beginning stages, which makes McCloud's 2014 prediction both ironic and troublesome. Ironic, because while he accentuates the plethora of women joining the field of comics writing, a paucity of women is actually represented; and secondly, because his argument of "raising readers" seems to be predicated on what he calls "the growing importance of all-ages comics" (McCloud 75). He is referring explicitly to the newest generation of manga and YA comics readers. Why might this be troublesome to use as an indicator of more female creators entering the public sphere? It is because McCloud is reinforcing a tie between genre and gender, a problem that has hounded women in traditional print publication for generations.

Female writers have long been considered to be primarily authors of domestic narratives, such as stories centered around relationships, romance, and issues of personal identity. All the while, male authors are credited for writing about the world at large such as politics, war, and other social issues. With these stereotypes embraced by publishers and their marketing teams, work from women is very often relegated to the category of "women's writing," and largely ignored by critics as trivial or not literary. Simultaneously, when male writers employ family themes, and even exhibit stylistically sentimental approaches, they more frequently receive critical acclaim for that work. We see this in traditional prose literature, such as Jonathan Franzen's *Freedom*, a novel about family, but also in comics literature, such as Craig Thompson's *Blankets*, with its themes of teen identity and romantic love. And just as Franzen's domestic novel was favored to win the 2011 Pulitzer Prize against a non-domestic tome by Jennifer Egan, Craig Thompson's graphic novel likewise shot to the top of national reading lists. It would seem that male authors are praised for embracing "women's themes." Meanwhile, female team Mariko Tamaki and Jillian Tamaki's graphic novel *Skim*, which employed similar themes of teen identity and romantic love, received far less attention. In an interview with Michael Cavna, McCloud discusses the lag time existing for female comics creators and singles out Tamaki's work.

> There's sort of a generational lag where women are concerned in comics. Women as part of the [comics] community are getting very close to 50 percent. But there's also that lag time where artists like Crumb or Daniel Clowes or Jaime Hernandez have been at it for 30 years. Artists like Jillian Tamaki just haven't been at it as long, so when Tamaki's work just really blossomed ... you're getting a sense of just how much potential energy is located in these creative minds. You realize that [roughly half] of the creative community is a volcano that hasn't necessarily erupted yet.... And so, the revolution is already here. It's just revving up over the course of the next decade or so. (Cavna n.p.)

It is difficult to reconcile McCloud's use of the word revolution when it seems that female artists are being recognized at a plodding pace at best. McCloud fails to mention any lag time for newbie males such as Craig Thompson, as there wasn't any. *Blankets* was Thompson's sophomore effort, following a successful debut entitled, *Good-bye Chunky Rice*. Nor does McCloud address the idea that work from a male comics creator might have an inherent market value that female creators must earn over a period of decades through extreme persistence rather than skill alone. The gender-genre binary continues to pigeonhole female creators, while it propels male creators forward. Interviewed in the *Daily Crosshatch*, Brian Heater asked Craig Thompson, "What do you think it was that resonated with not just comics fans, but also places like *Time*?" Thompson responded, "Probably the things that I was reacting against in the comics medium. I was reacting against all of the over-the-top, explosive action genre—I guess alternative comics have been doing that, for a while. But I also didn't want to do anything cynical and nihilistic, which is the standard for a lot of alternative comics" (Heater n.p.).

If we follow the gender-genre construct, in which female comics creators primarily create narratives outside of the "over-the-top, explosive action genre," then why don't their works resonate as deeply with comics critics and large venues like *Time* magazine, which awarded Thompson a #1 best book ranking in 2003? One might counter that a few women do receive such recognition, and point to Alison Bechdel's *Fun Home*, ranked #1 by *Time* in 2006. But here we are talking about a female creator who had already worked in print comics for decades. This example serves to reinforce McCloud's lag time theory for female creators, rather than acknowledge a systemic privilege afforded to male creators and their narratives. We might conclude that working within established gender-genre boundaries serves only to limit female comics creators.

Before discounting the impact that feminism has had on the comics industry in general, and on the publication of women's narratives in particular, we might bracket the matter for now to allow more time to pass—after all, social progress across the board has been uneven. Perhaps, as indicated by VIDA, mainstream print opportunities will gradually widen for women to publish. This would suggest an evolution rather than revolution.

However, at least one female comics writer, discussed in the interview portion of this chapter, does not attribute greater distribution and reception of her craft to the women's movement. Instead, she gives credit to the marvel of technology for providing greater opportunity to express her views through text and image. In other words, to the expanding and liberating space made possible by the World Wide Web. So here we can consider another hypothesis to explain the expected increase in public space for women's narratives, and one that suggests we put aside the slow-revving kind of change proposed by McCloud. With the emergence of open online publishing platforms, the restrictive boundaries of print publication cease to censor, mediate, or relegate the creative work of women to a category of "female writing." Internet publishing is fairly democratic. It does not discriminate based on race, gender, age, or income. As a (mostly) free and public space, the web is open to anyone wishing to publish by bypassing the evolutionary generational-gender gap in the print publication scenario referred to by McCloud. While McCloud sees a growing number of women in print happening in another decade or so as a result of more females reading and studying comics, the internet offers an immediate alternative to the status quo. Women, for the first time in history, have means of transitioning from a private creative sphere to a public one in a matter of seconds, rather than decades. A leap of faith in one's abilities is all it takes. Well, almost. While the digital revolution creates an instant space for women, it does pose its own challenges.

One concern related to the single-bound theory of female artists and publishers is the effect of the internet on the work itself. Literature scholar and writer Caleb Crain proposes that literary style changes as it goes online because the internet is "inhospitable" to the kind of quietness typically lent to private reading. Crain describes the online reader as sharing a reading space with millions of other readers and wondering about the author, "Who is this guy? Why aren't there any links? And, more damningly, is anyone else reading this?" Crain attributes the authorial styles that thrive on the internet as belonging to authors who post frequently, write about people and topics in the headlines, and identify with or address a group of people. Crain explains what he calls the concept of "groupiness."

> I would say that writing on the internet tends to be more popular when it satisfies the reader's wish to be connected—the wish not to miss out. The writer, too, may have such a wish. I admit that I love it when another blog links to mine; there is great consolation in the feeling of having a posse. And of course many readers online are also writers there. Perhaps these feelings of "groupiness" explain a few more traits of internet style. . . . One also finds more flattery and more insults online, another hint that online readers are more interested in affiliation and in the feelings associated with including and excluding other people. (Crain n.p.)

Regarding groupiness, is it possible that women publishing online would speak to each other and to engage in a creative conversation that is more immediate, and possibly more organic, than the one they could have by publishing privately? Such a phenomenon could certainly fuel the "women in the creative arts" movement, and provide support where little existed before, but an online community can just as easily, and swiftly, turn against the individual. Crain continues:

> whenever a writer expresses himself he also chooses how he will present himself—even if he chooses to keep his personal self out of view, insofar as that is possible. A writer is someone who has turned his self-presentation in language into an art or a profession, just as an actor has his self-presentation in person. Feelings and social context—or rather, linguistic effects that suggest feelings and social context—may be as crucial to a writer as metaphor and diction. (Crain n.p.)

It may be advisable, then, that as women leap forward in a single bound from private to public by engaging in the one-click revolution, they take care to understand the social context in which they are participating and acknowledge that their public persona, whether created or hidden, will determine if readers connect to or disengage from the content of their work. Comics are literary works, of course, and thus we would expect the internet to have similar influences on narratives with a strong graphic component. Will online social pressure cause female comics creators to alter their style, content, or persona in an attempt to gain greater support for their work? Two women working in the medium of comics comment on their experiences and allow us a peek into the role that technology plays in creation. Before introducing them, however, I will discuss my own experience as an online publisher of graphic narratives.

III. A Case Study: *inkt/art* and Creators Online

In 2007, I registered the domain name inktart.com and founded an online comics journal dedicated to publishing women working in or writing about comics. As a writer and fledgling cartoonist, I had already noted the lack of representation of women in the field. Having worked previously in an editorial capacity for print publications, I immediately appreciated the unlimited potential of the internet. The freedom offered in page layout, continuity of narrative, detail enlargement, and color appealed to my background in art history, and my additional background in English literature compelled me to adopt a literary approach, publishing comics submissions in categories such as poetry, fiction, and nonfiction. In my first attempt to create an online journal, and with no knowledge of programming or online formatting, I designed each page from scratch, right down to the navigation buttons. It was a colossal feat, but if I could do it, most any other person can too. I sent out a call for submissions via national and international Craigslist ads and through schools of art. Another perk of the internet is the ability to freely solicit work from every corner of the earth, and the response, like most things on the internet, was immediate. For the first issue, I interviewed Trina Robbins, the previously mentioned cartoonist, women's comics historian, and participant in the female underground commix movement of the 1970s. The journal made a quiet online debut. The reading community and contributors were pleased with the effort but I found that for the long-term, designing the journal page by page, button by button, to be an arduous approach for any person operating alone. In addition, I had no reasonable means of archiving the work. I then put the project behind me, considering it a one-off publication. Over time, the journal's online pages dissolved, developed bugs, and the links became unlinked. I dedicated myself instead to finishing my Creative Writing MFA thesis—a graphic collection of women's narratives—and I was thrilled that the first story in the collection was published by *Witness* in 2011, online and in color. This success reminded me again of the promise of online publishing and so I began in earnest to recreate a comics journal dedicated to women. I discovered the open publishing platform WordPress, with its bug-free and easily navigable magazine templates, and decided to launch *inkt|art* again.

The original pages from the 2007 venture are lost to the ether of cyberspace, but the current version of the journal is free, online, and archived since 2013. The mission of *inkt|art* is two-fold: to increase exposure for female creators and to promote literary comics. This is an effort to raise critical perceptions of the medium itself as well as to break down stereotypes of gender and genre. As opposed to identifying contributor's work as "women's comics," a label that suggests content that falls within narrative stereotypes, the journal publishes literary comics that are created by women, regardless of theme. Like a traditional print journal, *inkt|art* divides work into categories of fiction, poetry, nonfiction, essays, and interviews. It is not a self-publication site such as *deviantart.com*, or other online platforms that publish one's own work; *inkt|art* incorporates a submission and review process that includes acceptances, rejections, and revise-resubmits. Contributors are not paid, because, unlike many print publications, *inkt|art* does not solicit sponsors. The online journal simply exists to create space and visibility for women producing quality work in this medium. It is my hope that the gendered aspect of *inkt|art* will soon become irrelevant, as female creators continue to stake their claim with authority in both print and online publications.

I recently asked two regular and popular contributors to *inkt|art* to comment on their experiences and challenges publishing online, as well as their thoughts about working in a male-dominated publishing industry. Nicole Hollander is a veteran cartoonist who began the comics strip *Sylvia* in 1980. *Sylvia* was nationally syndicated in US newspapers for thirty years. Hollander ceased creating the newspaper strip in 2008, and began publishing her work online. Reflecting on this shift, Hollander noted:

> I feel freer online because I am not bound by the strictures on language or subject that apply to someone working in a newspaper. Newspapers have editors and they might decide that the word "orgasm" is not proper for a family newspaper. [Also] I was working four weeks ahead. This meant I couldn't comment on Chicago politics. A scandal was over before it started in terms of my four-week deadline. The

blog is very different. No one regulates what I say now. I write for publication every week. The drawings relate to the writing and everything is done very quickly.

At the time, Hollander was working on a graphic memoir of her childhood in Chicago. She also publishes a blog called Bad Girl Chats, in which she archives *Sylvia*, writes about politics, and publishes drawings. As she considers the changes in where and how she creates comics, she explained:

> My audience is a community and the community comments on much of what I do online. They provide suggestions and links to relevant topics. The communication is less idiosyncratic. I miss getting letters from my readers. There was an intimacy to the communication in those letters because they were private. No one saw them but me. My readers now are communicating not only with me but with the blog community.

Comics creator Noel Franklin comes from quite a different background. Franklin is a rising comics star who was first published by *inkt|art* in 2012. Since then, her work has been included in several comics anthologies, and she recently ran a successful Kickstarter campaign online to raise funds to print her work for the small press expo (SPX) in Seattle. Despite her substantive grounding in online platforms for sharing and distributing her work, Franklin acknowledges that she has a different relationship to her readership and community than what Hollander described:

> I really could do a better job of using the internet to build a community of readership. My strongest community is Facebook, which I use to link to online material and used exclusively to run a successful Kickstarter campaign. While I do enjoy online publication—for the ease of exposure and the potential extended reach—I do love printed material, so, I suppose online publication is just a middle ground for me. Eventually, I'll publish every online story in print. But I love how you can get people from all over the world to enjoy your stories via the internet, whereas it's hard to get a printed mini-comic into that many hands and eyes.

Despite this recognition that she can do *more* with the tools and resources of web-based publishing and distribution, Franklin also sees her career's future deeply intertwined with the web:

> Because I am so early in my comics career, it has been an absolute boon to have comics online. I tell the stories that I feel need to be told, the ones that live in me, which have nothing to do with the mainstream comics market. Yes, it is amazing

to get paid for your work, but I know that financial compensation follows reputation, and it's been great to be able to send potential funders, publishers and clients to stories that have been published by online journals. It provides third-party validation, and I've used the online exposure to support the sales of my self-published mini comics. I have been using the internet almost exclusively to get published in journals and anthologies—both online and in print. I research opportunities and submit online. I've had stories accepted in 11 journals over the past 24 months, including publications out of Canada, Serbia, England and Norway.

Looking across these comments, there are key commonalities and differences between how both of these creators interpret the role of online publishing in their careers. Both Hollander and Franklin anticipate that their online work will build an audience for print projects. Where Hollander is using the online forum as a space to create and publish sections of her in progress graphic memoir, Franklin uses the online forum to gain exposure as an artist in the hopes of building a platform for additional print work. Similarly, both women intend to republish what appears now online in a future print format. Importantly, both women identify themselves online as women and rendering their lived experiences as females is central to their work. Hollander explains, "I did and do identify as a feminist. If you ask me what I am, my country, my religion—it's all secondary to my being a woman and identifying with what happens to women because they are women."

Hollander's experience as female comics creator at the onset of her syndicated comic strip speaks to the many challenges women have faced in the industry. "My experience as a female creator might have been on another planet compared to the experience of a woman cartoonist now. For a short time, I sold my own work to newspapers. I was told once that since they carried *Cathy* there was no need for another woman," she says. Concurring that her gender also matters, Noel Franklin says,

> I absolutely identify myself as a female creator from start to finish with potential publishers and readers. My publishing entity is 'Gone Girl Comics' and—because of the gender neutrality of my name (Noel) I make sure to mention something about being a woman in comics in every introduction and online bio. As my stories are about my experience as a woman in this world, it's likely easy to tell that I am a female creator regardless, but that's not always the assumption people make. There are quite famous stories about women's lives that are written by men.

Both women are also in agreement that the liminal space of the internet affords them freedoms in terms of style and format, as well as ease of publishing. Additionally, the women seem to agree that online gender discrimination has not been a problem for them while print media has, and still does, present obstacles. Hollander has been discriminated against by newspapers, and Franklin feels that while she has not yet experienced gender discrimination online, local print publications have yet to support female creators in the capacity that they support males. She says that, "I do, however, feel that there is a dose of discrimination in my hometown, Seattle, which is said by some to be the center of the alternative comics world. You just don't see the level of female creators being supported as much as their male counterparts in local publications."

The women also shared different perspectives on the role of online publishing. Hollander embraces the nonrestrictive nature of internet publishing, in terms of form and content, using color now where she has not in the past, and exploring nontraditional narrative continuity. Franklin still works primarily in black and white, and does not alter her approach from print work to online work. Instead, she creates works that she knows can be republished, unchanged, in print form. Hollander engages with her online readership, while Franklin has not focused on community-building, instead working on her artistry and using the internet to find publishing opportunities. Finally, veteran cartoonist Hollander's online work is political and uncensored in nature. Meanwhile, Franklin's work addresses only those topics that she feels comfortable sharing with the world at large at this early stage in her career. Franklin explains that her focus comes from "a non-fiction standpoint, either auto-bio or comics journalism. Themes include iconic female friendships, bizarre incidents from childhood, overcoming fears and also the loss of my friends." In short, neither artist credits the women's movement or a liberating sociopolitical environment for their successes. Instead, both artists acknowledge the internet as an unprecedented force for creating wider opportunities for publishing their work.

IV. Conclusion

Optimism about the future of women's literary work, and of female comics creators particularly, appears widely shared. This paper explores two possible explanations for what appears to be a trend in growing public space for these artists. The first suggests that the feminist movement itself, with campaigns across the board for reforms, has for decades made varying impact on nearly every aspect of political and social life. The literary world may not yet have caught up with demands for gender parity, but some observers note that changes are afoot, albeit not quickly. A second and perhaps more plausible explanation for why we may find female artists more visible rests on the revolutionary impact of the internet. Immediate and unlimited publication opportunities portend a flood of literary work presented to us from previously marginalized authors. As cyberspace offers a new platform for comic creators around the globe, it is perhaps most revolutionizing for women working in the medium. The emergence of free and unrestricted space means that female creators are no longer limited in terms of color, page size, format, or length. Furthermore, in open space, there is no room for critical claims that women's narratives are not (or should be) commercially viable. The freedom to both create meaning in the medium of their choice and to seek out a global audience through social media has drawn female comics creators out of the shadows. The paper herein shares personal reflections from two such comics creators and the author herself about leaping into public space by a single bound.

There is significance in this account for educators, of course. The use of comics and graphic novels as pedagogical tools is becoming more widely appreciated across disciplines, much in the way that film and video has already been embedded in curricula. There is considerable potential for comics to build visual literacy and reading skills, foster critical thinking and creativity, bridge in-school with extracurricular experiences, and to motivate students to learn who have a natural affinity for the genre. There are numerous sources for teachers to drawn upon for recommended readings. For instance, Art Spiegelman's *Maus* about the Holocaust and Joe Sacco's *Palestine* remain staples in many reference lists for English or social studies lessons. In keeping with pedagogical goals of fostering diversity in instructional materials and classroom discussions, let's not neglect the contributions of female comics creators. Classic works such as Marjane Satrapi's *Persepolis* and Alison Bechdel's *Fun Home*, could be complemented with more recent projects such as *Syllabus: Notes from an Accidental Professor* by Lynda Barry, and *Ms. Marvel* by series creators Sana Amanat and G. Willow Wilson. Perhaps, too, we should keep in mind webcomics, such as those by Kate Beaton and others, that truly illustrate how the Web has enabled female comics creators to leap from private to public in a single click, and in doing so we, as teachers, might help foster a more diverse reading list and perhaps inspire the next generation of women to create their own super-stories through comics.

WORKS CITED

Cavna, Michael. "Best American Comics 2014: Guest Editor Scott McCloud Illuminates the Range of Modern Brilliance in New Must-Read [Q+A]." *Washington Post*, October 7, 2014.

Crain, Caleb. "Twilight of the Books." *New Yorker*, December 24, 2007. https://www.newyorker.com/magazine/2007/12/24/twilight-of-the-books

Franklin, Noel. Personal Interview. December 27, 2014.

Heater, Brian. "Interview: Craig Thompson Pt. 1 (of 2)." *Daily Cross Hatch*. May 7, 2007. http://thedailycrosshatch.com/2007/05/07/431/2007-05-07.

Hollander, Nicole. Personal Interview. December 27, 2014.

Kartalopoulos, Bill. "Discovering International Comics." *World Literature Today*. March 2016. https://www.worldliteraturetoday.org/2016/march/discovering-international-comics-bill-kartalopoulos

King, Amy. "The Count, 2013: Lie by Omission: The Rallying Few, The Rallying Masses." *VIDA*. February 24, 2014. http://www.vidaweb.org/the-count-2013/

McCloud, Scott, ed. *The Best American Comics 2014*. Boston: Houghton Mifflin Harcourt, 2014.

Riesman, Abraham. "The 10 Best Comics Series of 2014, the Year Feminism Conquered Comics Culture." *Vulture*. December 18, 2014. www.vulture.com/2014/12/10-best-comics-series-of-2014.html

Ro, Christine. "More Women Than Ever Are Marvel Creators, But Does that Matter? *Vice*. March 8, 2017. https://www.vice.com/en_us/article/z4kn7j/more-women-than-ever-are-marvel-creators-but-

Teaching Typical Comics: Overcoming the Biases of Comics Pedagogy with Online Tools

—BART BEATY, University of Calgary

As a discursive phenomenon, the idea of a "classic" comic book is a relatively recent phenomenon. Within the confines of the earliest organized comic-book fandom in the United States, the notion of a "classic" comic book referred to individual issues that played an historic role in the lifespans of popular characters. *Detective Comics* #27 was a classic comic book that introduced Batman to the world, for example. The importance of these works was crystallized in the 1970s by fannish institutions like Robert Overstreet's *Comic Book Price Guide*, which opened annually with a listing of the most valuable comic books on the back issue market.[1] Around that same time, Marvel Comics would help reify the equation of "classics" with historical firsts through their publication of *Origins of Marvel Comics* in 1974, and comic-book publishers have continued to market certain of their product as "essential" or "classics" in a manner that is close to an economistic model of value.[2]

That this conception of importance should become so dominant within fandom is not surprising given the lack of competing forms of legitimation within the field. For decades, comics were deemed self-evidently not fit for educated audiences; they had no place in the college or university classroom or in the scholarly journals attached to academe. While it is true that in the period prior to the Second World War, idiosyncratic writers like the poet E. E. Cummings and the critic Gilbert Seldes identified George Herriman's *Krazy Kat* as a popular work of enduring aesthetic value, the near total dismissal of comics by cultural elites was a far more widespread viewpoint.[3] The art historian Clement Greenberg, writing in 1939, dismissed comics as a "product of the industrial revolution" that he termed kitsch (9), while Theodor Adorno and Max Horkheimer, writing five years later, decried "a system which is uniform as a whole and in every part" (1). It is true, of course, that comic books—and, to a lesser degree, comic strips—in the United States at this period *were* the products of industrial models of production. Assembled in studios by packagers, comic-book stories were created by teams of writers, artists, letterers, and colorists working to tight deadlines on a piece-work basis. Indeed, so prevalent was this model that Michael Chabon could create an epic novel rooted in the fantasy that a single, heroic cartoonist might reject it.

Today, more than eight decades into the history of the American comic-book industry, the assembly-line model of production remains the norm. Of the thousands of comics published in the 2010s, for example, the overwhelmingly vast majority rely on an industrial division of labor. That is, they are the works that are least likely to be valorized in our culture and, by a wide margin, the least likely to be taught. While teaching in all fields of cultural undertaking is highly selective (and, I will argue, selective along the same ideological lines), classes on comics are especially so. Specifically, comics in the American university and college classroom are predominantly taught as single-authored, stand-alone graphic novels produced since 1986. This distortion does our students a disservice insofar as it obscures the historical complexities that have shaped the development of the American comic book, which is, after all, a predominantly industrial art form. Given the fact that the landmark works that launched American comic books into college classrooms (Art Spiegelman's *Maus*, *Watchmen* by Alan Moore and Dave Gibbons) were self-conscious reactions against the industrial history of comics production, it is frankly dishonest to write industrially produced comics out of the history of the form. In what follows, I will consider the biases that have created the current predicament in comics pedagogy and offer a few classroom exercises that I have used to try to counter those biases.

Round Up the Usual Suspects

The Open Syllabus Project (opensyllabusproject.org) is a big data research undertaking led by Joe Karaganis at Columbia University. The OSP team has collected more than one million publicly accessible syllabi for university-level courses in the United States dating back to 2005 and has extracted course readings from them. This allows them to provide data on the actual number of courses in their database that assign a specific work (with the important caveat that their database, large as it is, has captured only a very tiny percentage of all university-level courses), a "teaching score" within the field, and an overall ranking of texts both within and across fields. Further, the OSP uses metadata to demonstrate which texts are most often assigned in courses with other texts (for example, it will surprise few readers to learn that Aristotle's *Ethics*, one of the most widely assigned texts in the database, is frequently taught alongside works by Plato, John Stuart Mill, Immanuel Kant, and Thomas Hobbes). Despite the many reservations about the completeness of its data, the OSP provides a rare opportunity for scholars to move beyond the anecdotal in discussions of canon-formation in teaching.[4] Drawing on this data set provides some needed empirical support for my contention that comics studies has been predominantly concerned with atypical works that tend to define importance in ways that are at odds with the historical norms of the field.

What may surprise some readers is the fact that Scott McCloud's 1993 comics textbook, *Understanding Comics: The Invisible Art*, ranks in the top one hundred works taught on American campuses with nearly twelve hundred courses using the material.[5] It is not only the most widely assigned comics work, but its neighbors on the chart are among the most famous works of literature in the English language (Jane Austen's *Pride and Prejudice* immediately above it, William Shakespeare's *MacBeth* below). That this is the highest-ranking comic book is probably not surprising, but that any comic should chart this high possibly is. With regard to the centrality of McCloud within comics studies, it seems likely, based on this data, that an enormous plurality of comics studies courses require that students read the whole book or individual chapters of it, or, alternately, assign it as recommended reading. Indeed, it is striking that for almost every other highly ranked comic book on the list, *Understanding Comics* is one of the most commonly paired books, which indicates that when any comics are taught in a class, McCloud is taught alongside them.

McCloud's book, of course, is highly atypical. A first-person comics essay focused on the operations of the art form—there are few other comics like it. Nonfiction comics have been a decided minority in the history of American comics production, and personal essays are only a tiny sliver of even that population. As a comics textbook, particularly for introductory courses, *Understanding Comics* has the considerable advantage of readability. Despite the fact that many of his conclusions and presumptions have been widely critiqued by academic work in the field, McCloud is widely cited and taught precisely because his work serves as an entry point for those coming to the field for the first time. Note, for example, that one of the most widely cited academic English-language studies of formal operations in comics, Thierry Groensteen's *The System of Comics*, is ranked 78,347th in the OSP database, assigned in only ten courses. Moreover, *Understanding Comics* is widely taught outside of the confines of comics studies and in other fields. Among the noncomics that it is widely assigned alongside are Tracy Kidder's *The Soul of a New*

Machine about computer engineering and James Surowiecki's *The Wisdom of Crowds*. *Understanding Comics* is the fifth most assigned book in courses that also teach Edward Tufte's *Envisioning Information*, suggesting that it has a life in courses on information design, marketing, computer-interface design, and other cognate fields not generally considered to be parts of comics studies.

The second most widely taught comic book in American universities is, not surprisingly, also the one that is most widely studied by scholars. Art Spiegelman's *Maus* is, as I have argued (with Benjamin Woo), the most prestigious comic book in the history of American publishing: the most praised, the most studied (by a wide margin), and also as it turns out, the most taught (Beaty and Woo 17–26). It is, in short, the *Hamlet* of comics studies. While *Understanding Comics* is more widely included on syllabi, it seems likely that it is also more partially taught and more widely recommended. Notably, the OSP is top-heavy in textbooks; its most widely included work is William Strunk's *The Elements of Style*, a work that is much more commonly recommended than actively taught. The position of *Maus*, as the most generative "graphic novel" of all time and the spur for the boom in graphic memoirs, atop the field is undisputed. At the time of its publication *Maus*, a long-form graphic memoir about the Holocaust, could arguably be considered the most atypical comic book ever released in the United States; importantly, it paved the way for comics to enter university curricula in an era that predated courses on comics, and it was the linchpin for hundreds of articles about how comic books had finally "grown up" (Biff! Bang! Pow!). It has been widely taught in courses on world history and political science, and it is central not only to the study of comics but to the study of the Holocaust and related fields like memoir and trauma studies. The OSP demonstrates the way that *Maus* sits in multiple fields at once: among the books most commonly taught with it are Elie Wiesel's *Night* and Steven Levi's *Auschwitz*; Marjane Satrapi's *Persepolis* and Alan Moore and Dave Gibbons's *Watchmen*; and Toni Morrison's *Beloved* and F. Scott Fitzgerald's *The Great Gatsby*. In order, this suggests that *Maus* is equally at home in courses about the Holocaust, in courses about comics, and in surveys of twentieth-century American literature. *Maus*'s atypicality means that it is the one "serious" comic book that can be taught alongside even the most canonical American fiction.

Marjane Satrapi's *Persepolis* occupies the third position on the OSP, charting in various forms and under different titles depending on the edition. Combined, *Persepolis* appears on 482 syllabi in the dataset, about half as frequently as *Maus*, the work with which it is most closely associated. As a graphic memoir strongly inspired by Spiegelman's book, *Persepolis* was, at the time of its publication in France and, later, the United States, less atypical; it fit snugly into the category that had already been carved out by Spiegelman's example, narrow as that might be. Of course, the book has decidedly different dynamics, and while there is considerable overlap in the works that they share syllabi with, Satrapi—an Iranian-born cartoonist who created the work while living in Paris—clusters around a different set of contemporary novelists than does *Maus*, including Chinua Achebe (*Things Fall Apart*), Kate Chopin (*The Awakening*) and Sherman Alexie (*The Absolutely True Diary of a Part-Time Indian*). Situating *Persepolis* among other works that are frequently taught as feminist or post-colonial is, of course, not surprising: Satrapi's work proudly adopts these interpretive frameworks. In many ways, *Persepolis* performs a role that is akin to that of *Maus* but with a different emphasis.

The highest-ranking work of comics fiction in the OSP database is Chris Ware's *Jimmy Corrigan: The Smartest Kid on Earth*, which charts at number 650 in proximity to George Eliot's *The Mill on the Floss* and William Faulkner's *Absalom, Absalom!* In many ways, Ware's book is less likely than *Maus* and *Persepolis* to be taught alongside other comics. While it is most frequently taught with McCloud, the next fifty books that it shares space with are non-comics. *Jimmy Corrigan* is most widely affiliated with American modernist fiction: Carson McCullers, Paul Bowles, Walker Percy, John Steinbeck, E. L. Doctorow, and Pete Dexter. McCullers's *The Heart Is a Lonely Hunter*, with which it appears on a remarkable 271 syllabi (an astonishing 76 percent of all syllabi teaching Ware also teach McCullers), certainly frames the way that Ware's work might be read as focusing on outsiders and social misfits. As I argued in *Comics Versus Art*, Ware is among the most celebrated of living cartoonists, and also one of the most widely studied, but again, his work is highly atypical (211–26).

Finally, the only comic book to crack the top five of the OSP dataset from a popular genre also happens to be the least typical work in that genre: Alan Moore and Dave Gibbons's *Watchmen*. Released as a "graphic novel" at the same time as *Maus*, *Watchmen* broke most of the rules surrounding the publication of superhero comics: it was a limited series with mature content (almost unheard of at the time of its publication, although quite common now in the wake of its success) and self-consciously literary, philosophical, and political themes. So uncommon was *Watchmen* that it helped usher in, alongside *Maus* and Frank Miller's *The Dark Knight Returns* (number nine on the OSP list of comics), both the graphic novel revolution of the 1980s and the interest in comic books for adults in the United States. *Watchmen* stands apart from the four comic books ranked higher than it on the OSP list insofar as it is most commonly taught alongside other comics (including those four). Where it does share space with noncomics, those tend to be genre fiction

(William Gibson's *Neuromancer*; J. R. R. Tolkien's *The Lord of the Rings*) or postmodern literary fiction (Don DeLillo's *White Noise*).

We could, of course, go on. As we move down the OSP rankings the number of comics become more numerous, but the range of works does not become particularly more diverse. The next five highest charting works include Neil Gaiman's (and various artists) *Sandman* and Frank Miller's *The Dark Knight Returns*, which fit nicely with *Watchmen* into the category of postmodern superhero comics; Alison Bechdel's *Fun Home* (which shares many similarities with *Maus* and *Persepolis*, alongside which it is commonly taught), Gene Luen Yang's *American Born Chinese*, and Dan Clowes's *Ghost World*. Strikingly, there are no comics at the top of the list that were originally published before 1986 and only two feature work by multiple creators (such as an artist-writer team). The strong bias towards the self-contained, author-driven graphic novel is one of the strongest impressions that one takes from the OSP data, and it notably confirms the "literary" bias of comics studies as it is taught in contemporary college classrooms.

In his 1991 book *Making Meaning*, film scholar David Bordwell notes "academic humanism's omnivorous appetite for interpretation rendered cinema a plausible 'text'" (17). In its earliest period, Bordwell suggests, film studies could have been subsumed by sociology or mass communication studies, but it was not; rather the study of cinema entered the academy through the humanities, primarily through departments of literature. The same can surely be said today of comics studies. While one might have imagined that, with their strong visual elements, comics would enter the university classroom through departments of art and art history, or, because of their historical association with the newspaper and magazine industries, communication studies, the reality is that, as with film, it was departments of literature that were most receptive to the possibilities of comics studies. One significant impact of this development has been the shaping of teaching about comics. For comics to find a home in the contemporary university they had to be rendered plausible, which is to say that they must be made to align with the generally traditional and conservative values of departments of literature.

The bias in comics pedagogy, which is plainly apparent from the OSP data, stems from the field's adoption into departments of literature and can be best understood in the way that it has developed notions of "classics" that are at odds with those that have long prevailed amongst comics fandom. The comic books that are widely assigned by teachers are those that are presumed to be "self-evidently" worthier of classroom time than are other works. They are, in short, the most plausible texts in the field. The pedagogical notion of what constitutes a "classic" in the scholarly study of comics is ridiculously consistent and narrow: it is those comics, most commonly deemed "graphic novels" or "graphic narrative," that best resemble contemporary literary fiction with pictures, and which have been produced by solo authors over the course of the past thirty years. The teachable graphic novel is a work of comics that is most clearly at odds with traditional conceptions of the form: they are the least typical works in the field. This is, of course, perfectly normal. Indeed, it is expected. Departments of literature routinely select works to teach precisely *because* they are so unlike other works, and "genius" is conferred on writers who are most at odds with the conventions of their time (what book could be less typical of the writing of the 1920s than James Joyce's *Ulysses*?). At the same time, the concept of the "classic" within comics studies is already highly calcified, with works sharing generic conventions pertaining to psychological depth, authorial expressivity, and narrative strategies.

The Biases of Comics Pedagogy

Debates around curricular issues relating to the teaching of "classic works"—or the canon of Western literature—date to at least the nineteenth century, but in their current iteration came to forefront a quarter century ago during an explosion of debates about "political correctness" on campus. Works like Allan Bloom's *The Closing of the American Mind*, E. D. Hirsch's *Cultural Literacy*, and Dinesh D'Souza's *Illiberal Education* all sought to defend a restrictively traditional notion of the cultural centrality against what they perceived to be the evils of cultural relativism. Although the inclusion of comics on college syllabi was not a major concern for conservative thinkers during this period, it is noteworthy that the debate reached its highest public profile at a time when comics—particularly Spiegelman's *Maus*—were beginning to be widely taught for the first time.

In his 1974 book *Popular Culture and High Culture*, sociologist Herbert Gans grouped common arguments against "mass culture" around four poles. Inverting these condemnations of the popular, not surprisingly, offers an implicit validation of cultural elitism in the modern era, a stance that runs across ideological lines from the aristocratic conservatism of Matthew Arnold and José Ortega y Gasset on the political right to the Marxian vanguardism of Theodor Adorno and Antonio Gramsci on the left. Gans notes that "mass culture," which explicitly included the categories of comic books and comic strips, was perceived to be a negative influence on the individual (psychologically corroding, addictive), on society (contributing to alienation and anomie), on high culture (from which it was derivative and competitive), and, ultimately, simply defective as a commercial enterprise (1–77).

Gans counters these arguments during the process of discussing them, and Pierre Bourdieu, in *Distinction*, goes even further in countering the notion of the Kantian expression of disinterestedness in the evaluation of culture (3–90). Nonetheless, arguments about the value of restricting the consideration of culture to "the best that has been thought and said" (xi), in the words of Arnold's famous preface to *Culture and Anarchy*, often rest on a series of simple assumptions. First, it is asserted that widely taught works in the Western tradition are self-evidently great, that there is, in point of fact, a sublime in the Kantian sense that certain works attain. One must teach *Maus*, it would be argued, because *Maus* is so self-evidently among the best comics ever created that to fail to do so would constitute a form of pedagogical malpractice. Second, if mass culture can pose a threat to individuals, then great works are a boon to them. Reading difficult material, which *Maus* is presumed to be (at least relative to other comics), enhances mental faculties and allows students to think and feel more clearly. Finally, teaching the classics is regularly posited to benefit society as a whole when those works are alleged to contain and distill "universal values." That is to say, proponents argue that works commonly held to be "the best" have contributed to the triumph of enlightenment values. That each of these, and other, contentions is a self-interested ideological construct should go without saying. Arguments that certain works are self-evidently meritorious, and especially those that do not explicitly state assumed criteria of judgment, are, following Bourdieu, mere expressions of personal tastes in a circularly reinforcing expression of social power. While scholars and teachers working in a variety of humanities disciplines have done remarkable work in deconstructing the ideological operations of "common sense" notions of race and gender, the fact remains that conceptions of "quality" are not always regarded as ideological constructs. For Louis Althusser, ideology imposes "obviousness as obviousness" (116). In the domain of comics, nothing is more obvious than the fact that some comics are better than others, because structures of taste dictate that, for any given individual, some works are preferable to others. It is a simple leap for many teachers from personal preference to cultural truism.

At the same time, however, the objection that certain biases in comics pedagogy are more practical than ideological must be acknowledged. There are, in point of fact, many mundane reasons that comics classes are shaped as they are. A large number of factors influence the texts that are assigned in any classroom: the level of the course and assumptions about the types of students (and their familiarity with the material) who are likely to enroll, the availability of reading material in inexpensive editions, and the instructor's goals for the course. One truism about courses in comics studies is that they are frequently taught as stand-alone offerings; that is to say, many (most?) universities that teach a course specifically on comics teach only one course on comics—courses that ladder in the forms of programs are the exception to the norm. If a course on comics is stand-alone, an instructor is faced with the serious dilemma of deciding what to include on the reading list: they may feel a responsibility to cover the history of comic strips, comic books and graphic novels, formal approaches to the study of the form, and also cover major genres and themes all in a single semester of twelve to fifteen weeks. While this is an impossible task, the feeling of "duty" can often compel instructors to try to shoehorn in everything. In these cases, the reality is that works are often selected not because they are "great" but because they can be made to serve multiple purposes. If I want to teach students to read the formal complexity of comics *and* I want to teach at least one superhero comic book then perhaps *Watchmen* is an obvious choice. If, on the other hand, I want to teach superhero comics *and* I want to teach diversity issues then *Watchmen* is probably a terrible choice, and I may look to *Ms. Marvel*. If I decide, rightly, that at least half of my assigned texts should be by female creators I may have eliminated the vast bulk of comic books produced prior to the 1970s. And so on. Adding the complication of finding works that are in print can further complicate the issue.

The issue of availability has long been a limiting factor in comics studies, but recent developments in the online curation of comic books have rendered that objection less problematic, though by no means obsolete. It is true that, until recently, scholarship and pedagogy on the history of the American comic book was controlled by publishers and collectors. In the absence of substantial library collections, few options existed to expose students to the wide variety of the early comic book. In recent years all of this has changed. Online resources like the Digital Comic Museum (digitalcomicsmuseum.com) and Comic Book Plus (comicbookplus.com) have made tens of thousands of public domain comic books from the 1930s through 1960s available to our students for the first time. Comic books from publishers that have been bankrupt for decades now exist online in the form of high-quality scans, making the production of Ace Magazines, Ajax-Farrell, American Comics Group, Archie-MLJ, and Avon Periodicals (to cite only the As) available to a new generation of readers. Moreover, this work is available to students as free downloads (with an account) or it can be read online in a browser. With more than thirty thousand comic books available online, the opportunity to better situate our understanding has been provided to us through access to the comics version of Margaret Cohen famously termed "the great unread" (23).

Synchrony, Diachrony, and the Great Unread

How might we utilize online collections of industrially produced comic books in order to underscore the culturally constructed notion of importance and better illuminate the complexities of the history of the comic-book format? It is a reality that scholars working in most fields of cultural endeavor are unable to conceptualize the entire scope of the field in which they work. The sheer volume of cultural production, particularly in the twenty-first century, means, first, that no one has actually engaged with the entire scope of the field, and consequently that as scholars and teachers we operate under certain suppositions about history that are easily disproven. We fail when we envision in our syllabi the history of American comic books as the following.

- A vaguely defined nascent period in the 1930s
- The superhero boom running from June 1938 until the end of the war
- A brief vogue for crime comics, romance comics, and horror comics ended by the Comics Code Authority
- A return to superheroes leading to the "Silver Age" and characterized by Marvel Comics
- The consolidation of the superhero as the dominant genre
- An adult period giving rise to the graphic novel and "mature" superhero comics

This facile history, while possibly familiar, is of course almost entirely false. Any close reading of the actual output of comic-book publishers in the so-called Golden Age of the superhero, for instance, will instantly demonstrate that the genre was dwarfed by funny animals and other comics targeted at very young readers. Does our potted history take into account that, in 1979, there were ten times as many comic books published with the name "Richie Rich" in their title than "Superman" in the title? Do our histories account for the ways that horror and crime comic books postdated the creation of the Comics Code Authority?

As teachers, one of the most important lessons that we can impart to our students is that we need to build our histories from primary data, and the availability of digital comics from the 1930s and 1940s (and later) is one of the best methods for doing so. Following the example provided by Ferdinand de Saussure in his *Course in General Linguistics*, we could address comic books, like language, as a complete system to be studied at any given time (synchrony) or as a system evolving over time (diachrony). In what follows I will offer some thoughts on in-class assignments that have proven productive for me in the past that utilize both of these approaches.

I have found that a synchronic study of dozens of comic books published in the same month can reveal profound insights about the development of the American comic-book industry. Three examples follow that have worked well for me.

i) The origins of the American superhero. When I first began teaching superhero comic books of the 1940s I did so by assigning inexpensive and selective DC reprints of Batman and Superman stories such as *Batman Chronicles v1*. The problem with these collections is that they limited the focus to a single character from a single publisher and, moreover, stripped the stories from their original publishing context. More recently, I have begun breaking a large class into smaller groups and assigning them various comic books from a random month in 1940. In this way, students read issues of *Banner Comics*, *Fight Comics*, *Heroic Comics*, *Target Comics*, *Whirlwind Comics* and dozens of other similar titles. What they discover is that superheroes were much more diverse, and often more interesting, than they were heretofore led to believe during the period of the genre's coalescence and, also, that superheroes were generally only one type of adventure genre in anthology titles that frequently also included jungle comics, pirate comics, pilot comics, police comics, and other varieties of the adventure genre. Significantly, this helps reposition the superhero within American pulp traditions and figures like Superman and Batman seem far less like radical breaks with prior storytelling norms and much more akin to established conventions.

ii) The comic-book peak. As Jean-Paul Gabilliet has pointed out, the American comic-book industry peaked, in terms of units sold, in 1952 before beginning a downward sales trend as it lost the competition with television for media attention (46). Again, by adopting a synchronous view, students studying a single month in 1952 are able to come to term with the scope of comic-book storytelling that existed at this time. A unit addressing itself only to comic books published in any random month is able to emphasize the limited heterogeneity of the field, including the way that it ranged widely across genres and visual styles in the production of comics for disparate audiences. A unit focused on these resources produces a more accurate understanding of the evolution of the comic-book format over time.

iii) The debate about the Comics Code. The history of the Comics Code Authority is frequently reduced to a battle between Fredric Wertham and Bill Gaines at EC Comics. Our understanding of this debate has, for decades, been distorted by the fact that the entirety of the "New Trend" EC Comics have been comprehensively reprinted on multiple occasions and remain widely available (presently, in artist-centered editions from Fantagraphics and as book reprints from Dark Horse Comics). As a result, contemporary understandings of the postwar horror-comics debate have been understood almost exclusively through the lens of EC reprints; the availability of EC comic-book reprints shifted that publisher from a peripheral to a central role in our understanding of the controversy. Today, however, a wide range of work from dozens of publishers across hundreds of titles is available to researchers and students on the web. Similarly, a unit on horror comics can now offer students a sampling of work from dozens of titles in addition to those published by EC, enabling a consideration of how, exactly, the work in EC Comics was considered so "atypical" of the period and better allowing students to adjudicate the concerns of postwar parents about content in comic books targeted to young children.

While it is true that it is not possible to conceptualize the entirety of a field as large as comics, the tools provided by online comics collections can allow students the opportunity to apprehend the scope of comics production *at one particular moment in time*, dramatically enlarging their understanding of the logics of the field.

One of the central problems of the "great book" approach to the teaching of comics is not simply that it can contribute to a degree of ahistoricism but also that it frequently fails to provide the proper context to deliver on promises of "greatness." For many years when I first began teaching comics, I struggled in class sessions over the work of Jack Kirby (according to the OSP data, one of our least taught cartoonists).[6] An attempt to teach *Essential Fantastic Four* v. 1 completely failed when students found the material "ludicrous." When I refined the selection to only the three issues spanning the "Galactus Trilogy," the material fared little better. What I realized was that students born in the 1990s and 2000s had always known superhero comics to be post-Kirby; that is, the visual dynamism in Kirby's work described by Charles Hatfield was opaque to students who had only read comics that had already adopted his innovations in new ways. Kirby's work only seemed radical in comparison to the work that preceded it. Relative to the work that it inspired, it seemed old-fashioned. Teachers who have tried to impress on students the novelty of Jean-Luc Godard's jump-cuts in an era of music videos, or the shifting uses of irony on sitcoms in the wake of *The Simpsons*, will recognize the problem that aesthetic innovation is relational.

The diachronic approach to the classroom provided by online comic-book collections goes a long way to addressing notions of change. Specifically, in my classroom I have used group projects to discuss:

i) Historical periodization. The history of American comic books, broken down into historical "ages" by fans, is well-noted for offering almost no analytic validity (Woo 268–79). While there is little agreement among fans and scholars who have adopted fannish terminology about precisely when, for instance, the Golden Age ends and the Silver Age begins, it is clear that comics released in 1950 and those circulated in 1960 are considered to be representative of differing eras. What then can we make of the fact that comics from this period appear so similar to each other? Assigning students a wide range of comic books from periods separated by a decade or more reveals interesting results. Students are quick to note, for example, the way that comic books from these two years are most often collections of short stories, that stories tend to fall into a narrow range of lengths (generally five to eight pages), and that the formal operations of comics pages (number of panels, number of tiers, types of borders, prevalence of captions or sound-effects, word density within panels) is not considerably changed. What, they wonder, is the use of arguing for a different periodization if it does not mark a substantial change in form? Access to a large online repository of comics is ideal for driving questions about the way that we write the historiography of comics.

ii) Changes of focus and emphasis within individual titles. When Archie Andrews debuted as a comic-book character in December 1941 in the pages of *Pep Comics* #22 it was as one of eight stories included in that issue, and the sixth overall. There was, in fact, little to suggest that Archie and his gang would become iconic characters or that they would eventually take over the title, forcing characters like the Hangman, Sergeant Boyle, and Danny in Wonderland into obscurity. The online archive of *Pep Comics* from the 1940s, however, allows students to read the evolution of that comic book over a period of a decade, charting the shifting relations among the features as the Archie stories move towards the front of the book, are featured on the cover, and eventually take over completely. The diachronic approach in this instance lays out the kinds of production issues that comic-book creators faced during a period of rapid audience growth within the industry.

iii) The complicated nature of comic-book continuity. One of the most productive classroom exercises that I have regularly used relies not on the free online comics repositories but makes use of the Marvel Unlimited app.[7] Here I have asked students to read outside of continuity by selecting a run of comics spaced ten years apart. For instance, students have read issues from a single month in the same superhero title in 1963, 1973, 1983, and so on. Reading just six issues, spaced decades apart, can be an intentionally disorienting experience in a genre that has strong soap operatic narrative elements. This exercise challenges students to struggle through the effects of continuity change over time. In a large-cast series like *The Uncanny X-Men*, for instance, readers encounter seemingly inexplicable cast changes, as well as the deaths, rebirths, and transformations of characters and their relations, providing an opportunity to address one of the most unusual narrative effects of serial comic-book series. The same exercise with a title that is more sharply focused on a single character (Spider-Man, for example) generally forces the students to pay greater attention to shifts in formal properties as well.

A significant advantage of the enormity of contemporary online comic-book collections is that it offers so many varied ways to demonstrate shifts in practice within the field through group work and individual assignments, steering students away from a repetitive focus on thematic analyses and towards a very different kind of understanding of comic-book history.

The Open Syllabi Project is a powerful tool that allows us to map the teaching of comics in American colleges and universities beyond the strictly anecdotal. What it demonstrates is the remarkable homogeneity of comics that are taught to students, and the rapid coalescence around a small number of "important" comics that represent an extremely narrow—and completely unrepresentative—slice of total production within the field. Nonetheless, the resources made available to teachers and students by the Digital Comics Museum and Comic Book Plus allow us to develop holistic view of the history of American comic books in a manner that better illuminates the traits that have made comics such an important part of our cultural life. Frankly acknowledging the institutional and ideological biases that structure our teaching, and adopting tools that help us to illuminate their structures, allows us to better serve our students by providing a more complete understanding of the history of the comics field as it developed over time.

NOTES

1. The 1977 *Comic Book Price Guide*, for instance, lists the top ten as: *Marvel Comics* no. 1, *Action Comics* no. 1, *Whiz Comics* no. 1, *Detective Comics* no. 27, *Motion Picture Funnies Weekly* no. 1, *Superman* no. 1, *Batman* no. 1, *Captain America* no. 1, *Action Comics* no. 2, and *Marvel Mystery Comics* no. 2.

2. See, for example, Benjamin Woo's note on DC Entertainment's 2016 pamphlet, *Essential Graphic Novels and Chronology* 2016 (Woo, Benjamin. "What's An Essential Graphic Novel?" *GreatestComicBook.com*, http://www.greatestcomicbook.com/blog/?offset=1456162955558)

3. Both essays are reprinted in Heer and Worcester. Indeed, the entirety of the first two sections of this collection are useful on this point.

4. One of the best critiques of the OSP is offered by its own FAQ section, which discusses data limitations at length. http://opensyllabusproject.org/faq/

5. The OSP gives *Understanding Comics* a count of 935 but also gives the book under its full title, *Understanding Comics: The Invisible Art* an additional 244. The combined score for these two iterations would rank the book 71st overall.

6. In the OSP data, Jack Kirby's highest ranking work comes in at number 512,226.

7. My students have generally been excellent at finding free trial offers for this service.

WORKS CITED

Adorno, Theodor, and Max Horkheimer. *Dialectics of Enlightenment*. Translated by John Cumming. New York: Herder and Herder, 1972.

Althusser, Louis. *Lenin and Philosophy and Other Essays*. Monthly Review Press, 1971.

Arnold, Matthew. *Culture and Anarchy: An Essay in Political and Social Criticism*. London: MacMillan, 1896.

Beaty, Bart. *Comics Versus Art*. Toronto: University of Toronto Press, 2012.

Beaty, Bart, and Benjamin Woo. *The Greatest Comic Book of All Time: Symbolic Capital and the Field of American Comic Books*. New York: Palgrave-MacMillan, 2016.

Bloom, Allan. *The Closing of the American Mind*. New York: Simon and Schuster, 1987.

Bordwell, David. *Making Meaning: Inference and Rhetoric in the Interpretation of Cinema*. Cambridge, MA: Harvard University Press, 1991.

Bourdieu, Pierre. *Distinction: A Social Critique of the Judgement of Taste*. Translated by Richard Nice. Cambridge, MA: Harvard University Press, 1984.

Chabon, Michael. *The Amazing Adventures of Kavalier & Clay*. New York: Random House, 2000.

Cohen, Margaret, *The Sentimental Education of the Novel*. Princeton, NJ: Princeton University Press, 1999.

D'Souza, Dinesh. *Illiberal Education: The Politics of Race and Sex on Campus*. New York: Free Press, 1991.

Gabilliet, Jean-Paul. *Of Comics and Men: A Cultural History of American Comic Books*. Translated by Bart Beaty and Nick Nguyen. Jackson: University Press of Mississippi, 2010.

Gans, Herbert. *Popular Culture and High Culture: An Analysis and Evaluation of Taste*. New York: Basic Books, 1974.

Greenberg, Clement. "The Avant-Garde and Kitsch." *Partisan Review* 6, no. 5 (Fall 1939): 34–49.

Hatfield, Charles. *Hand of Fire: The Comics Art of Jack Kirby*. Jackson: University Press of Mississippi, 2011.

Heer, Jeet, and Kent Worcester. *Arguing Comics: Literary Masters on a Popular Medium*. Jackson: University Press of Mississippi, 2004.

Hirsch, E. D. *Cultural Literacy: What Every American Needs to Know*. New York: Vintage, 1988.

Woo, Benjamin. "An Age-Old Problem: Problematics of Comic Book Historiography". *International Journal of Comic Art* 10, no. 1 (2008): 268–79.

Woo, Benjamin. "What's n Essential Graphic Novel?" *Greatest Comic Book*, http://www.greatestcomicbook.com/blog/?offset=1456162955558

Put Some Light into the World: Interview with Brian Michael Bendis and David Walker

—JOHNNY PARKER II, Animo South Los Angeles High School and Neat-O Comics

Three weeks after the 2018 San Diego Comic Con, I had the chance to sit down and discuss education and diversity in comics with David Walker and Brian Michael Bendis. David Walker is an accomplished comics and film writer who has penned such titles as *Power Man & Iron Fist*, *Occupy Avengers*, *Luke Cage*, *Cyborg*, and *Shaft*. His film works include, but are not limited to, *My Dinner with AJ*, *Damaged Goods*, and *Black Santa's Revenge*. Brian Michael Bendis is a bestselling comics creator who has written *Jinx*, *Torso*, *Powers*, *Ultimate Spider-Man*, *New Avengers*, and *Superman*. Both gentlemen are currently professors at Portland State University, where they teach a course on writing comics. I, Johnny Parker II, am a thirteen-year veteran high school English teacher, as well as a comics writer, my work including titles such as *Black Fist & Brown Hand*, *Broken*, and *Death's a Bitch!* As we began our discussion over Skype, it was fitting that a heatwave was affecting Los Angeles and Portland, just as a political heatwave was dividing the comics community. In the weeks leading up to our interview, several notable comics creators and actresses had been attacked on social media by angry "fans," forcing some to take down their profiles. Inclusion and comics had become a hot button issue, and as someone who has a great deal of respect for David and Brian, I was eager to hear what insights these seasoned creators had to share.

Johnny Parker II: Let's start with representation—as fans, creators, scholars, and educators. How do our roles affect our understandings of comics?

David Walker: For me, it starts out with my role as a fan. As a kid, there definitely was a lack of representation in what I wanted to see and what I really

---

* All interviews in this volume have been edited for clarity and length.

needed to see. Now that I'm an adult and a creator, a lot of what drives me is not only what I wanted to see but what I want to leave for younger people to inspire them. I'm constantly thinking about young people and what they're going to see in comics, and wondering if they will feel as left out as I did. When you're growing up on the playground and everybody's picking who they get to be, you don't get to be anybody because the response is always, "Oh, well, he's white and you're, you know." You're left sitting there moping. To me, it's always about how is it going to impact a young person in a positive way.

Brian Michael Bendis: A lot of people focus on seeing yourself represented, a truth that you know from your world represented on screen or in fiction, but when I was growing up, as a little white boy reading books, I always gravitated to everyone's story that wasn't like mine. I was looking for representation of things that weren't my life. I think that's why I like the *X-Men*. It was filled with a bunch of people, completely different lives, completely different lifestyles, completely different backgrounds, coming together and hanging out. I want to hang out with people that have things to tell me that I would never know. So, I think for those of us who write and teach, it's our job to say, "You know what? This story that is very true. Yeah, put it down on paper because the truth to you will be truthful to someone else." We have to tell our students, "Yeah. You think growing up in your house with your crazy mother isn't interesting, but it is!" Everyone has a crazy mother and that's why people constantly gravitate towards crazy mother stories in fiction. We all relate to it, and even the people who don't will connect with you.

Walker: I would say that as an educator, one of the things that we run into a lot when we tell our students to tell your story and find the truth, we always hear, "Oh, I don't have anything to say. I don't have a story." And I'm like, "That's a load of crap!" Every single day something interesting happens to you, even something that seems boring and uninteresting can spin into something interesting.

Parker: I can totally relate to that. I teach and the very first thing we do at the beginning year is a creative writing/narrative unit. Every time, my students say, "I don't have anything to write about. My life isn't interesting," and my response is always, "Dude, you're growing up in South LA. That's not everyone's reality. Many people don't experience that, but many people want to read about that. They want to read about the world they don't live in. You have something to say."

Bendis: Exactly.

Parker: Speaking of giving readers insights to other perspectives, comic books, comic strips, and cartoons in general have played important and often unsung roles in history and politics. How do you see your role in public conversation around policy and politics?

Bendis: Politics is poison to me other than writing about politics being a poison to society. It's hard to generate an empathetic story about politics. What I end up writing about a lot is society. Politics is a part of society, but what I see in society. Sometimes I'll see something in society and I'm like: "Well, that's bullshit. I'm going to write about it." And a year later I look at it and go, oh, look what was bothering me and thank God I had an outlet. So that's how I see politics in my writing. Also, because I'm a little older, I'm aware of myself. There's some things I'm more aware of now, that I may not have been aware of as a younger creator. And I try to tell that to our students as well. . . . I know that as a father of two black girls, I'm constantly looking to do whatever I can, just put stuff out there that'll make the representation a little better. And like I'm not saying I'm fixing everything and obviously I'm not. But you know what, that's where Miles Morales came from. After seeing what is fed to my children from other authors. I can't help but go, okay, these are the flavors they're getting. But there are so many more flavors, and these flavors that I've seen and observed as their father would be a lot of fun to put out there. My work, it's less about politics. I see a society filled with families of different shapes, sizes, and racial mixes. I have a multiracial family, so I write a lot about multiracial households and adoption; it's a very normal thing that can easily be demystified to people who don't understand it, but it will also be there for my kids and other kids to read and go, "Oh, this is like us."

Walker: I've been accused of having a political agenda in my writing. It's actually not a political agenda. It's a human agenda. It's a storytelling agenda. As of late, I've been writing nonfiction stuff. I have a book coming out about the life of Frederick Douglass, and you know, you can't write about Frederick Douglass and not write about the Civil War. You can't not write about slavery. You can't not write about all these things. Is that political? No, that's true. That's America. And so then the question is which truth am I going to tell? Am I going to tell the slanted truth that we often get? When I'm talking about the Civil War, am I going to just gloss over it and say it's about state's rights, or am I going to get into the truth? The sad thing is, the articles of secession for every state that left the union and joined the confederacy is public record, and every single state that left the union said the same thing: "We're leaving because we want to keep our slaves." There's nothing political about putting that in your comic. One of the things we talk about, as educators and as creators, is that we have to find our truth with a capital T. But if you're telling a story that's nonfiction, where you have to find the truth free of propaganda and rhetoric, it becomes very simple—this is what happened, this is what they wrote, and this is what they did. The truth is always more compelling and stranger than fiction. People are always going to read between the lines, and they're always going to fill in their own blanks. I can't control that. Brian can't control that. You can't control that. All you can control is how you paint that picture. Then they are going to see what they see. They're going to read what they read.

Parker: I'm curious what role your education plays in your work. How has becoming an educator impacted your creative journey?

Bendis: First of all, most people in their lives on a creative journey know the journey never ends, that school is never out. You never graduate, it just continues on. So, I decided to become an educator. I've accumulated all this information—let me help those behind me and give it to them because it took me a long time to gather all this. Let me give it to you. That way you can get to a higher place than I got. The other thing is that we're constantly evolving as creators, even while we're teaching, the teaching is part of our evolution. It gets us back to basics and it gets us thinking about the things that we're teaching. As an educator that writes, you'll find that your friends that are writers will be a little lost in the weeds because they don't think of the basics as often as educators. We're constantly thinking about, why is my character doing this? Honestly, sometimes writers can get lost in that, because there are things they are thinking in loftier terms. But the basic tenets of writing, we revisit them every day for every class. It makes us do it right.

Walker: I've only been teaching a little over two years. You know, Brian was one of the two people that dragged me into it and you know, I've learned different things. I'm constantly learning stuff from Brian and other writers, asking them questions and the difference being, okay, I'm a published writer, I'm an educator, but I still want to learn stuff. You should never be done learning.

Parker: In your classrooms, you have a very powerful presence upon your students. Were there any classes or courses or teachers that had a big impact on you, that helped develop you into the person you are now?

Bendis: When I went to the Cleveland Institute of Art, they didn't have a comic-book program; they didn't understand what the hell I wanted to do. It hadn't made it into the culture like it has right now. Now, I think it'd be much easier to walk up to your professors and say, "I have a dream and it involves comics." But back then it was—I had a professor that I showed Dave McKean's work on *Black Orchid*. He equated it to the cartoon strip *Andy Capp*. And I was like, "Oh, you don't see the difference." That's a bummer. So, they gave me an independent study and let me sit in a corner. Now we're trying to be the teachers that weren't there for us. I'm literally trying to teach the comic-book, graphic-novel class that we wanted. Like, here's all the information I wish someone would have turned to me and said, "Here's how you do this, this, this, and this. Go!" I don't mean this in any sarcastic way, but there are teachers that helped me because they were great and there are teachers that helped me because they sucked. And both of them inspired the way we teach our class.

Walker: I had a very similar thing, but it occurred when I was younger. I had a teacher early on look me in the eye and tell me I wasn't going to amount to anything, that gets into other issues of race and class during the 1970s. It still scars me to this day when I'm struggling with something, I hear this woman's voice telling me I would never amount to anything. But I was fortunate enough in high school that I had a teacher who recognized that I had a problem. He pulled me aside and said, "You're smarter than what your grade reflects. What's the problem?" And it was the first time a teacher ever asked me what's the problem. I said, "I don't care about the stuff your teaching. I've already learned this before." He said, "What do you want to know about?" I remember this so clearly because it was 1985 and the tenth anniversary of the fall of Saigon. In the high school I was going to, there were a lot of Southeast Asian refugees, and I said, "We should be learning about these kids that are in this school, that are here with us right now. We should be learning about the Vietnam War." And he looked at me and he said, "Okay, you teach us." And that was the beginning. I was a junior in high school, and that was the first time that concept of independent study kicked in and that you can be learning something other than what the school taught. And now I'm a huge fan of the concept that there's more than one way to learn. When we were kids, you couldn't do a book report on a graphic novel. Now you can. To be a part of the process of not only teaching and using those as teaching tools, but helping educate people to create their own is like a dream come true. When I think back to my old high school, back then there wasn't a single comic related thing in the school library. Now they have an entire bracket. It's awesome.

Parker: In my own classroom, I try to use graphic novels on a regular basis. Recently, I used *My Black Friend* by Alan Sitomer to help teach storytelling structure as well as different forms of oppression to my students. And so, my question for you gentlemen is how do you use graphic narratives in your classrooms to help teach students?

Bendis: Quite a few ways. Number one, their first assignment is autobiographical. They have to do a deep dive into themselves and into the art form. We tell them to write that anecdote that always kills at a party. Tell that story that represents you that has a beginning, middle, and end. It allows us to read their stuff and see where they are as writers and who they are as people. And then the second thing that we do, which might seem like a little show and tell-y, but it actually works and blankets the entire semester, we make them bring in their absolute favorite graphic novel and their absolute least favorite graphic novel. We take our work out of the running, to spare them the instincts of being the smart ass who hates my *Avengers* run or tries to kiss our butts, like, "Oh. Mr. Walker, *Shaft* is the best thing." We're off limits. But we tell them to bring in your favorite and least favorite graphic novel. And get in front of the class, introduce yourself and talk about both books. Again, we get to know them a little bit better. We get to know where they are in their graphic novel literacy program at PSU. The students are encouraged to talk about what they like and don't like, and what's fascinating about this is sometimes the same graphic novels will be brought in as someone's favorite and someone else's least favorite. So, then they feel that they have to get up there and defend this, and it's always *Watchmen* or *Walking Dead*.

Walker: Someone will say: "I love *Watchmen*." And someone else will say, "This is the worst thing I've ever read."

Bendis: Yeah, and I remember someone had both and I was left there thinking: "Ooh, I wonder which is which. I have literally no idea what they're going say." Also, what's fascinating, and I tell this to any author that will listen, almost every semester at least two people bring up the work of the same author as their favorite and least favorite. Like this author brought them to the heights of heights and the same person disappoints the shit out of them, but the point is that they are now engaging us in their conversation about graphic novels. Often they bring in manga and other sub-genres that we may not have the encyclopedic knowledge that we have on other stuff. So, we're now opening up the conversation to what did you grow up with. Sometimes it's not even a physical comic, it's a webcomic, or they only know one manga and they love it so much, it made them want to make them. All of these conversations get brought into the classroom, and then the punchline of course is that we're now telling you this truth.

Walker: And the only way you're going to get that feeling is to complete it. For better or worse. You've got to complete it. As difficult as it is to struggle and to get through, it's easier to do that, than to live with the regret of having given up. The moment you give up, you don't necessarily understand that. In terms of graphic novels, we use Will Eisner's books in teaching. For me, it's about making sure that students also understand the history of the medium. So, we show a couple of documentaries about the history, because a lot of people come into loving the medium because of a love of another medium. They love all the Marvel movies or they love a show like the *Walking Dead* and then they discover comics. But their knowledge of comics doesn't go quite as far back as it needs. A lot of it is just about also making sure that there's literacy, that they understand not just the language of comics, the art of comics, but there's also an understanding of the history. One of the reasons Will Eisner is important in what we teach is because he was a part of almost the entire history.

Bendis: Will Eisner has a very interesting journey as a creator with representation. He actually had severely problematic representation issues with some of his most classic works and then addressed them decades later after the war. He came back and said, "Why was I drawing people in such a horrible caricature?" And then he did a whole graphic novel about Oliver Twist, which deals with the dual nature of the moneylender, the Jewish character. I'm Jewish, and so this struck a chord with me—that Eisner did a whole graphic novel trying to figure out why this great author did the same thing. Eisner asked the question: why was there an evil Jewish character in the middle of this great work of art by someone who clearly has observed the world through better eyes, right? So, here Eisner was raving about, "Why did I do it? Why did he do it? Why is it even in us?" And he was just asking the question, which is so much more than most people can ever get to. That gets us back to truth. Are we being truthful with ourselves, are we writing our truth, are you writing your truth? Then, it goes to the Will Eisner story of when he figured it out. He went to the army, and he met them, he met black people. And he went: "Oh wait, I'm way off!" Immediately, he tried to fix everything he did wrong. What that tells you is, go learn. Go out there, get out of your skin, get off of Twitter. That's not what the real world is going through. Talk to people. If you don't know something but you're fascinated by it, go learn whatever you want to know. Whatever that culture is, I promise you, people will share it with you. Anything you want to know about, there's someone who's the expert in it, and they're dying to tell you about it. Go find out and you'll just become a better creator.

Walker: A better human being, a better member of the world. The other thing too is that then Eisner goes into education. We could argue that he mastered his craft in terms of being a creator. He tackled his own foibles, his own weaknesses, started to reassess what the truth was for him, and then he went out and was like, "I need to start teaching this to other people." Ended up going to school, visual arts, hoping to take courses with them. But that was the late seventies, early eighties. That was the beginning of comics education in America, and he's one of the founding parents of that. So again, it's very fascinating and it's always interesting because over half of the classes we teach, they're like we never even heard of this guy. And to me it's like if you're studying film and you never heard of Orson Welles, never seen *Bicycle Thieves*, or never watched a Kurosawa movie, in my mind, you're not that serious about your craft, even as great a filmmaker as Spielberg is, Orson Welles made *Citizen Kane*. If you want to be a filmmaker and haven't seen that, there's a problem.

Bendis: Well, we're getting to that age where we bring up *The Matrix* and they refer to it as a classic. My point is that also, this Will Eisner documentary is highly recommended because it tells the story of a creator who made problematic choices and then realized that and then asked the question out loud.

Parker: As you mention, Will Eisner asking that question out loud, it makes me wonder how he would have asked that question in today's world. Would it have been in a 280-character tweet or maybe a picture posted to Instragram? Today's technology allows for direct access between creators and audiences through blog comments, Twitter, Facebook, various social media. In your professional opinions, what are the advantages and disadvantages of interacting with your audience and even students through social media?

Bendis: When I grew up, I was the only kid reading comics. My friends were happy for me, but they weren't into comics. So now, no matter what thing you're into, you can reach out and there's someone in the world who is into it too. It's a very special thing when you find that connection, but when the group turns into a mob, that's when things get awful. I'm grateful in a way that I've experienced some of the worst of it because I can stand up. I've experienced the feeling of Twitter just becoming a Nazi rally in my face and it feels like the world has shifted. There's positive and negative.

I will tell you, for someone who has experienced death threats and all the negative that you can do, it's doesn't outweigh having the world come together and celebrate Superman or celebrate Miles Morales. My point is that there's a lot of darkness, but I'm telling you—the light is every day. It's constant. It's all over the world. People are connected through characters, through truth, through love of craft, just a love of comics. It doesn't even have to be representation; it's just, I love looking at word balloons and you do too and I just want to share that feeling with you. It's so intimate and I know how special that feeling is.

Walker: I agree with all of that and you know, to add a little extra to it, I think back to the things that my grandparents, my great-grandparents, my great-great-grandparents went through and all I have to do is stop and think about the fact that when my great-great-grandfather was five his mother was sold to another plantation and he never saw her again. That's a difficult life. The fact that some people on Twitter hate my guts and are calling me nasty words. Forget about it. Sometimes the stings hurt a little bit more, but at the end of the day, they're just words.

Bendis: I'd just like to go on record and say I regret my entire answer after hearing his answer.

Walker: Let me reject negativity and find some positivity, let me put some light into the world because that's ultimately, I can't speak for Brian, but what I am doing is I'm trying to put a little light into a very dark world. I look around at all my friends who have kids, and it goes back to what I said earlier, how can I help make this world a slightly better place for young people.

Bendis: I'm literally the writer of Superman and my job is to write the character that reminds you that everything's okay, and that can be difficult. That can be, you know, when everyone's yelling at each other all the time about everything. Again that gets back to our initial job of what do I teach young creators. I'm not backing down, and I'm not changing my tune, and I'm not going to not create what I want to create, or write what I want to write. I'm so often reminded from good people where the good path is. Let's just keep going. Keep going.

My point is to teach by example, not only if you're writing but by behavior. I really try not to get into Twitter battles or get down in the mud. The conversations up here are all about truth and beauty. You guys want to be part of it. Come on in, we're having a great time.

Parker: Given everything that's happening in the world today, what shifts in comics culture do you see affecting your creative works?

Bendis: Well, I find myself writing more universal hope, more good guys winning because you definitely see that we're not getting that in the real world. So let's give them something that they're not getting, which is Superman will win, the bad guy's going to jail. It's also just, you know, more analyzing. I find my work getting more intimate, writing less about the world and more about people relating to each other. Maybe having an intimate moment. I know that it has a lot to do with my life and my lifestyle. I like intimate relationships, so that seems more powerful to me than going, "The president sucks." So, I'm constantly looking to tell a story of a character that I'm not seeing every day. I figure you want to take your break to take from the crazy in the real world and come visit our crazy.

Walker: I think that hope thing is such a big thing to me these days because there's such a feeling of hopelessness. There's a project that I've been working on for several years that I've been slowly but surely building, and then, after this last election, I was like, I can't do this project right now. If I do it, I have to find a way to give it more hope, because there's just not enough of it. In fact, Brian and I had a conversation very recently. We were laughing, we were chopping some stuff up and throwing some ideas back and forth, and I came up with this thing that was kind of dark and cynical, and he was like, hey, that's great idea, but here's why it's not going to work. I had my arms crossed and didn't really want to hear it. But there was a truth there. And the truth was, not only do we need the hope, but as writers, we think we've read it all. Yeah, we read all the *Harry Potter* books and we get that version of Hero's journey, and we've seen the original *Star Wars* movies. So, we get that version of heroes doing that. We've read Spider-Man, you know, but out there, there's some kid, maybe ten, twelve years old, maybe even a little younger. They haven't read those books yet. They haven't discovered that with great power comes great responsibility, and we're not writing to middle-aged readers so much as we're writing to these young people and giving them that sense of hope, especially in a time where there isn't nearly enough.

Bendis: But at the same time, I love telling students: "You pissed man? Then punk rock this comic. Just vomit on the page, scream your head off." I do it because I feel like I'm kind of lying a little bit, because yeah, I write hope and I also wrote a book called *Scarlet*, which is about a young woman who is on the streets of Portland, and she started the next American revolution because of the corruption of the police department pushed her and pushed her and pushed her until it pushed so hard that it started a revolution. So, I'm writing on the alternate history where we've had enough, so I'm doing both. But even in that, I feel it is hopeful. So, going back to telling the students these things, write what you know but also write what you want.

Parker: How have you seen comics studies change over the years?

Bendis: Over the eight years I've been teaching, and I know it's completely anecdotal, but it's also undeniable that the makeup of the class has shifted. At the beginning it was about 80 percent dudes and now it's about 70 percent women.

Walker: Yeah.

Bendis: And for Portland, it's pretty ethnically diverse, and with that comes us talking to each other differently, us communicating about creativity differently. The comics industry is gonna be interesting in about ten years. Look who's taking the class, look who's interested. Of these twenty-five people, if two and a half of them make it, there's a better chance that two and a half of them are women. This is interesting.

Walker: I think it was the first semester that I taught with Brian. One of those students is now an editor at Oni Press, and there's another student who's an associate or assistant editor at Dark Horse. There's a student that I had that is now working in production at Dark Horse. Brian taught Josh Williamson. I would say that the last year, four semesters, there's a lot of women, a lot of transgender women in the class, and it's just fascinating because, you know, there's now schools with master's degree programs in comics. And you realize, if there's a true future within this industry, the groundwork is being sewn right now.

And, it reminds me of like if you studied film history, things really shifted in the late sixties, early seventies. And that was when the first serious film studies program started in the universities here in the US. The students started making the films, so you got your Coppolas, your Spielbergs and your Lucas and that's what you got. And so, like ten years from now, we're going to see a lot of that coming out of comics. We're going to start seeing,

"So-and-so graduated with their MFA in comics from University of Oregon or whatever school is teaching it in California." And, I think that there's a very bright future in that regard. And I'll share this with you because this is sort of along those same lines. Recently, there was a third-grade class that asked me to come in. They have a comic book club/class where they make their own comics. So, I came in for the day as the guest instructor. The teacher was there and they had parent volunteers, but none of them knew about comics and none of them knew how to teach comics. I realized in the moment that this is what's missing. You can't hand a third-grade teacher McCloud's *Understanding Comics*. So, I started looking at all the books on how to create comics and I realized there isn't anything out there.

And so I've been thinking about that a lot lately; we need to get to a point where we can teach teachers to be more literate about comics. Comics is such a strong visual medium, but you're not going to be able to start out drawing like John Romita or drawing like John Buscema, so let's look at how we teach visual composition and tell kids that stick figures are fine.

Right now, there's two types of teachers teaching the comic studies programs. There's people like Brian and myself who are working professionals, and then there's more like the theoretical instructors that have never created a comic in their life and, they're breaking out *Maus* and *Persepolis* and going, "Okay, so we're going to do something like this!" And that's starting a little steep. Let's look at *Hyperbole and a Half* and talk about how that's a bit more easy to work with.

Parker: You talked about how your classrooms have changed. You see more women, more trans folk, more people of color in general. So, it's a two-part question. One, what do you think has caused this change? And number two, how do we continue this change?

Bendis: I know for a fact that the representation that we put into the books matters. The Milestone Comics guys were doing it before us. There's always been someone fighting this fight, but we need more characters like Miles Morales, Riri Williams, Kamala Khan. The conversation about these characters riled up a bunch of people, but it also made a bunch of people go, "Hey, there is a place for me. There is a place for my voice. And you know, God bless Brian, he's doing the best he can, but I'm a black creator, and I'm going to do him one better." I'm all for this.

At the same time, Kelly Sue Deconnick and everyone around her making The Carol Corps not just a beautiful fan thing, but a, "Hey! Comics are for women. Comics are for women creators!" There is no debate. This is a fact, and the door is open. In the few years since, I have felt this beautiful rush of female energy in every facet of our creative field, and it's great.

Walker: I'll add to that. So, I just got back from San Diego Comic-Con. This was my nineteenth year going, and my first year going, you hardly ever saw any obviously black people or black women for that matter. But if you saw like a black man or a black creator, it was almost like we would avoid eye contact. There were a lot of people that acted as if, well, if I acknowledged my own blackness or your blackness, then I'm not going to belong here anymore, and I'm not that sort of person; twenty years ago, I was reaching out to everybody. That's how I met Robert and Jeremy Love and Dawud Anyabwile back then known as David Sims. Him and his brother did a comic called *Brother Man*. I'm reaching out and connecting with these people, and somewhere along the lines is how I met Dwayne McDuffie and Denys Cowan. And in going back to what Brian said about the Carol Corps, suddenly there was this level of empowerment where you felt like it's okay not only for me to be in this space, but it's okay for me to be seen talking to other people like myself. Whereas before there was sort of this fear like someone was going to say, "Oh, you don't belong here."

So, the last few years we've done the Black Heroes Matter flash mobs at San Diego, and this year was such an amazing thing. Every time I saw a black person on the convention floor, I stopped and talked to them, and I was like, "Hey, do you know about the flash mob this year?" Most of them didn't know. I explained it to them, and I'd also tell them about a pop-up event that was happening outside of the convention. And then I said, "I hope you don't mind me interrupting you, but you know, we're building a community here and I want you to know that, as far as I'm concerned, you're part of this community if you want to be part of it." It's about not being afraid to say that.

Going back to what Brian said about women creators, I want to work with the best creators, and what I'm discovering is that some of the best creators possible are people who've been left outside of our industry for a long time.

Bendis: Yeah. But also there's the Black Heroes Matter movement matters for this simple reason. Comic creators are faceless and even with social media, no one ever particularly knows what anyone looks like. So, you may very well be David Walker's biggest fan and not know what he looks like. I had this experience with another creator, who I was working with, who is a very successful mainstream creator, who happens to be black, but they don't have a black-sounding name. In this one instance, when we were signing together, a young creator literally didn't see us until it was his turn in line, and when we saw us, he was stunned. You could see his whole world had shifted right in front of us. And it's not just, hey, we're here, it's like you can make it too. The door's open, come on in, and some people just don't know that until they see it. So that's why I love the Black Heroes Matter flash mobs because I've seen the power of visibility with my own eyes.

Walker: This year they did rally for Rose. Nerds of Color did a rally for Kelly Marie Tran who plays Rose in *Star Wars: The Last Jedi*, and I didn't know about it till after the fact, but you know, I saw all these people with their Rose t-shirts and I asked, "Where do I get one?" I just bought one. I was talking to Keith Chow, who was the guy who organized the rally for Rose, and he didn't say anything to me about this at the time, but then I read an interview with him where he said: "Oh yeah, it was David Walker and the others that did the Black Heroes Matter that motivated me to do the rally." This is what I'm talking about, in the face of all these people that are trying to tell us we don't belong. It's like you gotta stand up and say, "Yeah, we do."

Bendis: So, going back to your question, we need more of everybody's pitching in representing their truth, no matter what it is, where you come from, you're helping create a stew of truth, a diversity of truth, a diversity of perspective and experience. That's what we need more of. You need everyone's experience and everyone's perspective.

In the last few years, we've seen the shift. Now I can't even imagine what it's going to look like in the next five years. Look who's in our class and I happen to know there are classes all over the country. They're doing this now, right? That's why we're having this discussion. What's it going to look like six years, ten years from now, when these creators are now part of the pool? That's why we teach. I want everyone to have a real chance. I want more people to have a chance. The chance out of the gate is still not equal, so as educators we try to do everything we can to level that playing field.

PART II

COMICS PEDAGOGY IN PRACTICE

Every day, students of all ages sit in classrooms that are shaped formally and informally by the power of comics. From wayward doodles in the margins of pages to pedagogical moves to shift the role of comics beyond these margins, image-based meaning-making is an integral part of some students' lives. For a growing number of teachers—from elementary educators to professors engaged in graduate seminars—comics have become a powerful force for how students are taught and how complex ideas are made manifest. In our ongoing work presenting workshops on comics pedagogy and through continually learning from the scholarship and shared lessons of other comics scholars, what comics *in practice* actually look like is often muddled. There are a plethora of educators who are excited and convinced that comics pedagogy can transform the possibilities of classrooms but who are seeking further support and guidance in taking the step toward fully engaging in a comics pedagogy.

The six chapters in this section focus on the *practice* of teaching and learning with comics in classrooms. Spread across various different contexts, these contributors share very different approaches to what comics *mean* and how they are a part of the instructional goals for the classroom. Importantly, these chapters also center comics in several key ways. Both Ebony Flowers Kalir and Nick Sousanis consider how *producing* comics can shape how educators approach the learning goals in their classrooms. As scholars that have also produced comics professionally, both Kalir and Sousanis speak to the role of production in their capacities as artists, authors, educators, and scholars. Working hand in hand with these production-centered chapters, the contributions from Ben Bolling, Benjamin Villarreal, and James Kelley focus on how comics function as texts for various—and interdisciplinary—subjects. From analyzing comics for lessons tied to science literacy to connecting texts to Victorian literature to exploring the transmedia motifs *across* various instantiations of Batman, these chapters apply very different pedagogical uses to the comics medium within classrooms. This variety is one we want to underscore within this volume's vision of a comics pedagogy; there is no single, "right" way to teach and use comics within the classroom. Finally, influential comic book force Lynda Barry reflects on the role of pedagogy within her own classroom practices as professor; her words here complement the varied nature across the chapters in this section and her diverse array of publications.

Despite our emphasis for this section on contexts and approaches to teaching, we want to offer two guiding caveats for readers. First, although these chapters emphasize the *practice* of teaching with comics, this is not divorced from the powerful theories of learning and instruction that undergird these authors' classroom decisions and plans. In fact, we want to underscore these chapters as synthesizing the interwoven relationship of powerful *praxis*, the integration of theory, practice, and reflection (Freire). Pedagogical growth in educators comes from theory-building, applying new ideas within classrooms, and adjusting one's teaching from these experiences. This cyclical process is one we name to recognize the intellectual traditions of teachers as knowledge producers and not simply as disseminators of someone else's curriculum.

Building from this caveat that *all* teachers possess the capacity to build meaningful new dimensions to our understanding of comics pedagogy, we want to recognize that there is not a one-size-fits-all approach for using comics. As such, we did not seek and these authors do not offer specific lesson plans, handouts, or other materials for immediate adaptation. Put simply, teaching successfully hinges on relationships. Knowing the needs of students and the conditions under which a class is taught shapes the specific texts, prompts, pace, and atmosphere through which a (comics) pedagogy will develop. In this spirit, we hope these chapters inspire and act as guiding beacons for readers to find their own way through the varied pathways on which comics can be leveraged in classrooms.

On Copying

—EBONY FLOWERS KALIR, University of Wisconsin–Madison

THE LIVELINESS PARTLY COMES FROM NOT KNOWING WHAT KIND OF PICTURE YOU ARE DRAWING AT THE SAME TIME YOU ARE DRAWING. IT ALSO COMES FROM SHARING THIS EXPERIENCE WITH OTHER PEOPLE.

THIS KIND OF COPYING GIVES STUDENTS A CHANCE TO GET TO KNOW THE DIFFERENCE BETWEEN DRAWING TO WATCH WHAT HAPPENS AND DRAWING TO ILLUSTRATE A PREMEDITATED THOUGHT OR MENTAL IMAGE.

 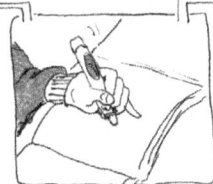 

THIS DISTINCTION, WHICH I LEARNED FROM MY TEACHER, LYNDA BARRY, IS THE PRIMARY BASIS FOR HOW I MAKE COMICS AND TEACH A MAKING COMICS COURSE.

FOR THIS ROUND, YOU WILL CO-CREATE THE PICTURE. THIS MEANS NO ONE IS LEADING THE DRAWING.

THERE'S NO TALKING. YOU CAN'T DISCUSS WHAT YOU'RE GOING TO DRAW. YOU'LL FIGURE THAT OUT AS YOU TANDEM DRAW.

"THIS GUIDELINE HELPS CARRY THE STATE BETWEEN THINKING AND NON-THINKING OVER TO LOOKING AT A PICTURE. I AIM TO TEACH STUDENTS THE DIFFERENCE BETWEEN SEEING A PICTURE AND WATCHING IT."

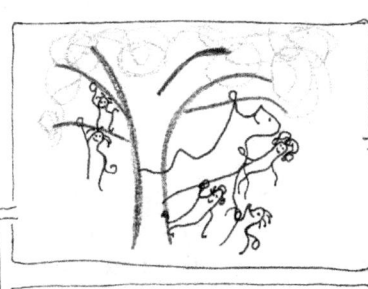

"THE LINES A PERSON DRAWS TO MAKE A COMIC CREATE A PICTORIAL LANGUAGE THAT DIFFERS FROM SPEECH OR TEXT. TANDEM DRAWING IS AN INTIMATE CHANCE TO EXPERIENCE AND KNOW ANOTHER PERSON'S PARTICULAR LINE AND HOW THEY MOVE TO CREATE THEM. SOME PEOPLE CALL THEIR UNIQUE WAY OF DRAWING A LINE THEIR STYLE. LYNDA BARRY LIKENS IT TO AN ACCENT. AN IMPORTANT PART OF MAKING COMICS IS LEARNING HOW TO TOLERATE YOUR OWN AND OTHER PEOPLE'S PARTICULAR PICTORIAL ACCENTS."

Thinking in Comics:
All Hands-On in the Classroom

—NICK SOUSANIS, San Francisco State University

Comics let us say things we can't in other forms. This principle is at the core of my approach to teaching comics, which focuses on the form's potential for multimodal communication and on how the combination of textual and visual elements has the ability to unlock both new ideas and creative responses to old problems. Therefore, even in the more traditional theory or education-based courses I have taught, in which my students tend to describe themselves as nondrawers, I always put hands-on comics-making front and center. By taking these novice drawers through various comics-making exercises, I want to give students a first-hand understanding of what the form is able to express while also showing them how much more capable they are at visual communication than they realized before entering the classroom. These lessons, I hope, are carried with my students into their other classes and beyond—as future teachers, scholars, and even sometimes practicing cartoonists.

Before delving into the specifics of these courses, I want to note how my prior noncomics teaching influenced what I would do in my comics classrooms. First, as a teenager right up until my final year of doctoral school, I taught tennis to players of all levels and ages. It is, to say the least, imperative that practice be a significant part of learning on a tennis court—you can't talk about how to hit a forehand—you have to move your arm, your feet, watch how someone else's body does the motion. Theory isn't unimportant—I introduce analogies such as likening the way air flows over an airplane wing that provides lift in relationship to how topspin makes a ball dive—but ultimately this is something you have to feel to understand. My other primary teaching experience was an undergraduate public speaking course at Wayne State University that I taught for several years. I saw my role as not unlike what I did on the tennis courts: I provided structure, prompts, feedback, coaching, and lots of encouragement, but so much of the time I sat in the back of the classroom as each student performed, and I watched them grow on their own over the term. (I might add, on a theoretical note, as a doctoral student, I was quite taken by Jacques Rancière's *The Ignorant Schoolmaster*, which drew lessons from the story of an eighteenth-century schoolteacher who couldn't speak the language of his students and how this acknowledged ignorance on the part of the authority figure led to an emancipatory learning experience for the students.)

Despite these earlier experiences and a strong belief in the importance of making as essential to understanding, it still took me a little longer to fully institute this practice into my comics courses. Initially I think I treated hands-on practice as more of an add-on than a central focus. And perhaps with comics, where they are perceived as less than "academic," I felt a certain defensiveness, a need to come to their rescue with heaps of theory. In my first comics and education class at Teachers College, I conceived of a number of exercises (which remain part of my repertoire and will be discussed later)—activities to get students comfortable drawing and making their own explorations to connect back to theory. They were a lot of fun, but in looking back, I clearly framed them as supplement. The third time teaching the course, some of the texts we were planning to use were backordered and late in arriving, so I flipped the course and started with the comics-making activities. A few weeks into the course, when the texts still hadn't arrived, I started to apologize to the students, "sorry that we hadn't learned anyth—" And I caught myself. Here I was in the midst of drawing a doctoral dissertation as comics to make an argument that this form could offer as much intellectual rigor as its textual equivalent, and in my own class, while I had them making, I was undervaluing it—seeing the process of making as support and not as core.

And that was a profound realization.

Through these simple comics-making exercises we'd been doing together, they had been teaching themselves and gained a tremendous wealth of understanding that, I believe, far exceeded what they would've attained at this point from readings. One example prompt: tell the story of how you got here (interpreting this as the student wished—the literal commute to the university or how their life path landed them there), and do so in two ways: a three-panel comic strip and also as a two-page comic. What sorts of decisions do you make when working in the three-panel format that you did differently in two pages? What were the challenges of moving one from another? What kind of affordances did you have with two pages in contrast with three panels? Not only could they compare their two distinct versions, but there was a whole classroom of students who'd all tackled the project from their unique vantage point, and now we could look at all of these together, for inspiration, to get ideas, learn new strategies, discover things that weren't working, and see clearly how much they already knew about making comics unfettered by any expectation of a proper way to go about it. Those experiences were revelatory and set the stage for them to engage with scholarship and read professional works with new eyes. They were hungry for new material to inspire their own works and filled with a desire to transfer this understanding to their students.

From this crucial realization, I would make practice the first thing—and in all the different settings I've taught comics, we start with practice and continually circle back to it as the foundation for deeper understanding. In my experience, all of my students are able to make comics and frequently really interesting ones—no matter what their drawing skills—and that practice aids them greatly in getting a handle on the medium. They hit on sophisticated concepts in their making that they later are attuned to observe in the comics we study. And they have so much fun—something we shouldn't undervalue. Play matters and is too infrequently present in our classrooms. These activities reawakened something every student did as a child. In regards to assessment, for all the quick activities I have them do in class or at home in their sketchbooks, I evaluate entirely on completion, not skill. They are encouraged to try everything. Inventiveness, curiosity, and willingness to vigorously immerse themselves matter most. By making the class a space for them to play—I watch them take risks, work harder than I asked them to do because it's theirs and there's a deep sense of satisfaction in seeing it done well. And I suspect they make discoveries many of them might not if it was about their grade.

To accompany some of the practical exercises in this chapter, I want to share two students' personal perspectives, one here and the other at the close. This is from a student in my introductory comics course at San Francisco State University. Kyleigh, a first time comics maker, reflects on the experience of making her final project, a personal narrative:

> I had never made a comic before, and I was surprised by the sense of accomplishment I felt after using this medium. As an English major, I love to use language to tell stories. . . . Drawing pictures that represented my story actually forced me to manipulate my language. It created a cycle of positive feedback that surprisingly strengthened my skills as both a writer and illustrator. In the beginning, I was really nervous about my comic because I am a perfectionist and I do not feel like I am a particularly good artist; I feared that I would get so hung up on how imperfect my drawings were that I would lose sight of the story. The opposite actually happened. The meaning of my comic became much more significant to me than my sketching, and I finally realized that that's one of the benefits of comics—it does not have to be hyper-realistic to be a successful story.

Drawing comics allows you to really sprawl your thoughts out on paper. Writing allows me to translate my experiences into feelings and words, but drawing my experiences forces me to reflect on how the physical images of my memories influences the way I think and act. In the case of my particular narrative, I think comics' ability to generalize a story was very effective because this is a relevant, commonplace occurrence.

Kyleigh's experience rings true of what I've seen throughout all of my classes—no matter their skill level or prior experience drawing, the act of making affords deep insights. (See figure 1.)

And with that in mind, let's take a tour through some of the specifics.

Because comics accommodate such disparate kinds of drawing styles and skills (consider as a pairing of extremes, the lush, dense hyper-realism of J. H. Williams III to the spare poetry comics of John Porcellino), I've shied away from focusing much on drawing technique. This extends even to my more recent courses within the comics studies program at San Francisco State that are designated "Making Comics." Instead, I'm always looking for ways for students to engage and play with form, to give them a range of ways of using comics to express what they want to say. To this end, I find that constraint-based exercises, as with the three-panel and two-page example above, help them explore and hone in on what works best for them. The constraint limits the focus to one particular aspect of working in comics, but the prompts are open enough to allow all sorts of material from the individual student to make its way onto the page. And it does.

While I prefer to come up with my own assignments, I definitely borrow and adapt from others whenever I can. Cartoonist-teachers Jessica Abel and Matt Madden have come up with tons of great exercises (available in their book *Drawing Words-Writing Pictures* and website of the same name, as well as Matt's "OuBaPo" constraint-based comics-generating rules). I'm a big fan of their brilliant, massive collaborative activity "Panel Lottery," where Abel and Madden provide three characters that anyone can easily draw on model, and prompt participants to draw on three different index cards, one, two, or all three of the characters doing or saying something on each card. The group (or separate groups within a class) then works together to create a coherent narrative from these randomly generated "panels." It's a fascinating activity that offers terrific insight into how to construct a sequential narrative from otherwise disconnected scenes. In all the times I've run it, it's been a wonderful way to get students drawing with no barrier to entry, and working and laughing together as they learn about comics! It's also the sort of thing future

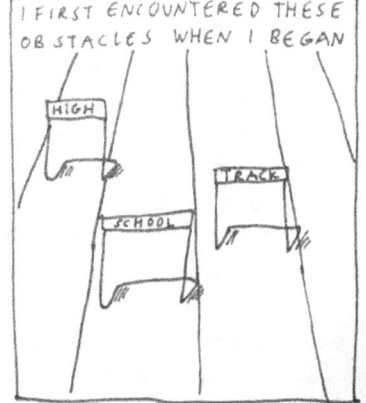

Figure 1a: Kyleigh's final

Figure 1b: Kyleigh

teachers latch onto to see how they can use it with their own students and invent variations for their particular purposes.

The first time I taught my comics class, I wanted an exercise that got students quickly thinking about the entire space of the comics page as a maker does without them being stymied by a lack of drawing skills and confidence. I came up with "Grids and Gestures," which has taken on a larger life beyond my classrooms (I've done it in numerous workshops and as a Twitter challenge (#gridsgestures, for detailed instructions www.spinweaveandcut.com/grids-gestures, Sousanis, 2015) and it has become the touchstone for how I set the tone in my classes. To summarize in brief, I set it up by having everyone look at the ceiling tiles and other features in the room, and imagine putting them to music. Long notes, staccato beats, all of those time signatures represented by the organization of space. We then bring this back down to the comics page and how in comics, time happens in space. I share examples where page layout is integral to the narrative. Then I instruct them: on a single sheet of paper of any size, organize the space into some sort of grid-esque composition that represents the shape of your day (that day, your average day, a particular day), and rather than drawing *things* in it, inhabit those spaces you've drawn with lines, marks, or gestures that represent what you were up to or how you felt in those moments. I give them about seven minutes to complete it, and then we share and discuss. As with many of my prompts, I try to explain the exercise so that it's deliberately somewhat ambiguous to allow everyone to bring their own take to it but also providing enough structure so that they aren't lost at the same time. Students not only start thinking about the compositional structure of a page, but more importantly they realize how much they all already know about drawing. It's a starting point to begin to get them past the fear of "I can't draw" and to remain open and imaginative in finding their own ways to explore comics creation not limited by a particular conception of what they think drawing should be. I've expanded on this by making it into a diary exercise for them to do over the course of a week. Grids and Gestures sets up other basic conceptual exercises—one where I work with how much expressional content can be in a single line, and more involved exercises using construction paper cutouts to portray relationships with abstract shapes, color, and composition, and moving onward to more general concepts.

Before outlining the other exercises, I want to highlight some key activities I do that aren't specifically comics-making but still focus on getting students comfortable communicating visually. This includes "sketchnotes" (as coined by Mike Rohde), which consists of taking notes using a mix of words, simple drawings, and diagramming. (See figure 2.) It is, as Rohde insists, not about

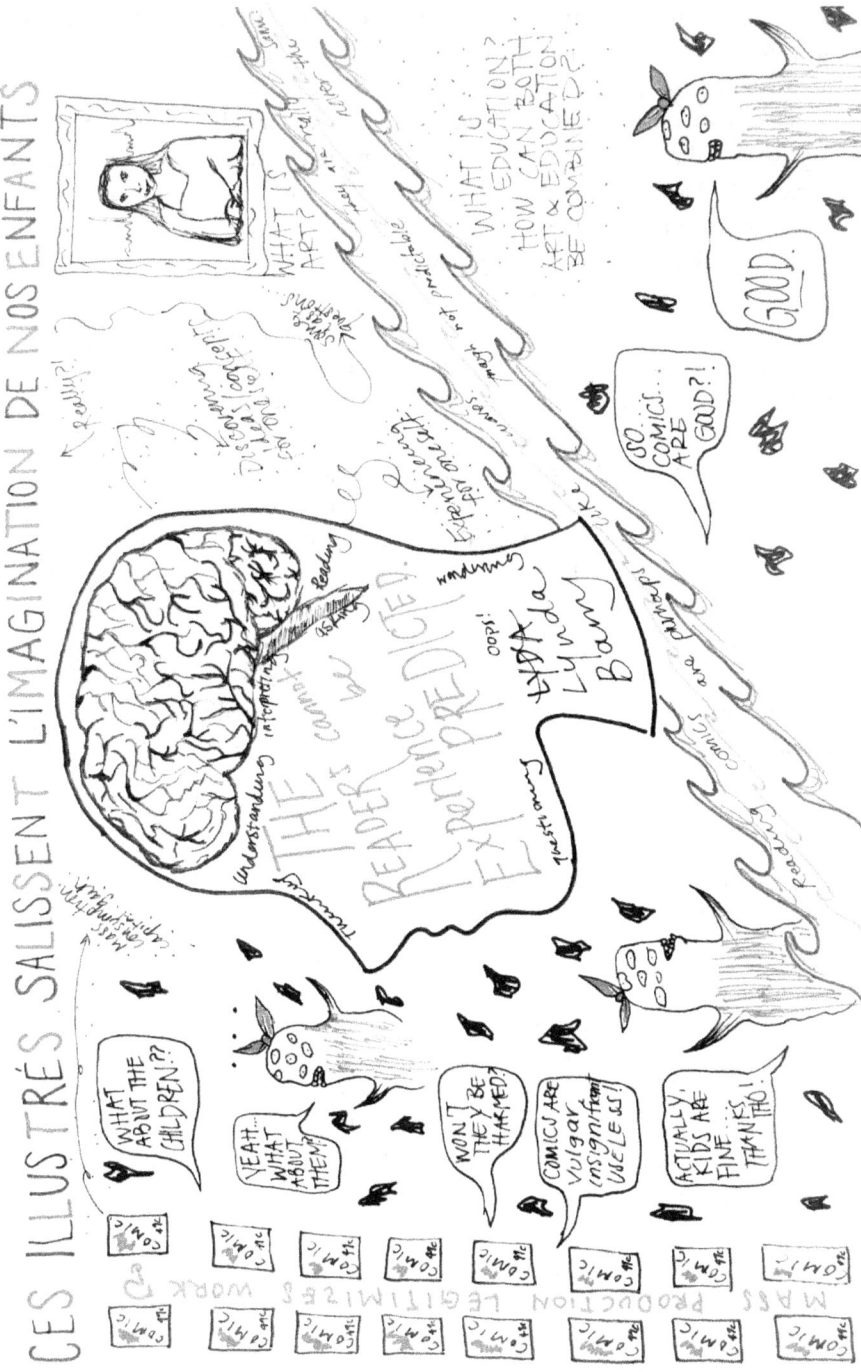

Figure 2: Sketchnotes example

making good art but getting ideas down. I have students make sketchnotes in all my classes and have them do it in at least one of their other classes. The mix of words and pictures is comics-like, visual notetaking as a means of retention is well-demonstrated, and many students continue using this method for taking notes in their classes going forward. Additionally, at the start of semester, I frequently have students make a sketchnote to map out what brought them to the course and what they want to take from the experience. Sketchnoting gets them mingling words and pictures off the bat with no pressure and has been a great way for everyone to get to know one another.

As a means of prompting group discussion and keeping the focus on comics as a visual medium, another key activity involves having students visually analyze and annotate comics pages. I have them do this with every reading, as well as for a few more involved projects over the term. I keep the format wide open—I suggest they trace, redraw, or photocopy the page, perhaps layering over it with tracing paper or acetate, anything that lets them engage with the art in an intimate way. Drawing directly on the composition is the key! This active interaction with the comics page invites them to start noticing everything the authors employ to construct meaning. When I do this for a larger standalone project, I provide a set of pages for them to choose from that I've selected, all of which are particularly interesting in a formal way such that I'm certain they can't help but find things to notice. I tell them that if they spend at least half an hour moving their hand and eyes over a page, they will absolutely start to discover all sorts of things about the maker's choices and the creative decisions within that were not immediately apparent. After they cross this threshold, some switch seems to flip and all sorts of things start to spill out—they find every square inch invested in meaning. The results are frequently this beautiful and insightful explosion of thinking. Students develop their own coding strategies, work in multiple layers, diagram, redraw key elements—find ways to draw out and bring to light elements of the page we'd otherwise be unaware of. As I've been collecting them over the years, I now briefly share some past examples with new students, which has often led to attempts by students to outdo earlier classes, by being more inventive in their formats and more exhaustive in all they bring to light.

As I said, I provide them with particularly complex pages, which pretty much guarantees they will come up with something interesting; but as they get better at this, they are able to do the same with even the most straightforward composition in rather run-of-the-mill comics. Sometimes we turn this analytical spotlight on their own, relatively novice works. And while initially, they may think their pages will be of little interest, here too it turns out that the student can bring to light a treasure trove of inspired decisions. It's important to distinguish this from doing analysis solely based in writing. It's not that this can't be extremely insightful (of course it can), but in my experience, I strongly believe that the act of drawing on drawings—this direct physical response with the hand and guiding of the eyes through the page—opens students to seeing in ways they couldn't otherwise. The resulting annotated page could, of course, be subsequently turned into an essay if so desired, but the thinking is in that direct spatial engagement.

I'm reluctant to require specific textbooks on process—not that I don't have several and share from them to develop the course—I want to have students see a wide range of approaches in order to develop their own. I certainly draw heavily on Scott McCloud's *Understanding Comics*: it was a huge influence on me, it's brilliant and accessible, and it's exciting in opening up what comics can be. But as McCloud says, it's the start of a conversation, and I want them to keep adding to it. In my making courses, where we don't have regular readings, I frequently pair Matt Madden's *99 Ways to Tell a Story*, in which he makes a one-page comic of a completely mundane event and then proceeds to revisit it ninety-eight times in different variations and styles, alongside Lynda Barry's *Syllabus*, which offers a glimpse into her course on teaching comics for nondrawers at the University of Wisconsin–Madison. Madden's book, in its relentless exploration of form, page after page offers tremendous insight into how comics do their thing. We do a few activities inspired by it, including to imagine we are adding to his book by making a variation of his base story in a way that he didn't. For another, they tell a mundane story of their own in a one-page comic, and then make three different versions of it, where they play with style, storytelling, and distort form (including things that we may no longer even consider comics), challenging themselves to be inventive and question the very structure of conveying a narrative. We tackle a few of Barry's exercises in class; her "let's draw Batman" in successively shorter intervals from three minutes down to five seconds, is always extremely helpful, particularly with nondrawers in seeing how much they can draw, and I find it aids all of them in developing their own styles. Much of it I have them explore on their own—and I see it really help students in getting past their fears and finding inspiration for their own creative process.

Because of this reluctance to have a specific textbook, in my making courses I've been having them make their own "Recipe Book" of sorts, where each student contributes a short, single chapter highlighting some element of comics creation that they feel is particularly important, unique to their own way of working, and was helpful to them in learning to make comics that they want others to benefit from the experience of. Students have focused on elements of technique, ways to organize their work space, inspirational activities, and other tips in a variety of illustrated and other forms. It lets them take charge of what's important to their own learning in a real way and they get really into it.

Much like the three-panels/two-pages activity, I do an exercise where students partner up and share a brief story about themselves (either in conversation or sometimes via email). Then, without further collaboration or sharing anything visually about their stories, each person makes a comic representing their partner's story and a comic telling their own story. So each person will have created two comics, and there will be two versions of each person's story. We end up with this great look at their distinct approaches to the same story—what took prominence, what was left out—all the different solutions they came up with, which in turn highlights the myriad sorts of approaches one can bring to telling any story.

Some exercises are fairly straightforward, at least in prompt. We create short wordless comics, with careful consideration for the different ways we can do something wordless, but not necessarily silent—so substitutes for dialogue, sound effects, and such. (I highly recommend David Berona's article analyzing Peter Kuper's wordless *The System*, in which Berona breaks down several different approaches to wordless comics: http://ireadpictures.com/david-a-berona-on-the-system-by-peter-kuper/.) We explore comics-poetry and the links between comics and poetry, and students make works either adapting an existing poem (found or their own) or something entirely new, with the emphasis on form and the interdependency of text and image—as opposed to illustrating text. (The comics-poetry anthology *Ink Brick* offers a wealth of inspiration: http://inkbrick.com/.)

After hearing Scott McCloud talk on airline safety instruction manuals, I've become quite fascinated to see how they might be reimagined in a comics class. It's an exercise that can be helpful in working on clarity of narrative and could potentially be quite useful as future explanatory materials. Essentially, after looking at existing manuals (and things like IKEA instructions), we discuss what's working and what we feel could be improved, and then they try their hand at it at anything from shoe-tying to recipes.

Many of the exercises I come up with spring from thinking about a particular page design or storytelling choice, and some from things in my own work. One such is an exercise playing with metaphor and visual-verbal resonance, a central feature of my approach, which was sparked after reading Alan Moore and Melinda Gebbie's short essay comic "This Is Information." I've done a number of pages where I use a single visual metaphor to talk about something else altogether—well-known fictional rabbits to talk about games, roses to talk about the name "comics," a "show of hands" to talk about the process of voting, and so on. I want them to explore both the metaphorical potential of comics and the process of allowing words and images to co-generate one another. As I've described the assignment (which is best understood after sharing a few specific examples), make a one-page multipanel comic in which you select a single thematic element to use metaphorically or literally throughout as a way of linking the piece together. A short way to think about it is to talk about one thing in terms of another. Keep the metaphor running in some way for each beat of the narrative. A favorite example came from a student using horses (and a zebra) to brilliantly work through her thoughts on her racial identity.

I have students do something with their storytelling that could only be done in comics. This can include taking advantage of the spatial nature of comics, it might mean exploring time in a particular way, playing with the concept of simultaneity across panels, using panel-breaking, or the role the very structure of the composition can play on storytelling. Sometimes the prompts have an additional constraint—as with one that was to be rooted in the place they lived that highlighted time in some way (as in things like Chris Ware's *Building Stories* or Richard McGuire's *Here*).

In my first several years teaching, I hadn't done a lot with minicomics, besides showing students templates for making them. That changed when we Skyped with legendary former Dark Horse editor Diana Schutz, who shared stories about how she greatly appreciated the minicomics she was given by creators at conventions. She could easily take these home with her, and thus they were a great way to get someone to remember you. That idea of something easily shareable, cheap to produce, and finished appeals to students, and I've since made it a staple of class, with students producing both straightforward and wildly experimental minicomics.

I'm a strong believer that we learn a lot by studying and copying other creators. I frequently mimic other artists in my own work to play with styles and approaches (see "A Life in Comics" and "Bi(bli)ography") and am a big fan of R. Sikoryak's perfect adoption of another artist's look to tell his own stories (see his "iTunes Terms & Conditions" or *Masterpiece Comics* for great examples). With these examples in mind, I have them make a short comic about themselves using at least three instances where they directly reference the style from three different artists they admire or were influenced by as a way of telling their own narrative. The results for this have been amazing—their work often makes a significant leap with this project from what they glean from their "muses," and they tell insightful stories about themselves along the way.

"22 Panels That Always Work" is a fabled thing in the comics industry—an illustrated "cheat sheet" by cartoonist Wally Wood, as he put it "or some

Figure 3: Carmen's twenty-two panels

interesting ways to get some variety into those boring panels where some dumb writer has a bunch of lame characters sitting around and talking for page after page!" These include such things as "extreme closeup," "down-shot—cast shadows," "back of head—part of head," and so on. After sharing his original twenty-two drawn panels along with numerous adaptations of it by various artists over the years, I have students create their own set, so that they now have this handy reference guide done in their unique styles. We then turned it into a game where I drew numbers one through twenty-through out of a hat (usually around seven in total), and they made a one-page comic based on the sequence I'd selected. (See figure 3.) As with the example above, I witnessed their comics grow in significant ways as following Wood, they were invested deeply in thinking about the particular composition of each panel in a way many of them had not done prior.

 I do a few variations on script-to-page translations. For one, we start with a script to a single page (for which I also have the finished comic), and they break it down and thumbnail the page. To give them a good sense of how this works, I share a range of different scripting styles (often the extreme density and descriptiveness of an Alan Moore script alongside the closer to more spare theater directions of Neil Gaiman). When they've made their pages, we can compare the solutions they came up with to one another and against the page from the original comic. We've expanded on this where they pick an existing comic, write a script from a page of it, then give that script to someone else to produce a page, and again compare the results. They learn about what's necessary to put into a script and provide enough instructions to get what you're hoping for—or let it be wide open and surprised by the result. (Often to humorous effect—one student wrote a script for a page from *Pride of Baghdad*, which features lions as main characters, a fact he forgot to mention in his notes for the second student!) These sorts of telephone games are great interactive learning experiences and students delight in them. I've continued to introduce variations in my making courses—chopping up the whole process of producing a page—as in, person one shares a story, the second does thumbnails, the third person makes the actual page, and still further breakdowns. Each variation gives students insights into the process without having to be bogged down with telling just the right story—the collaboration and time constraint facilitate quick growth. (See figure 4.)

 One of my favorite things to do, which works really well both in class and in workshops with large groups, is an independent-collaborative three-person exercise. The instructions are super simple. The first person takes a sheet of paper and proceeds to quickly (in maybe two minutes) compose a blank panel structure. The paper is then handed off to a second person (without

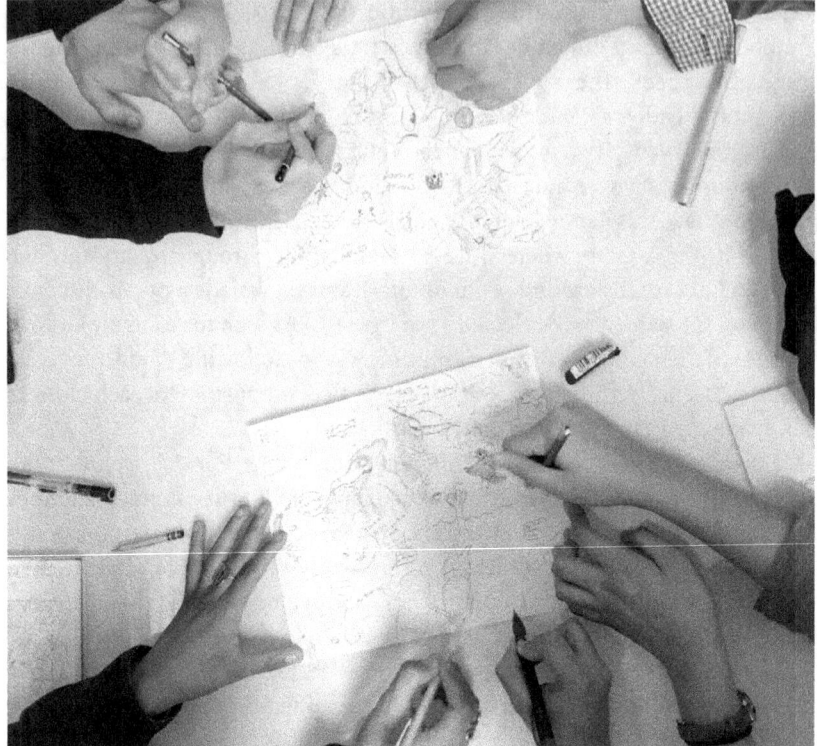

Figure 4: Making comics together

further comment from the first) who adds words to the page—in the form of dialogue in word balloons, thought bubbles, captions, or sound effects (in five or so minutes). It is then passed to the final person who draws everything. (My first time testing it out, I had them do the drawing second and words last, but it proved less generative.) There's something almost magical about how the disparate elements come together with these, and I think it speaks to the importance of constraints and collaboration to accelerate the creative process. I find in my own work, the more rules I build around the work, the more free I become to explore and arrive at unexpected places. I've increasingly made in-class collaboration a part of my courses. These fast switches, dividing up the labor, frees them from having to think of something perfect that they've invested too much in. They can get their hands moving and thus their minds working, and the results are frequently thrilling. And the energy in the classroom while they're doing this is such a treat to behold.

At the Angoulême Comics Festival in France, I watched a live drawing performance where two teams of cartoonists take turns making a comics page—one team draws a panel all at once and then they pass the page to the "opposing" team to continue the story in the next panel and back again. I immediately wanted to try with my students, though I was slightly concerned it might not work as these were all seasoned professional cartoonists and my students were almost all novices. But to the contrary, students dove in and tackled their panels with abandon! To make it simple, we divide a piece of paper into four equal quadrants, make teams with two to three students each, and pair them off. Unlike what I'd seen in France, I didn't give students a rest while the other team was drawing. We have two pages being worked on at the same time. Both teams start in the first quadrant on their respective pages. After five minutes, the teams exchange pages and work on the next panel, and then pass again until they've filled all four. I've added different wrinkles—sometimes we do it silently, other times with a specific theme to incorporate throughout, and always it's produced terrific energy in the room. (See figure 5.)

Watching students grow leaps and bounds in their comfort level working together in these quick-paced activities has kept me experimenting. I pull out some feature from a comic we've looked at, and then try to reverse-engineer it to make an exercise that constrains for whatever unusual thing the comic did. One might expect for the comics produced under these conditions to be more or less throwaway formal exercises. To the contrary, I'm constantly surprised by how often these formal rules generate unexpectedly meaningful stories. I'm not asking them to discuss their emotions or personal stories, but I think a space opens and the stories flood out almost by accident. A few examples: "Zoom"—an exercise where someone draws whatever they want in the first panel, and then the next person draws their panel by zooming in or out directly from the prior panel, and so on. Sometimes panel layout is arranged at the start, and I've also tried it where that too is developed as each panel is drawn, which adds another layer of complexity, especially for the person at the end. We do an exercise where I ask them to sketch out a three-page fight scene and also, separately, a conversation. I prompt them to have an arc of ups and downs and moments of resolution (without any further specifics) and have them focus on page turns and the lower right corner of each page (to build anticipation for the next page). Story material pops out in comics crafted in minutes! One final exercise, something I'm calling "Zithers," which is intended to get students thinking about the way a comics maker can control the reader's movement through the page diverging from strictly left-to-right, top-to-bottom reading patterns. I set it up by drawing a curving, possibly looping directional arrow for everyone. Students are to then try and "solve" this pathway, by coming up with a page composition that follows the reading order that the arrow suggests. They

Figure 5: Reverse engineering

can use panel arrangement, overlapping panels, introduce a character leaping across a border, use the placement of text boxes or sound effects, anything they can come up with to get the reader to go in the desired direction. Solving these is hard enough (I don't have anything in mind when I draw them), but they not only figure out solutions but come up with genuinely interesting pieces all from me drawing a looping arrow! I keep trying new things to push them, expecting that some exercises will likely be a bust—but that's rarely been the case as students are always up for these odd challenges and rise to the occasion.

Everything I've been doing in my classroom is shaped by and influences my work, where I argue that comics should be taken seriously in academic settings. When I give public talks, I frequently get a response along the lines of, "I buy your argument, I see that it works for you, but I can't draw." To make the case in a way that I find is more succinct and powerful than all my intensely involved drawings, I have for the last few years taken to sharing an excerpt from one student's work. Let me introduce Odessa—a shy student who spoke very little in our "Comics as a Way of Thinking" course at the University of Calgary. The sketchnote she made about herself at the start of the semester revealed a lack of confidence in her drawing skills but an openness to explore. Throughout the semester she did a number of intriguing comics that did fascinating things with panel breaking, which in turn sent me to gather up additional examples to share with the class. I've thought about her work a great deal over the years since I've begun sharing it, but it was only the occasion of writing this chapter that prompted me to ask her about it directly.

As with her smaller pieces over the semester, this comic she created for her final project is highly involved in exploring form. She plays with the comics panel as window, as support, as tangible presence, and she manipulates the very way we read, reinforcing her point in the narrative by beautifully winding her words around and asking the reader to rotate the page to follow her thinking. It demonstrates an extremely sophisticated understanding of the comics form and it powerfully speaks to how working in visual ways allows us to make discoveries and understand things about our subject and ourselves that we couldn't without it. (See figures 6a–6e.)

I think in looking at her work, we would still agree, this is not the work of a trained drawer in the ways we conceive of that. However, I think it is impossible to miss that what she created is a profound piece of thinking. It shows that visual thinking isn't about technical training, but about understanding the properties of the form and drawing on our natural ability to understand space. It means an enormous amount to me each time I share it, and I see its impact with others whenever I share it. All of them are deeply moved by what she created. (A fact Odessa found to be wild!) I asked her what she was able to express in comics in ways perhaps not available in other forms.

> I've never been very good at talking about myself. The anxiety in me makes me think that, when someone wants to know about me, they only ask so they can make fun of me later. Anyway, I never felt like that in comics class. I ended up writing about myself without really realizing what I wrote was about me until about halfway into the semester. It is a lot easier to draw a silly comic about pink elephants then it is to go up to someone and say, "Hey, I'm pretty sure I have social anxiety, sorry if that's weird and sorry if it's not." Being able to draw and visualize something like that let me look at it and say, "You know what? That pink elephant is kinda silly." I'm forever going to deal with the elephant but it's oddly comforting to have something to point at and tell it to shut up. I have come pretty far on that issue in the last couple years. It's nice.

Of its genesis, she describes having the phrase "this is a story" stuck in her head and working with it to see where it went:

> Then I got part way through and went "oh whoops" because apparently I'd dug a little deeper than intended and ended up finding the memories of being bullied. I didn't know that it was bullying at the time but now I look back and go, "No, that was not okay." So, there is that. Also, I was coming to terms with the fact I have zero interest in stereotypical "life" stuff like kids or marriage. While I didn't know it at the time I made the comic, though I suspect it helped me figure it out, I am bisexual. Which would explain whenever I tried to convince myself I was straight or someone tried to make fun of me for being gay I felt like I was being stuffed into an ill-fitting box. I spent a lot of time that year wondering who I am and who I should be and it turned out the answer was "who cares?" *I'm me and I'm pretty cool. That's what matters.*

Comics let you say things you couldn't in another form and learn things about yourself along the way. I connect Odessa's experience of discovering her own creative potential to an observation I made in response to someone in a workshop I ran. One initially reluctant participant made this incredibly elaborate three-dimensional metaphorical cutout construction, and then she said, "I'm not usually into artsy-craftsy things." I responded that it wasn't a piece of art, "that's a piece of thinking." Working in this way is available to everyone, and I think the flexibility of comics to allow a broad range of approaches in how we use images, words, and space makes them particularly inviting for anyone.

Figures 6a–6e: Examples from Odessa

And while I certainly want my students to leave class knowledgeable about comics—theory, history, and craft—I mostly want them to be better be able to understand and express their own thinking. By incorporating making, I think we can achieve both.

To those who are onboard but worried you don't know that much about comics and definitely don't have the skills to draw them or (therefore) to teach them, I say it's ok to acknowledge your ignorance and to trust your students. Start trying things and let them lead the way. You'll figure it out together.

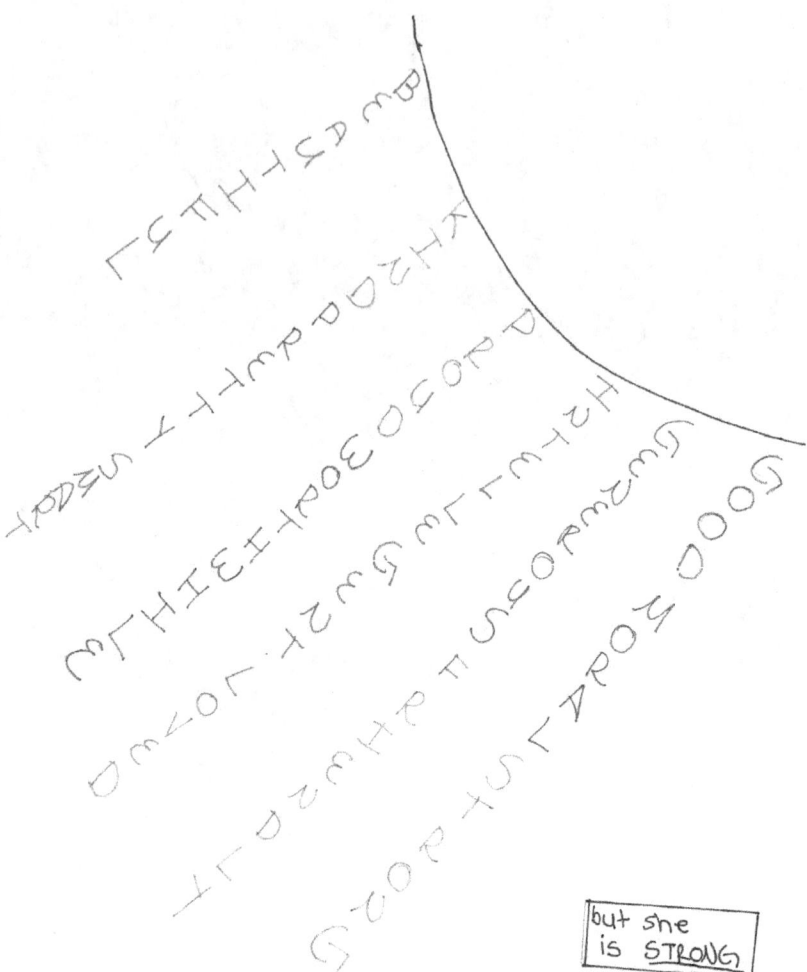

Figure 6b

Figure 6c

Figure 6d

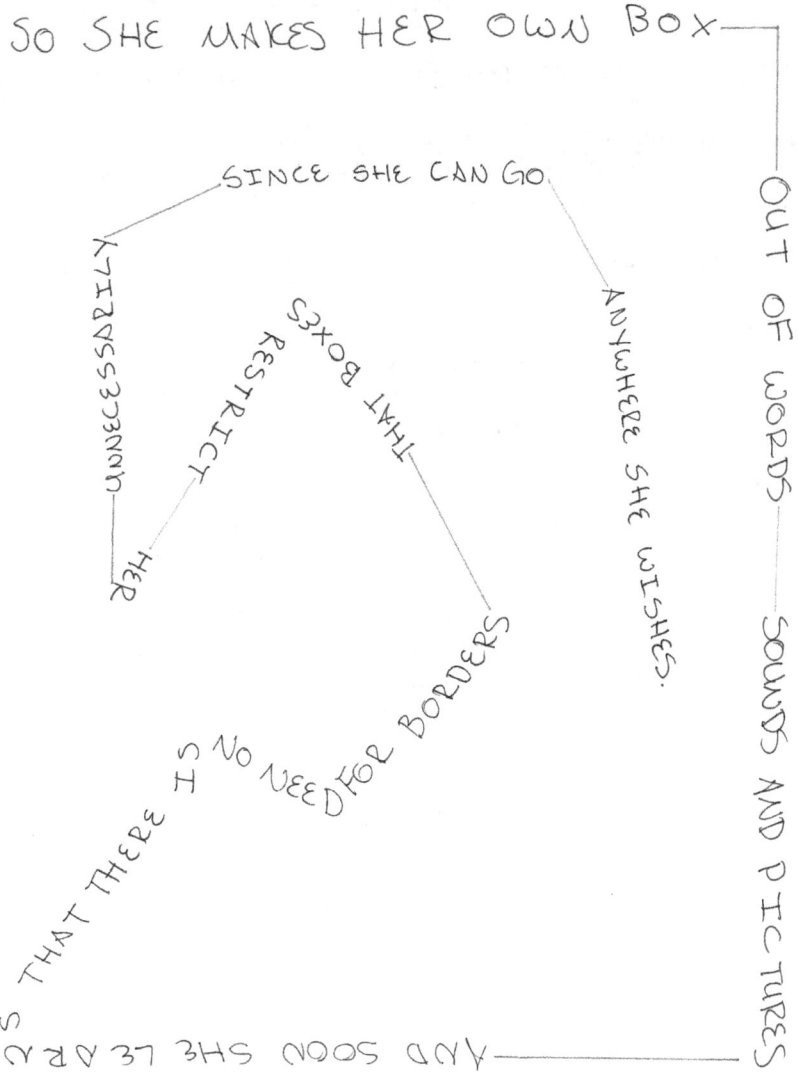

Figure 6e

WORKS CITED

Abel, Jessica, and Matt Madden. *Drawing Words and Writing Pictures*. New York: First Second, 2008.

Barry, Lynda. *Syllabus*. Montreal: Drawn and Quarterly, 2014.

Gallwey, W. Timothy. *The Inner Game of Tennis*. New York: Bantam Books, 1978.

Madden, Matt. *99 Ways to Tell a Story: Exercises in Style*. New York: Chamberlain Bros., 2005.

McCloud, Scott. *Understanding Comics: The Invisible Art*. Northampton, MA: Kitchen Sink Press, 1993.

McCloud, Scott. *Making Comics*. New York: Harper, 2006.

McGuire, Richard. *Here*. New York: Pantheon Graphic Novels, 2014.

Moore, Alan, and Melinda Gebbie. "This Is Information." In *9-11: Artists Respond*. Milwaukie, OR: Dark Horse Comics, 2002.

Rancière, Jacques. *The Ignorant Schoolmaster: Five Lessons in Intellectual Emancipation*. Translated by K. Ross, Trans. Stanford, CA: Stanford University Press, 1991.

Rohde, Mike. *The Sketchnote Handbook*. Berkeley, CA: Peachpit Press, 2012.

Sikoryak, Robert. *Masterpiece Comics*. Montreal: Drawn and Quarterly, 2009.

Sikoryak, Robert. *Terms and Conditions*. Montreal: Drawn and Quarterly, 2017.

Sousanis, Nick. *Unflattening*. Cambridge, MA: Harvard University Press, 2015.

Sousanis, Nick. "Grids and Gestures: A Comics Making Exercise." *SANE journal: Sequential Art Narrative in Education* 2, no. 1 (2015):.

Sousanis, Nick. "A Life in Comics." *Columbia Magazine* (Summer 2017): 28–33.

Ware, Chris. *Building Stories*. New York: Pantheon Graphic Novels, 2012.

OTHER RESOURCES

To see examples of the student activities detailed above, along with his syllabi, readings, more exercises, and other resources for using comics in the classroom, please visit Sousanis's Comics Education website http://spinweaveandcut.com/education-home/ or www.thinkingincomics.com.

Jessica Abel and Matt Madden's website *Drawing Words/Writing Pictures*: http://dw-wp.com

Panel Lottery—a great collaborative comics-making exercise by Abel and Madden: http://dw-wp.com/2010/05/panel-lottery-an-exercise-in-narrative-juxtaposition-and-editing/. PDF (with instructions): http://dw-wp.com/wp-content/uploads/2010/05/lib-workshop-panel-lottery.pdf.

Transmedia Superheroes, Multimodal Composition, and Digital Literacy

—BEN BOLLING, University of North Carolina at Chapel Hill

In the spring of 2015, on the first day of "Networked and Multimodal Communication: The Transmedia Batman," I prepared three broad topics for discussion. Immediately after sorting through first class business, I drew the following image on the board and asked, "What does this mean?" (See figure 1.)

There was a little hesitation before someone ventured, "It's the Batman symbol." I said, "Great. That's one answer. What else does it *mean*?" For fifteen minutes students offered ideas, all of which I clustered around the image. And then via a show of hands, we voted to determine the five most popular ideas, which were (in descending order) Batman, justice, hope, hero, and tragedy. I then told the class about one of my favorite high school English teachers who, returning to school after the summer of 1989 somehow unaware of the pop culture juggernaut that was Tim Burton's *Batman*, found herself beset by t-shirts featuring what she perceived as a menacing set of gleaming, golden teeth. The anecdote led to my second prepared question heuristic: "So how do you know that this poorly drawn image is the Bat-Signal and *not* a menacing mouth?" That line of questioning threw my humanities majors into a semiotic crisis, so I asked each student to take a moment and think about the different texts—comics, films, video games, etc.—that constituted their cultural fluency in Batman. With the exception of two self-identified comics readers, the vast majority of students reported that the Christopher Nolan Batman films—*Batman Begins* (2005), *The Dark Knight* (2008), and *The Dark Knight Rises* (2012)—were their primary or *only* points of reference for the Batman mythos. I still wondered, "Are any of you Batman people? Batman fans?" No one spoke up and I admitted that, although I read comics as a fan and a scholar, I wouldn't consider myself a Batman person either. This admission also led me to my favorite and final question heuristic: "So why take this class?" A few students were pursuing the University of North Carolina's

Figure 1: Regardless of their familiarity with the Batman mythos, most students recognize the "Bat-Signal" and attribute multiple layers of meaning to it.

minor in Composition, Rhetoric, and Digital Literacy (CRaDL), and a couple of business school students were looking for communications-intensive classes to fill out their general education requirements. Most folks avoided eye contact. Finally a brave student offered, "Three of the four required books were comics. How hard could this class be?" We all laughed and most folks agreed that comics—and particularly the superhero genre—were among the least challenging objects of analysis anyone could imagine.

This essay gives my auto-ethnographic account of "Networked and Multimodal Communication: The Transmedia Batman," an undergraduate course in which students critically analyze the expressive potential of various media while building digital composition skills to engage the discourse communities that constitute their primary texts. In the following pages, I offer pedagogical context for the course design, provide an overview of learning objectives and class activities, and reflect on experiences and student feedback to formulate best practices for blending more conventional literary analysis with multimodal composition. Ultimately, I argue that grounding transmedia analysis in a sprawling pop-culture construct like the Batman mythos subverts the "hermeneutics of suspicion" that too often dominate literature courses. Paul Ricouer identifies a hermeneutics of suspicion in his analysis of the "masters of suspicion," Karl Marx, Sigmund Freud, and Friedrich Nietzsche, whose philosophical and critical writings underpin much of the literary theory and critical approaches of the last century. To the point, Rita Felski describes the hermeneutics of suspicion as "a distinctly modern style of interpretation that circumvents obvious or self-evident meanings in order to draw out less visible and less flattering truths," limiting the value placed on affective responses to a text to traits aligned with the most distrustful consumer. As the anecdote above from my first day of class suggests, my students were not intimidated by Batman and from the first class proved largely resistant to the idea that a superhero narrative might have obscure meanings lurking beneath the surface of the text. That initial class meeting drove me to complicate the seeming unsophisticated nature of superheroes for my students throughout the semester, but also encouraged me to consider the wide range of affective responses that may prove instructive in the literature classroom. Most significantly, I contend that the massive Batman intellectual property—constituted by texts in almost any medium, form, and genre imaginable—provides students a wide range of examples to analyze while they work to build an aptitude for participating in the media in which these stories are told.

With regard to methodology, I draw upon my daily lesson plans and notes for many of the anecdotes in this essay. The syllabus, assignment descriptions, grading rubrics, student evaluations, and other course materials referenced below may be accessed at benbolling.com/teaching/transmediabatman. The class also used a password-protected Tumblr page where students posted assignments and discussed course content. Although I will reference content from Tumblr in some anecdotes, I do not provide open access to the page to protect student anonymity. On the aforementioned teaching website, I do share some examples of student work with the permission of the creators. This course was the first that I designed, taught, and organized using the Scrivener application rather than a Mac Finder folder, an idea I first encountered in a post by Ryan Cordell on the *Chronicle of Higher Education*. Scrivener is a word processing and research tool popular for its robust formatting capabilities, dynamic composition modes optimized for long-form projects, and its integration of research into the word-processing interface. As Cordell and others[1] have noted, the application allows teachers to organize a wide range of media files from lesson plans to student projects in an editable "project binder." For the purposes of developing and implementing "The Transmedia Batman," Scrivener provided an adaptive and intuitive means for organizing a class split between textual analysis and digital composition.

I developed "The Transmedia Batman" under the aegis of "English 149: Networked and Multimodal Composition," a course in the Department of English and Comparative Literature at the University of North Carolina–Chapel Hill. UNC's online course catalogue describes the class as a study of "contemporary, networked writing spaces. The class will investigate electronic networks, linking them with literacy, creativity, and collaboration. The course also explores multimodal composing. Students will develop projects using images, audio, video, and words. Topics include the rhetoric of the Internet, online communities, and digital composition." After meeting with course architects Daniel Anderson and Todd Taylor, I determined two primary course objectives. First, students should develop a critical apparatus for engaging a wide range of media—particularly texts shaped for and by networked platforms like social media. The second objective, inextricable from the first, aims to build digital composition skills so that students may participate in networked discourse communities.

As I sketched a syllabus, I found Adsanatham, Garrett, and Matzke's research on digital delivery in teaching multimodal composition helpful as I prepared for the recursive, dynamic process of teaching and responding to digital texts. Claire Lutkewitte's *Multimodal Composition: A Critical Sourcebook* also provided guidance on topics ranging from adaptability in responding to student work to integrating online literacies via student-teacher collaboration. It's important to note here that I was a graduate student in 2015 and my dissertation work concerned serialized narratives—stories told incrementally. In the course of my research on reading methods in literary studies, I had been galvanized by Rita Felski's "Suspicious Minds," an essay that presaged her 2015 monograph *The Limits of Critique* and in turn inspired a vital discussion of critical and pedagogical concerns in the pages of *PMLA* in 2017.[2] In "Suspicious Minds," Felski critically examines the "hermeneutics of suspicion" discussed above, figuring the mode of literary analysis as a ubiquitous critical reading practice in which the reader-scholar approaches the text as an opponent that must be rigorously interrogated to expose repressed or purposefully hidden meanings (215). In considering an organizing theme for Networked and Multimodal Composition, Felski's essay inspired me to think about previous texts that seemed to open up the affective range of criticism in my students.

Even when teaching comics students coded as "more literary" graphic novels (e.g., Marjane Satrapi's *Persepolis* and Howard Cruse's *Stuck Rubber Baby*), I had noticed a more capacious criticism, an openness to a wider range of affective responses in critically engaging texts. For instance, when teaching *Stuck Rubber Baby* in the context of "Literature and Cultural Diversity," one student framed her critical analysis of the text's fractured depiction of a lynching via her own experience navigating the collapsing gutters in the comics' layout (Cruse 190–92). Overall, I had noted a willingness to be more *vulnerable* in students' engagement with comics, a shedding of distrustful critical reading in favor of analysis that allowed room for affective responses like wonder, bliss, and enchantment. In 2014 I was also working part-time at a comics shop and one day, while shelving a graphic novel celebrating Batman's seventy-fifth anniversary, I wondered if a mythos that began in the pages of *Detective Comics*—the detective who Felski wryly figures as the literary critic *par excellence*—might evoke the *least* suspicious response from my students.

With a theme for the course in mind, I began. When considering the digital composition skills I would integrate into the class, I decided to base my instruction in the Adobe Creative Cloud applications. I had experience with Photoshop, InDesign, and Premier Pro from my professional background in illustration and marketing design. Also the software was—and remains—industry standard in a range of fields, so skills-based instruction in the applications seemed worthwhile in this context. The Creative Cloud subscription bundle was relatively new in the spring of 2015, but UNC students were able to access most of the applications free of charge via a cloud-based server or in campus computer labs. When the entire twenty-person class tried to access an application to follow along with one of my application tutorials, however, we regularly crashed the server. Because of these frustrations, some students ultimately purchased a Creative Cloud student subscription noting that the software was more affordable than many textbooks. In the 2016–2017 academic year, UNC began providing all students with an Adobe Creative Cloud subscription, a luxury that made the sort of skills-based instruction described below much more student-friendly. The specters of expiring free trials, software subscription fees, and crashing servers were gone, opening up what I describe as a willingness to imagine a long-term engagement with the Creative Cloud applications.

Unlike my previous composition courses, I eschewed strict unit delineations when designing "The Transmedia Batman." The sequence I built into my syllabus sought first to establish a common critical and technical vocabulary. With the first reading, a selection from Umberto Eco's *Semiotics and the Philosophy of Language*, students parsed out definitions for key terms that we would use throughout the semester, including "icon," "index," "symbol," "medium," "form," and "genre." In small groups, students identified technical definitions in Eco's essay, paraphrased each concept in their own words, and generated examples to help ground the semiotic terms in concrete instances. I challenged students to think about some of these abstract semiotic concepts in the context of our discussion about the Bat symbol and its valences of meaning. For instance, we noted that like an icon, the Bat symbol does bear some resemblance to that which it represents, but the vast majority of meanings we associated with the signifier on the first day of class are *symbolic* in that they are not inherent, but must be culturally learned. Though one student notes in the course evaluations that he "didn't really like the discussion about signifiers/symbols etc., ... as we didn't really talk about it except for a single instance," overall I found students integrating these critical terms into written and oral analysis of texts throughout the semester.

I asked students to complete an "Assessment of Familiarity with Digital Composition Software," a short questionnaire that required them to describe their proficiency in applications used for word processing, image manipulation, sound editing, and video composition while accounting for the social media platforms they used. Although most students described their skills with word processor applications (primarily Microsoft Word and Pages) as "excellent," the vast majority of students marked "none" or "very little" when asked to describe prior experience with the Adobe Creative Cloud and even more user-friendly media-editing applications like Garageband and iMovie. The social media question revealed just how dispersed these students' attentions were across networked platforms, listed in descending order of popularity as follows: Facebook, Instagram, Twitter, LinkedIn, Tumblr, Pinterest, Wordpress, Yik Yak, Snapchat, Vine, Reddit, YouTube, and Google+. As editor Peter Carlson noted in feedback on this essay, students were far more fluent in modes of digital consumption than in applications that fostered participation or production. So, I decided to stake out a digital home for the course on Tumblr because most students were familiar with the interface, and it allows users to upload a wide range of media, including text, images, sound, and video. In an icebreaker assignment I asked students to post 140-character descriptions of their five "favorite" media texts (films, books, songs, television, etc.) to the class Tumblr, explicitly cautioning them to embrace what they *like* rather than what they think is most *culturally significant*. This assignment provided a better metric for sorting students into peer workshop groups than any activity I have ever used. Most importantly it opened up productive classroom conversations about expressing intimacy for a text—the act of *claiming* a text as one that induces a range of positive affective responses from delight to diversion—particularly in a networked platform like Tumblr.

We quickly began working to build dual proficiencies in two very different discourses: Batman and digital composition tools. For six class meetings, we evenly split the ninety-minute period between discussion of a text and a workshop on multimodal composition. The first assigned comic, Frank Miller and Klaus Janson's *The Dark Knight Returns*, provided an uncanny introduction to Batman-in-comics for most students. In my post-class notes from Thursday, January 15, I write, "They [students] recognized a lot of imagery in *The Dark Knight Returns* (Batman on that horse!!) and the ethos of Batman as a trauma-survivor vigilante from the Nolan films, but seem perplexed by the dystopian plot." I chose *The Dark Knight Returns* as our entry point into the Batman mythos because: a) the graphic novel is widely celebrated by critics and academics,[3] b) the 80s dystopian setting defamiliarizes some qualities of the Batman metanarrative, allowing students' culturally learned assumptions about Batman sharper focus, and c) in my ethnographic studies of comics fans[4] *The Dark Knight Returns* emerges as emblematic of a sea change in representations of Batman across media in the 1980s. On Tuesday, January 20, after students completed the graphic novel, I note, "No one seemed to care for or about the plot. Batman the character is what's important to the vocal majority. But what *defines* the character of Batman remains a moving target." *The Dark Knight Returns* also allowed for short lectures on Batman's publication history (with particular emphasis on the 1980s shift away from lingering camp associations with Adam West's television Batman to a darker antihero) and the intellectual property's development in media beyond comics. These discussions dovetailed nicely with Scott McCloud's *Understanding Comics*. Although I expected McCloud's work to inspire a more complex appreciation for the unique visual-verbal rhetoric of comics, I did not anticipate the work's long-term utility in discussing digital composition. For instance, ideas about the varied expressive grammars of line, light, and color that seemed purely theoretical in our initial discussions would reappear later in the semester when students reflected on their own visual and filmic compositions. We then moved to Miller and Mazzucchelli's *Batman: Year One*, another seminal text eerily recognizable to these students acquainted with the gritty Nolan Batman. With the second graphic novel students began to note incongruities in what comics fans might call continuity, or the inner logic and narrative history of the story world. My notes from Tuesday, February 3, suggest that "the class finds Batman a little more elusive than before? They like *Year One*, but struggle to make the Batman here fit with the character in *The Dark Knight Returns* and the Nolan films. A unified theory of Batman eludes us." I also note that the quality of textual analysis most akin to close reading in the conventional parlance of literary studies increased dramatically when students approached *Batman: Year One* with the concepts of *Understanding Comics* in mind.

Simultaneously, in composition workshops we began an overview of the Adobe Creative Cloud (CC) interface. In subsequent semesters, when all students had unencumbered CC access, I have used the introduction to the full range of applications to point students to library resources, authorized Adobe tutorials, and creator-made YouTube trainings. I then ask them to play; to learn a basic task in one of the applications we will use later in the class and make something. I also encourage students to explore the mobile versions of CC applications to compare mobile functionality with the computer software. I find that early emphasis on *play* is pedagogically invaluable. Play certainly connotes a lack of consequences, but as competent students encounter complex digital composition software—in many cases for the first time—deemphasizing quantitative evaluation in the learning process allows for greater freedom in the acquisition of skills.[5] Some students are inevitably unnerved by what they perceive as uneven skill acquisition. For instance, after two forty-five-minute demonstrations of image editing tools in Photoshop, I asked students to post their own photo manipulations to Tumblr. Some students became worried about assessment when they saw their products displayed beside their classmates. In response I developed a mantra that I have found uniquely helpful when teaching the range of composition tools in Adobe Creative Cloud in an introductory context: "Applications are tools just like a pencil. Some people use the pencil to write a sentence. Some sketch a figure. Some turn the pencil into a mast for a tiny sailboat. I just want to see you learn to use the pencil." So, although I devised methods for adjudicating students' understanding of key concepts like "layers" that span CC applications, in introductory assignments I set low evaluative bars for fundamental skill acquisition. During this initial composition workshop phase, technical difficulties required that I adapt my instruction to include not just in-class demonstrations, but also multimodal PDF tutorials and troubleshooting videos that inevitably engaged more learning styles and allowed students to review skills beyond the limitations of the classroom.

For the first major evaluation, students were tasked with researching a Batman text in any medium and creating a five-minute "pop culture review" style video that offered a brief narrative overview of the primary text, provided context and commentary from at least two secondary sources, and advanced a brief argument for the text's place in the overall Batman mythos. The grading rubric (see figure 2) asked students to couple specific video editing skills like "using scrolling effects to present *at least* five still images" with the "softer" public speaking skills learned during composition workshops.

By reviewing sample videos drawn from comics and entertainment blogs and critically analyzing the ways in which they did and did not meet the parameters of the assignment, students acquired a clearer understanding of the rhetorical situation. We devoted two class periods to review of and response to these first video compositions. In addition to providing students with a cursory overview of Batman narratives across a host of media, the process introduced the class to peer assessment skills we would build on throughout the term. After viewing their classmates' work, students wrote a brief response to each video including one piece of constructive criticism

Video Presentations: Tales of the Bat

Date Assigned: 1/13/15
Topics Must Be Approved by: 1/20/15
Date Due: before class on 2/5/15

A successful video presentation will:
- Be uploaded directly to the course Tumblr as an embedded video file before class on **Thursday, February 5th**.
- Provide a brief overview of the narrative presented in/by the primary text.
- Situate the text within a context. (For instance, if you chose to present on Alan Moore and Brian Bolland's *The Killing Joke*, you would want to tell us about the historical context in which the text originally appeared, how it has been received by scholars and critics, and how other texts have responded to it.)
- Offer the perspective/commentary from at least two secondary texts
- Give a brief account of how and why *you* think this text resonates through the Batman mythos
- Use audio and video editing techniques learned in class workshops to create a dynamic narrative about your source materials

Your video presentation will be graded according to the following rubric:

Requirements	Points	Comments
The video provides a brief, dynamic overview of the narrative presented in the primary text	25	
The video offers critical analysis, historical context, or commentary from at least two secondary sources.	20	
You provide a brief account of how and why you think this text resonates through the Batman mythos	20	
You use audio/video editing techniques learned in class workshops **Expectations:** (highlighted elements are present) • Video incorporates audio voice-over • Video uses scrolling effects to present *at least* five still images • Video uses footage from at least two other video sources • Video is synced to voice-over	25	
Speaker in video is clear, precise, and engaging.	10	
Total	**100**	

Figure 2: Sample grading rubric for the video presentation unit

with an idea for improvement and one point of praise. Peer responses and my own feedback were framed with revision in mind; in lieu of a final exam, students would submit a portfolio of revised projects with short essays accounting for their response to feedback and critical reevaluation of their own work. This "Tales of the Bat" video assignment proved one of the most effective for challenging students to hone skills in written, oral, and multimodal communication. Additionally, the *topics* of student videos—ranging from animated television programming to radio serials—fostered comparative media analysis in organic classroom discussions. For instance, after reviewing all of the video projects one student noted that Robin, Batman's sidekick, was typically featured as an adolescent or teenage boy in comics and animation whereas he is more often played by adult actors in live-action film and television—when the character appears at all. This student observation about what I termed "the Robin instability principle" became a touchstone in our discussions for the remainder of the term. When we examined the ways in which Batman was shaped by the formation of the Comics Code Authority in 1954, signifiers of masculinity embedded in the Batman mythos, and the rhetoric of female Robins like Carrie Kelley and Stephanie Brown, for the first time the class seemed to become more *generatively* suspicious that hidden meanings may lurk beneath these seemingly straightforward stories of good and evil. I suggested then that "the Robin instability principle"—the widely variant depictions of an underage vigilante apprentice—allows us to analyze representational idiosyncrasies in the media, forms, and genres of narrative delivery modes as well as larger cultural forces (from intended audience to hegemonic systems of morality) that shape the production of commercial texts.

Our conversations about Robin's incongruity across media transitioned into a discussion-intensive series of classes in which I offered an argument about the *resonance* of Batman. Much of my research on seriality draws upon Wai Chee Dimock's "A Theory of Resonance" to argue that texts do not remain unchanged by time, but rather accrue resonances of meaning in shifting interpretive contexts. Furthermore, I contend that serialized narratives, told incrementally over time, foreground the instability of narrative truth claims while revealing irreducible elements—storied aspects of a larger metanarrative that resist erasure in the process of retelling. One of the examples I often use when unpacking the concept of the irreducible element for students involves Martha Wayne's pearls. Whether they have read a Batman comic or seen a Batman film, most students can give a thumbnail sketch of the foundational trauma that led Bruce Wayne to become Batman. I challenged students in the Transmedia Batman to distill the story into its most essential textual elements, and they produced, "Wealthy family. Dark alley. Robber. Gunshots.

Orphan." I then asked them to fill in details they gleaned from various media. One of the first words offered was "pearls."

In a wide range of media depictions, Martha Wayne's pearl necklace, shattered by gunfire and scattered across the bloody pavement, has become a powerfully resonant symbol for the trauma that inspires Bruce Wayne to become Batman. Most students are surprised to learn that the deaths of Thomas and Martha Wayne were not part of the first Batman story (*Detective Comics* #27 in 1939); the now ubiquitous origin narrative was first presented on two sparse pages in *Batman* #1 in 1940. "The Legend of the Batman – Who He Is and How He Came to Be" opens on an armed robber as he confronts Thomas, Martha, and young Bruce Wayne, demanding, "I'll take that necklace you're wearing, lady!" (*A Celebration of 75 Years* 15). From that single panel, Martha Wayne's jewelry has become an irreducible element of the Batman origin. Miller uses breaking pearls to parallel the shattered psyche of Bruce Wayne in *The Dark Knight Returns* (24–25). In a host of other media, the scattered pearls are framed against the Waynes' spilled blood to signify Bruce's loss of innocence, the senseless destruction of life, and the sullying effect of gun violence.[6] But when I encounter the ur-text from *Batman* #1, I read Martha's necklace not as pearls, but as a chain with a pendant. Martha's choice of jewelry may seem inconsequential to some students, but I suggest that by analyzing the alteration of narrative details in long-form transmedia intellectual properties like the Batman mythos, we may critically engage questions of historiographic methodology and the ethos of narrative history.

The challenges of reading Dimock's "A Theory of Resonance" as a critical apparatus for engaging the juxtaposition of Adam West's Batusi-dancing Caped Crusader with Christian Bale's gravel-voiced Dark Knight led to the midterm assignment. This project required five-person peer workshop groups to produce a twenty-minute audio podcast in which they staged a roundtable discussion about the role of Batman in twenty-first-century popular culture. While testing students' ability to record and edit sound, I also required them to reflect on both previous course readings and texts presented in their colleagues video projects. In terms of oral communication skills, I argue that effective group management and interpersonal conflict resolution are some of the most valuable "soft skills" we can build in composition courses. And when students are prepared with group contracts, accountability plans, and understand that peer evaluation will be factored into their grade, they are much more likely to approach group composition projects with a positive attitude.

The podcast assignment allowed workshop groups to storm and norm ahead of a more complex exercise in multimodal composition. In 2015 I was the panel director of NC Comicon, a popular arts convention based in

Durham, North Carolina, co-owned by comics artist Tommy Lee Edwards. Edwards agreed to visit my class and provide feedback on students' pitches for marketing materials designed to promote NC Comicon in an array of media. I asked students to consider the tandem questions "Who consumes all of these Batman narratives?" and "How do you motivate those 'Batman-people' to attend an event like a comics convention?" In the context of their market research, students wrote brief analyses on topics ranging from hashtags to subreddits. Each workshop group then chose different target demographics, including "ages 5–12," "UNC students," "comics fans," and "parents." They were charged with creating one thirty-second video that might appear on a social media platform like Facebook or Tumblr and a small portfolio of complementary marketing materials in other media (including flyers, audio advertisements, memes, and other social media content). This assignment provided the first opportunity for group members to adjudicate one another's contributions and quality of work as a part of the grading rubric. After we reviewed and scored the materials as a class, two students were selected to present a curated selection of the class's work to Edwards. While this particular assignment may not be easily replicable in other contexts, the key objective, in which students compose marketing materials for the primary object of analysis, proves more adaptable. And for their part, students, like one commenter in the course evaluations, described this project as "closer to 'real world' scenarios, and more enjoyable." While I don't wish to imply that all composition courses should cater to occupational training, I would argue that by grounding aspects of the digital-composition skills-building process in recognizable rhetorical situations and professional discourse communities, we may, with certain tasks, model long-term personal and professional engagement with multimodal composition tools.

After a few weeks of composition-intensive workshops, I asked students to complete a survey in which they reassessed their skills in five categories of communication: written, oral, image editing, sound editing, and video editing. The class resoundingly ranked oral communication as their weakest skillset. So, for the final unit of instruction, I created a "pitching and networking assignment" that would require students to reverse engineer an "elevator pitch" for a Batman comic and present it to their peers in one-on-one sessions. To scaffold the assignment, I assigned Blake Snyder's *Save the Cat*, self-described as "The Last Book on Screenwriting You'll Ever Need." I adopted Snyder's book not because of its pedagogical value but because nearly every professional media artist I know—including screenwriters, comics artists, novelists, and podcasters—has read it. The text's ubiquity and bombastic claims to demystify commercial storytelling simply begged interrogation. So first students were charged with reading a Batman comic or graphic novel that we had not discussed in class. Then they attempted to fit the story into Snyder's "beat sheet," a fifteen-point schema akin to the hero's journey. Students were able to complete a conventional beat sheet with varying degrees of success, but the exercise led to a particularly insightful discussion about the role of convention and subversion in the composition of all media. For the primary assignment, students crafted a "logline," a pithy one-sentence summary of their chosen comic that outlined the central conflict of the narrative while promoting an emotional hook meant to "sell" the story. They then pitched their logline along with a longer two-minute "elevator pitch" detailing the finer points of the comic to each of their peers and me. In addition to my score and evaluative feedback on oral composition and presentation, students received both oral and written responses from their colleagues. While developing oral communication skills, this assignment also allowed us to explore an even broader sampling of Batman narratives beyond the confines of a uniform reading list.

The Transmedia Batman was the first syllabus I designed with a "to be determined" block at the end of the term. When discussing "Networked and Multimodal Composition" with Daniel Anderson, he recommended using the final weeks of the semester for a class project that would foster more specialized skills acquisition. So on Thursday, April 2, I prepared the following question for opening discussion: "For your final composition, you will work together as a 20-person production team to show me what you've learned in terms of multimodal composition skills and knowledge of comics studies. How will you do that?" The question prompted an open dialogue about my expectations, the logistical nightmare of coordinating twenty schedules beyond appointed class time, and what I describe in my notes as "a smart consideration of media, form, and genre." By the end of the period, the class decided to develop a web series comprised of three sample five- to eight-minute video segments. I suggested that I would act as the "producer" or "showrunner," approving drafts, guiding individual contributions, and providing direction to the overall project as necessary. To generate content for their short videos, students divided into three "segment" teams; one group decided to film a roundtable in which UNC comics studies faculty discussed their research, another chose to interview UNC students to create an ethnographic sketch of self-identified comics fans, and the final team wanted to create a video profile of artist Tommy Lee Edwards. Students delineated a "production department" to finesse the video segments into a coherent whole and assigned roles including "segment editors," "art/design manager," and "scheduling coordinator." Finally, a "web team" formed to create a delivery platform and marketing strategy for the web series.

Students voted to name the project "Speaking Graphically," and I conducted the next three classes like production meetings. We began the period with oral reports from each working group. I encouraged students to troubleshoot production problems as a group. For instance, when the "communications manager" and "scheduling coordinator" reported frustration with email response lag times, students began using the digital messaging service GroupMe for more timely communication. For my part, I found that the showrunner role allowed me to affect a more stern classroom persona so that when students flaked on group responsibilities I reminded them that in a professional setting they could be fired for their behavior rather than simply be docked a letter grade. The rhetorical situation fostered one of the most collegial composition environments in my teaching career. Most memorably, when the art manager presented a portfolio of logo designs and the sound editor debuted options for theme music, the class provided incisive, respectful feedback that inspired both individuals to hone their creative contributions. During each class meeting, after concluding our production meetings, we broke into smaller groups. I was able to devote class time to coaching these working groups through challenges unique to their projects while also providing more dynamic, one-on-one instruction in specialized composition skills using the Adobe Creative Cloud tools.

However, the opportunity for failure was one of the most significant outcomes of the "Speaking Graphically" project. For instance, when two faculty members failed to appear for the scheduled filming of the roundtable segment, students reacted quickly, filling the seats with comics retailers and refiguring the content of the video as an intersection of academic and popular discourses on comics. Before reviewing "Speaking Graphically" in its entirety, I asked students to submit a three-hundred-to-five-hundred-word essay describing their individual role in the composition, experiences working within smaller teams, and the quality of work they produced. The reflection essays allowed me to assess individual work more effectively while situating contributions within the context of the larger project. The throughline provided by this set of essays described various frustrations related to group composition and a range of behaviors for managing interpersonal communication. In general, students reported that the "Speaking Graphically" assignment allowed them to specialize, playing to their unique interests or perceived strengths while building skills in group management.

Our final class discussions allowed me to tip my hand as a literary scholar, presenting students with my argument for Batman as a highly unstable, but powerfully *resonant* narrative in twentieth- and twenty-first-century American culture. Simply put, I contend that what Batman *means* at any historical moment, in any medium in which the mythos appears, tells us more about the rhetorical context than the text itself. Rather, a few narrative memes—the deaths of Thomas and Martha Wayne, vengeance, the cape and cowl—remain persistent if not inexpugnable amidst the background cacophony of multimodal stories told over seventy-five years. As a class, we read a short comic by Max Landis and artist Jock in which the Joker celebrates the inconsistencies in his character and students offered a number of challenges to and questions about my theories of seriality that continue to shape my research. Finally, we read the "Endgame" story by Scott Snyder and Greg Capullo unfolding at that very moment in the pages of *Batman* #35–40. In what I may only describe as pedagogical kismet, our last class met on April 23 and the final issue of the "Endgame" arc, featuring an epic confrontation between Batman and the Joker, would not be released until April 29. Many students noted that, in the context of our sprawling investigation of Batman media, it seemed very appropriate to leave the discussion productively unfinished. I should also note that after finals season that May, I received emails from five students who sought out the final issue of "Endgame" on their own and wanted to discuss its maddeningly ambiguous conclusion.

For their final assessment, I asked students to curate a portfolio of revised compositions accompanied by short statements that outlined any changes made since the initial submission, provided an account of any feedback that informed specific revisions, and discussed any skills honed in the process of working on the assignment. I use a final portfolio grading system in most of my composition classes because I have found that in addition to modeling the rewards of revision, the portfolio encourages students to critically evaluate their own work while practicing composition skills in which they have received targeted feedback. In this class, many students chose to revise the first video-editing project, and both the revised products and the reflection statements testified to the value of time and practice using digital composition applications. I allowed five students to revisit their reverse-engineered loglines and elevator pitches and each of them wrote about very specific incidents of insightful peer feedback that helped them develop more effective organizational strategies for this specific genre of oral communication.

Blending comparative media analysis with multimodal composition may seem a tall order with divergent pedagogical aims. But my experience with the Transmedia Batman suggests that the combination was valuable to students, and teaching the course allowed me to formulate ideas for "best practices" that have influenced my praxis as an instructor in both subject areas. In course evaluations, one student notes that "Batman was a great vehicle for teaching complex skills and ideas," and I could not agree more. As I suggest earlier, students seemed *suspicious of being suspicious* of the superhero genre across media forms. Certainly as the semester progressed, students found a hermeneutics of suspicion invaluable as they sussed out valences of meaning in the Batman metanarrative, but they also developed a more open analytic apparatus that eschewed what Felski might describe as the more narrowly focused "critique." For instance, when one student tried to account for her affective response to the character Harley Quinn, she wrote, "I don't know why I'm drawn to her. She's ridiculous and I think I like feeling that sense of absurdity. She makes me feel like it's okay to be having fun reading." A number of class discussions returned to the spectral figure of the "Batman person" and what aspects of different texts inspired devotion in fans. Though our class conversations were often structured by conventional literary studies approaches like close reading, allowing for considerations of audience and affective responses other than critical suspicion opened up many productive avenues for analysis. When providing an introductory overview of multimodal composition tools like Adobe Creative Cloud, I contend that students are best served when exposed to a wide range of applications early in the semester. By emphasizing the value of both play and revision, we may model critical, long-term engagement with compositions and composition tools. I also suggest that integrating genres of professional discourse from "social media marketing" to "elevator pitches" into the composition curriculum encourages those practical, outcome-oriented students to extend their engagement with skills and knowledge presented in the course. And finally, I believe group projects are integral to building soft skills, from conflict mediation to time management, in the context of a multimodal composition course.

While reviewing my course evaluations, I noted that one student wrote, "I didn't think I was a Batman person. Now maybe I am . . ." I think I am too, but in the wake of the Transmedia Batman, I wonder if we all aren't Batman people of varying degrees, shot through with fragments of the Batman mythos. Like many of my students, I became aware of how difficult it is to account for all the sources of my Batman literacy—and just how pervasive Batman is in twenty-first-century American media. In conversation, comics studies colleagues have wondered if other transmedia superheroes like Superman, Wonder Woman, or the X-Men would prove an effective organizing text for a class of this nature. I imagine any number of superhero intellectual properties could anchor a comparative media and multimodal composition course, but in the early twenty-first century, especially in the immediate wake of the Nolan film trilogy, I doubt any other property would prove quite as productively unwieldy in its resonance as Batman.

NOTES

1. Bryana R. Campbell's "Course Planning with Scrivener," Josh Braun's "Scrivener as a Syllabus Tool," and Elaine Campbell's "How I Use Scrivener for Academic Writing" offer a range of insights for integrating Scrivener into course planning and academic writing.

2. See *PMLA* 132, no. 2 (2017).

3. For instance, in its March 5, 2009 issue, *Time* named *The Dark Knight Returns* one of its "Top 10 Graphic Novels" and in his *The Journal of Popular Culture* article "Complexity in the Comic and Graphic Novel Medium: Inquiry through Bestselling Batman Stories," Paul A. Crutcher identifies *The Dark Knight Returns* among a handful of other graphic novels as possessing that oft-elusive "Literary" validity.

4. See It Happens at Comic-Con: Ethnographic Essays on a Pop Culture Phenomenon from McFarland Press (2014).

5. See Blaine E. Smith's "Beyond Words: A Review of Research on Adolescents and Multimodal Composition" in *Exploring Multimodal Composition and Digital Writing* for a comprehensive synthesis and interpretation of seventy-six studies focused on adolescents' multimodal composition practices across contexts.

6. For a striking visual representation of the "scattered pearls" phenomenon, I recommend "Batman's Parents Dying: The Supercut" published on YouTube by *New York Magazine* in September 2014 (available at https://www.youtube.com/watch?v=jtpxEmInvfg).

WORKS CITED

Adsanatham, Chanon, Bre Garrett, and Aurora Matzke. "Re-Inventing Digital Delivery for Multimodal Composing: A Theory and Heuristic for Composition Pedagogy." *Computers and Composition* 30, no. 4 (2013): 315–31.

Batman: A Celebration of 75 Years. DC Comics, 2014.

"Batman's Parents Dying: The Supercut." YouTube, *New York Magazine*, September 23, 2014. www.youtube.com/watch?v=jtpxEmInvfg

Bolling, Ben, and Matthew J. Smith, eds. *It Happens at Comic-Con: Ethnographic Essays on a Pop Culture Phenomenon.* Jefferson, NC: McFarland, 2014.

Braun, Josh. "Scrivener as a Syllabus Tool." *Josh Braun's Blog*, September 15, 2012. https://wideaperture.net/blog/?p=3713

Burton, Tim. *Batman.* Warner, 1989. Film

Campbell, Bryana R. "Course Planning with Scrivener." *Smart Women Write*, September 19, 2016. https://smartwomenwrite.com/2016/09/19/course-planning-with-scrivener/

Campbell, Elaine. "How I Use Scrivener for Academic Writing." *Alawuntoherself*, October 20, 2015. https://alawuntoherself.com/2015/10/20/how-i-use-scrivener-for-academic-writing/

Cordell, Ryan. "Scrivener, Scrivening, Scriverastic." *The Chronicle of Higher Education*, March 8, 2010.

Cruse, Howard. *Stuck Rubber Baby*. DC Comics, 1995.

Crutcher, Paul A. "Complexity in the Comic and Graphic Novel Medium: Inquiry through Bestselling Batman Stories." *Journal of Popular Culture* (2011): 53–72.

Dimock, Wai Chee. "A Theory of Resonance." *Publications of the Modern Language Association of America* (1997): 1060–71.

Eco, Umberto. *Semiotics and the Philosophy of Language*. Vol. 398. Bloomington: Indiana University Press, 1986.

Felski, Rita. "Critique and the Hermeneutics of Suspicion." *M/C Journal* 15, no. 1 (2011).

Flaherty, Colleen. "The New, New Education." *Inside Higher Ed*, August 24, 2017.

Landis, Max and Jock. "The Sound of One Hand Clapping." *Adventures of Superman* 2, no. 14. DC Comics, 2014.

Lutkewitte, Claire. *Multimodal Composition: A Critical Sourcebook*. New York: Bedford/St. Martin's, 2013.

McCloud, Scott. *Understanding Comics: The Invisible Art*. New York: Harper Perennial, 1993.

Miller, Frank, Klaus Janson, and Lynn Varley. *Batman: The Dark Knight Returns*. DC Comics, 1986.

Miller, Frank, and David Mazzucchelli. *Batman: Year One*. DC Comics, 1987.

Nolan, Christopher. *Batman Begins*. Warner, 2005. Film.

Nolan, Christopher. *The Dark Knight*. Warner, 2008. Film

Nolan, Christopher. *The Dark Knight Rises*. Warner, 2012. Film.

Ricoeur, Paul. *Freud and Philosophy: An Essay on Interpretation*. Delhi: Motilal Banarsidass Publishers, 2008.

Satrapi, Marjane. *Persepolis I & II*. New York: Random House, 2008.

Smith, Blaine E. "Beyond Words: A Review of Research on Adolescents and Multimodal Composition." *Exploring Multimodal Composition and Digital Writing*. IGI Global, 2014. 1–19.

Snyder, Blake. *Save the Cat! The Last Book on Screenwriting You'll Ever Need*. Michael Wise Productions, 2005.

Snyder, Scott, and Greg Capullo. *Batman: Endgame*. DC Comics, 2015.

Truth, Justice, and the Victorian Way: How Comics and Superheroes Might Subvert Student Reading of Classic Literature

—BENJAMIN J. VILLARREAL, New Mexico Highlands University

Charles Dickens would have loved superhero comics. I became convinced of this several years ago, when I presented on the influences of Dickens on the comic *Batman: Noel* at the Comic Arts Conference, a part of my ongoing research into how English teachers can introduce canonical literature to new generations of students. With their orphaned protagonists' good intentions, faltered attempts at heroics, and inability to manage either their personal and social affairs, I like to think that Dickens would have admired the similarities that superheroes like Batman and Spider-Man share with the likes of Pip and David Copperfield. With both groups of works drawing on the structure of fairy tales and myths, it's easy to assume that comics are the descendants of Victorian literature's great works and perhaps give new means to introduce them to students.

After all, comics are full of orphans turned heroes, growing up weak or alone to discover mighty power that they must use to either lift themselves or others up: Spider-Man, Superman, and of course, Batman, among many others. Batman is particularly interesting because that power is simply his own resolve to use his wealth to make Gotham City a better place. Having studied comics and superheroes both as an undergrad and masters student, then, I was not surprised by Pip following a similar course in my first reading of *Great Expectations*. I started to chart Pip's progress on Joseph Campbell's hero cycle to see how similar Pip was to what I thought were his comic book brethren: the Call to Adventure, the Belly of the Whale, Atonement, Return, etc. (to name the key stages). I was looking for Pip to pave the way for Peter Parker learning to use his power for good by becoming Spider-Man. Similar to Pip, Peter Parker doesn't quite grasp Uncle Ben's last words at first: "With great power comes great responsibility." For Peter Parker, ignoring these words leads to his uncle's death and is the impetus to becoming a superhero. For Pip, not making the best of his great expectations (managing his funds modestly, working diligently to secure his assumed future as a gentleman) means failing in his dreams and, instead, just doing what he can to help his fugitive benefactor Magwitch escape the authorities before following in the parasitic Miss Havisham's and his benefactor's footsteps—namely, using their wealth to live a better life through a young surrogate. But where Peter Parker's hero story is just beginning when he realizes the error of his ways, Pip's is ending, meaning he doesn't succeed in Campbell's cycle like Spider-Man does.

Thus I began to wonder if these different outcomes despite similar beginnings explained my students' confusion over the heroes of other Victorian literature I had used in classrooms in the past; students would read *Dracula* or *The Strange Case of Dr. Jekyll and Mr. Hyde* but have difficulty understanding why it took so long for the "heroes" to do anything. Eventually, they would understand why these characters were heroes but not how they were heroic. Thus, after my own great expectations for Pip (earning his inheritance, marrying Estella, offering social support to his poor family and friends) were not met, I started looking for other templates through which to study his and later David Copperfield's adventures, while looking for explanations for their seeming lack of heroics (like those of contemporary heroes despite hard beginnings).

What I discovered was an ongoing debate among Dickens scholars over the success of David Copperfield and Pip: comedically useless or tragically beset by trials. While I won't venture an argument on which side is right, such research does suggest new ways for introducing students to heroes misunderstood next to the triumphant Oliver Twist and redeemed Ebenezer Scrooge, especially when other Victorian heroes seem to live on in comic-book superheroes. Further than helping students, Dickens seems to ask for this interpretation of his work, alluding to fairy tale-type tropes throughout them. Further still, this becomes problematic when these works stray from the formulaic tales from which they seem to draw. Hilary Schor refers to this as a kind of dark fairy tale (153). And Beth Herst writes that a society or culture creates heroes to champion what it holds dear (2). Both then suggest that it shouldn't be surprising if students have difficulty relating to the heroes of classic literature.

Indeed, Roger B. Rollin wrote about this as far back as 1970, himself pulling from Northrop Frye in decades prior, describing a student capable of waxing on about comic books but not *Macbeth*. Rollin's essay "Beowulf to Batman: The Epic Hero and Pop Culture" argues that students can be taught to draw parallels between "pop romance" (such as comics) and classic literature by learning about the commonalities of their heroes. Drawing on Frye's archetypal heroes, Rollin argues that by demonstrating how, for example, Beowulf and Batman are of the same hero archetypes, students can more easily enter into analysis of Beowulf. But what happens when students assume two heroes are of the same archetype (e.g., Pip and Spider-Man) when they are not?

This chapter begins with a description of my attempt at teaching *A Christmas Carol* and its contemporary adaptations, followed by analyses of *Great Expectations* and *The Personal History of David Copperfield* for how their Victorian heroics might not resonate with students more familiar with contemporary superheroes. It then offers a short theoretical explanation for why students' prior experiences with superheroes should be considered when teaching Victorian literature. Throughout, it will draw on my interpretation of attempts at these approaches with college English students.

Because so much popular culture media, such as comics and superheroes, exists as part of students' experiences and much of that media has been influenced by the fairy tales and archetypes that came prior, there are situations in which students may not know how to make sense of this literature. Superhero comics have shown readers time and again that children with tragic beginnings will rise above their circumstances in extraordinary ways. But Dickens and Victorian literature often subvert those expectations given their contexts. Helping students understand those differences, despite the mutual influences, then becomes key in creating space for student engagement with classic texts.

Using Pop Culture to Make Sense of *A Christmas Carol*

In an early attempt at studying this, I used Charles Dickens's *A Christmas Carol* in a six-week college English class, hoping that a story as ubiquitous as Ebenezer Scrooge's would enable students to engage the text through their experiences with, at least, the countless adaptations that have been produced since its publication. To my surprise, while most of the students were aware of Scrooge as a miserly penny-pincher, less than a handful had ever seen let alone read a version of the complete story. This, of course, challenged my purpose of choosing a text to which students could relate through their prior experiences and suggests that Dickens's relevance may be on the decline. Even among scholars, Dickens's nonfantastic works rank lower. In his introduction to *The Annotated Christmas Carol*, Michael Patrick Hearn writes,

> *A Christmas Carol* is the most popular work of England's most popular novelist, and it has had a remarkable life of its own beyond its author's vast reputation.

> Should all of Charles Dickens' marvelous creations, from *The Pickwick Papers* to *The Mystery of Edwin Drood*, be suddenly threatened with extinction, the story of Ebenezer Scrooge would surely survive. (xiii)

There is little question then whether the likes of *Great Expectations* or *The Personal History of David Copperfield* will remain (or are still) popular among contemporary readers—after all, neither of them have had a Disney adaptation. And if Herst is right that heroes are the "embodiment of the values, assumptions and beliefs" of the society that needs them (2), then Pip and Davy may have little place in the world of contemporary superheroes.

In light of this, my students' reading of *A Christmas Carol* was accompanied by many articles of critical pop culture study, and one in particular resonated with them, Linda Seger's "Creating the Myth"—a dissemination of Joseph Campbell's Hero Cycle (among other archetypes) for screenwriters. And while the article used several film examples (*Star Wars*, James Bond, etc.), older tales and myths were just as useful in making it all "click." My students were able to deconstruct Scrooge's story, trying to chart his progression as an archetype, analyzing both how the events of his life made him and what Dickens was trying to teach them. Much about this class challenged what I hoped I would find (and had found, in previous sections of the class, with different texts).

To start, after reading Seger's piece, I asked them to chart the journey of a hero of their choice and demonstrate the story's use of archetypes, in small groups. The only stipulation was that every member of the group had to be familiar enough with the hero to explain that hero's journey to the rest of the class. Examples ranged from Harry Potter to Jack Sparrow, but superheroes (particularly Batman and Spider-Man) were the most commonly chosen examples (likely because of their popularity in recent films). It's also worth noting here that I have used this same lesson when discussing Campbell's Hero Cycle in several classes, and Spider-Man is almost always an example students turn to as familiar, whether from film or comics. From there, applying the model to Ebenezer Scrooge seemed a simple step many students had no trouble following up.

With *Great Expectations* Comes Great Responsibility

I was pretty pleased with my students' work surrounding *A Christmas Carol*, in terms of their ability to analyze the text beyond its moral merits, so I looked to some of Dickens's other novels for classroom use. My own reading of *Great Expectations* and *David Copperfield* was informed by my students' reactions to *A Christmas Carol*; in other words, I tried reading as my students might, looking for ways "into" the novels. For example, my initial reading of Pip's hardships had me half expecting him to receive a letter from Hogwarts and likening the discovery of his disreputable benefactor to Darth Vader's fatherly revelation to Luke Skywalker. But in many ways, Dickens's young heroes seemingly fail in the ways their contemporary pop culture counterparts succeed.

Great Expectations follows the misadventures of young Pip, an orphan who is threatened into aiding a fugitive named Magwitch (for which he feels terrible guilt), abused by his older sister and guardian (for which he feels terrible guilt), and bullied by the upper-class love of his life (for which he feels terrible guilt) before the novel is even a quarter over. But when he is invited into the circle of his love Estella's adoptive mother and then discovers he is to inherit great wealth and be brought up a gentleman, he thinks his fortunes have changed and is set to live the high-life. He spends more than his allowance (after all, he'll have more than enough to pay it off in the end), tries wooing his love (because his benefactor must be her kind mother Miss Havisham), and never bothers taking up a profession (since he's going to be rich). Of course, then he discovers his benefactor is actually Magwitch, and his inheritance is seized; Miss Havisham marries off Estella to his nemesis, and he has no money or job. He ends the novel alone—unless you wish to read "I saw no shadow of another parting from her" (1481) to mean he marries Estella—working for a kind friend, attempting to raise his young nephew Pip to be a better man than he was.

Aside from perhaps the ending, Pip's story is very similar to classic fairy tales. With its sibling/surrogate mother abuse, transformation at the hands of a kind old woman, and sudden end to the dream of upward social mobility, *Great Expectations* holds much in common with Cinderella. In her piece "In the shadow of Satis House: The Woman's Story in *Great Expectations*," Hilary Schor writes that

> of all Dickens's fantastic accounts of boys' lives, all of them alternately fairy-tale and horror story, none more insistently plays with the story of the fairy princess, or more insistently rewrites that story's darker side, than does *Great Expectations*. Pip casts his own story as a romance, with Estella as at once the beautiful, cold, distant "light" of his existence and the reward for his trials. (153)

Schor suggests that Pip's story strays from the fairy tale formula because he assumes himself the hero of a fairy tale. Believing himself to be a kind of Cinderella with Miss Havisham for a fairy godmother, Estella in place of Prince Charming, and a large inheritance instead of a glass slipper, Pip misses out on all the clues that he is really in a horror story. It turns out, Miss Havisham was left at the altar and seeks to wreak her vengeance on all men by raising a perfectly "beautiful, cold, distant 'light'" to lure men to their doom—a siren whose beauty causes men to dash their ships on rocks. Instead of a kind, eccentric benefactor (inexplicably leaving her fortune and daughter to a blacksmith's apprentice), Pip is revisited by the frightening fugitive who once threatened his life. And rather than a life of leisure, he spends it toiling away monotonously though somewhat satisfied.

In his seminal analysis of fairy tales *The Uses of Enchantment*, Bruno Bettelheim writes that

> myths and fairy tales were derived from, or give symbolic expression to, initiation rites or other *rites de passage*—such as a metaphoric death of an old, inadequate self in order to be reborn on a higher plane of existence ... this is why these tales meet a strongly felt need and are carriers of such deep meaning. (35)

In other words, fairy tales are not only cautionary tales but moral guides—though Bettelheim grants they satisfy a certain degree of wish-fulfillment, too (36). In trying to assist Magwitch and his young nephew, Pip does become a better person by the novel's end, if not the hero he believed himself to be.

In the case of Cinderella in particular, Bettelheim notes that Grimm's title "Aschenputtel" refers to a "lowly, dirty kitchenmaid who must tend to the fireplace ashes" (237). He goes on to add that tending ashes "was a symbol of being debased in comparison to one's siblings, irrespective of sex" and that "there were stories in which such an ash-boy later becomes king" (236). This certainly applies to Cinderella, at first debased by her step-sisters but later marrying the prince. Pip, too, begins life as the brother-in-law and apprentice to a blacksmith while abused by his sister before discovering his fortune. But this only speaks to the wish-fulfillment interpretation of the novel.

Bettelheim explains that Cinderella is also a story that allows children to make sense of their world. He goes on to elaborate, "Every child believes at some period of his life—and this is not only at rare moments—that because of his secret wishes, if not also his clandestine actions, he deserves to be degraded, banned from the presence of others, relegated to a netherworld of smut" (240). In other words, children, according to Bettelheim, feel guilty for desiring something and relate all the bad things that happen to them to forms of punishment.

Similarly, though Batman's story has been rewritten many times in the last eight decades, the death of his parents at the hands of a criminal has been explored as his motivation in various ways, from a righteous sense of justice and sparing future children such a fate to punishment for surviving his parents. Returning to *Batman: Noel*, Lee Bermejo plays with this contemporary Batman's guilt in his retelling of Dickens's *Christmas Carol*. Here, Batman plays the role of Scrooge, obsessed with finding the Joker even on Christmas Eve and putting Bob (a lowly courier with a kid) to task to get it done. Visiting his past, he holds himself responsible for his parents' deaths, the "failure" he has spent his life trying to escape. We see this in his willingness to use Bob and his young son Tim as bait to catch the Joker; he puts them in the alley of his past, holds the child responsible for his father's actions, as he punishes himself. Like Cinderella and the children who read her, Bettelheim might say we read Batman in the same way—punished because he did something wrong.

As such, receiving the thing or action they desire (in Batman's case, catching criminals) is equated with forgiveness, since they must have deserved the thing desired. In this way, Cinderella demonstrates that rising above your abusers means you are not only above reproach (and therefore innocent of wrong-doing) but were probably abused out of jealousy—as she was by her step-mother and sisters. Pip, too, then is no longer a guilty wretch when he learns of his expectations but was deserving of them all along. And if he deserves them, he must only have to go through the motions to become a gentleman as Cinderella becomes a princess. It's maybe easy to see how he could have mistaken himself for a hero of his own romance, as Schor suggests. Further, if we follow Bettelheim's reasoning, because Pip's wishes do not come to fruition, we (and Pip) must assume that there was a reason for all his guilt for which he is being punished—just as Peter Parker blames himself for Uncle Ben's murder.

All of this connects to the notion of *Great Expectations* as a fairy tale or hero's journey, which often, like every *bildungsroman*, symbolizes coming of age. But Pip's sense of guilt keeps him from taking ownership of his story, which perhaps contributes to his failings as a hero. He doesn't want to get his hands dirty, but without his expected inheritance, that's his only means of being a hero.

While this is a very brief look at *Great Expectations* through the lens of the traditional fairy tales and myths with which it shares characteristics, it yields an explanation for Pip's character and perhaps those inspired by him. If Pip was Dickens's Cinderella, then superheroes may be our Pip—guilt-ridden, abused, but better for it. But we need deeper analysis so that we can better understand Dickens's and other Victorian heroes and their apparent failings.

These failings are often all too apparent to students, who may know only a contemporary definition of "hero," modeled by the men and women in tights on the pages of comics and screens of the movies. When I teach Victorian literature, students often just want to know how we got here from there; a common question is how *that* was considered heroic.

In this way, *The Personal History of David Copperfield* may already resonate with millennial and Generation Z readers: a young, poor student, unable to find employment after finishing school, begins an internship while trying to live the big-city high life with a rich buddy who has tons of followers and, enviously, seems to have everything figured out. But lest this look too romantic, Davy is also abused by his step-father after the death of his mother, spends much of his life either homeless or at least without a stable home, sees two of his best friends' honor tarnished, and becomes a widower shortly after his first marriage.

Schor was also writing about Davy when she remarked that all of Dickens's boys' stories are "alternately fairy-tale and horror story" (153), but she could have also been referring to all the orphaned superheroes overcoming their tragic beginnings, deaths of partners and family. However, Davy's story ends much better than Pip's, with a satisfying career as a writer (inspired by the stories he loved as a child) and marriage to a good woman (and childhood friend). Of course, Davy's story is Dickens's. But Davy and Pip begin life fairly similarly—guilty orphans unsure of themselves and frightened of the world—so why the change in ending? This is especially odd given that *David Copperfield* is just as steeped in fairy tales as *Great Expectations*.

In his book *Dickens and the Invisible World: Fairy Tales, Fantasy, and Novel Making*, Harry Stone studies the ways in which Dickens's work is inspired by fairy tales, in which Dickens borrowed from not only their life lessons but also their plot devices. To demonstrate Dickens's love of fairy tales, Stone begins his book by telling the story of the feud between Dickens and one-time colleague Cruikshank over a book of heavy-handed tales that Cruikshank published. Cruikshank's book featured retellings of classic tales with contemporary morals shoved in the reader's face. Dickens disliked the book, sacrificing his friendship for the stories that meant so much to him (much as they were young Davy's salvation): "The lesson, Dickens felt, was clear. In an age when men were becoming machines, fairy stories must be cherished and must be allowed to do their beneficent work of nurturing man's birthright of feeling and fancy" (5).

Stone devotes a whole chapter to *David Copperfield*, analyzing the fairy tale elements that begin in its first chapter, noting particularly that few have studied Davy's caul—an omen to protect the bearer from drowning at sea—or that the circumstances of his birth should merit the ability to see spirits, all of which sound conspicuously like the mythos of superheroes. Stone argues that

Davy does indeed see ghosts, those of the past and future in his own writing. Explaining this, he demonstrates that Dickens tells

> a truthful story about everyday life, and he is tracing the wonder and mystery that reside in that outwardly ordinary life. He wished to convey through the everyday, even through the sordid and the cruel, the same sense of magic, of deep half-understood connections, that fairy tales project. The novel is not to *be* a fairy tale, it is not to offend our sense of what life is, but while conveying reality, it is to help us see those hidden dimensions in life that go beyond the merely rational and mundane. (196)

Stone gives similar examples of the fantastic in Dickens's work—from the fairy-tale like trials his protagonists must face, to adding a sense of the magical to his descriptions, and even magical transformation. Stone's analysis is difficult to challenge, particularly given Dickens's documented love of fairy tales. Further, given *David Copperfield*'s autobiographical nature, it's clear that Dickens (possibly even as a youth) used fairy tales to make sense of life's cruelty. It stands to reason then that he'd want fairy tales, as well as his own stories, to be of similar comfort to his readers. Still, this doesn't explain why Davy's story ends so differently from Pip's.

Beth Herst begins her book *The Dickens Hero: Selfhood and Alienation in the Dickens World* by quoting Angus Wilson's "The Heroes and Heroines of Dickens": "To examine Dickens's heroes is, simply, 'to dwell on his weaknesses and failures'" (1). But Herst disagrees, arguing instead that Dickens's heroes run "within a sustained progression" that brings us "closer still to the heart of his imaginative world" (1).

To do so, she notes that any hero is simply an "embodiment of the values, assumptions and beliefs" of the society that creates it (2). And Dickens's time called for a different kind of hero than the "public great man or private paragon" of times past, for a different world—"'the great wilderness' of London" (6). In this, Dickens demonstrates that Victorian heroics are at odds with Victorian values. His heroes can only be heroic by self-actualization, "an achievement incompatible with social integration" (7).

Nowhere is this perhaps more apparent than in comparing David Copperfield to Pip, making Davy, perhaps, a better entry point for students. Spider-Man, again, becomes a relatable example of the hero whose very heroics keep him from social success. Spider-Man, even in his original incarnation, struggles to balance his superheroics with everyday life (keeping a job, girlfriend, good grades).

Davy, Herst notes, is particularly interesting in that he is a hero who does not use other heroes as models for his own heroic efforts, in spite of reading and enjoying tales of their exploits (43). Davy is also peculiar in that he's homeless—even when he has a roof over his head, it is not his own roof (47). Herst notes that many critics have used this as proof of Davy's snobbery, but she contends that this is merely his attempt at self-actualization (54). She ties this to the tradition of the *bildungsroman*'s "concern with the relation between social pressures and psychic needs, charting the interaction between world and self" (7). Further, Davy admits and is aware of his mistakes, proof of greater maturity necessary for a hero (64). In this way, finding his home by the novel's end makes him a successful hero: "Youth passes into maturity, and comes to a stop there" (7).

However, for all his similarity to Davy, Pip is doomed from the outset by his social status. Herst argues this is Dickens's social commentary on Victorian heroics: Pip is limited as a hero by society (117). This is the chief reason Pip does not mature by the end of *Great Expectations*; he misunderstands what's expected of him and follows that path rather than the path of self-actualization. Another reason, however, is that Pip never overcomes his guilt, again unlike Peter Parker.

In "The Hero's Shame," Robert Newsom makes an interesting move of using Dickens's life to analyze and make sense of Dickens's semi-autobiographical fiction—particularly *David Copperfield*. Doing this, he looks (as the title suggests) at the guilt felt by Dickens's heroes. He notes "that there are 'Two kinds of crime [that] form Dickens' two chief themes, the crime of parent against child, and the calculated social crime'" (Van Ghent quoted in Newsom 4). The former aids in the hero's belief that he (or she, in the case of *Bleak House*'s Esther Summerson) is guilty of something of which he is normally unaware. However, Newsom is careful to separate guilt and shame as separate emotions of Dickens's heroes.

For example, Pip feels guilt over helping the escaped convict at the novel's opening (he feels as though he's done something wrong, though he perhaps could hardly be blamed). However, he feels shame when made to cry by young Estella's cruelty over his unrefined nature and social class. This makes sense, and ties to Dickens's own childhood shame over working in a blacking factory and being the son of a debtor. Further than that, it explains all the reasons Pip fails as a hero when Davy succeeds: Pip was born too low, sacrifices himself for a social gain that society will not allow him to accomplish, feels guilty for being unable to accomplish it, but still does not mature to a degree that enables him to see the ways in which he was wrong, instead only seeing how he was wronged.

In the end, this explains not only a lot about Dickens's heroes and the misconceptions around them but explains the trouble students can have trying to relate to a text that they may be unable to understand. Dickens's heroes operated in a different time under a different set of social expectations. And in addition to that, Dickens tried to show that for all our love of fairy tales and the lessons we take from them, one's social reality can make reaching "happily ever after" difficult if not impossible. Taken together, they can serve a valuable framework for introducing new readers to these works, their protagonists, and the world they inhabit, at a time when their relevance can be questioned.

What this means is that Dickens's heroes cannot be taught in isolation from their setting but as a product of it. We can't ask students why Pip or Davy should feel guilty (when by contemporary standards, they shouldn't) without exploring the world that says they should. We can't ask why Pip isn't like Peter Parker without exploring how his world won't let him be. So I haven't. It became clear to me in this research that such questions would be difficult at best to adequately explore in the typical college English courses I have taught until recently—freshman-level writing courses. The students I asked to read *A Christmas Carol* had difficulty making meaning of its modern iterations beyond viewing them as adaptations. With limited time and resources, we could only look at aspects of Bermejo's comic, as well as a TV adaptation, and while they understood the moral lessons of the story, many treated it as a children's tale, so much so that rather than forcing them to continue analyzing the novel over the course of the semester, I gave them license to explore the themes raised in the story instead—capitalism, horror, what makes popular culture endure. And while many of them could expound on the story's virtues and vices, the story remained a separate consideration.

The Incredible Hyde

This creates a dilemma for educators interested in using films, comics, games, and other media of popular culture to help students better understand canonical literature. As Louise M. Rosenblatt explains in her seminal book *The Reader, the Text, the Poem*, readers' prior experiences direct what sense they make of new texts. As such, educators cannot ask students to read canonical literature, like Dickens and other Victorian texts, without acknowledging that students are going to try to make sense of those texts using what they already know.

In some ways, this is exactly what Roger B. Rollin hopes for in his piece "Batman to Beowulf." He wants students to use their knowledge of pop culture to understand the classic literature with which they may be less familiar. But Rollin also points out that readers relate to and understand different hero archetypes for different reasons. Pulling from Northrop Frye again, he argues that society looks up to heroes like Batman (hoping to be more like him), but relate more to the everyday heroes (he offers *Star Trek*'s James T. Kirk in this role; I suggest David Copperfield fits it nicely as well). For this reason, it's very possible students will approach a character like Davy or Pip expecting them to fill the same archetype as Spider-Man, only to find them wanting in different ways, Pip especially. His type is not even considered by Rollin, as he appears to fit Frye's description as "superior neither to other men nor to his environment" (quoted in Rollin, 434). As such, despite his similar backstory to superheroes like Batman and Spider-Man, Pip will not develop like them, possibly confusing or frustrating some readers (like me) at first glance.

Learning from my literary research into Dickens and choosing works more closely tied together, such as *The Strange Case of Dr. Jekyll and Mr. Hyde* and *The League of Extraordinary Gentlemen,* may be a closer fit for introducing students to Victorian literature through popular culture representations. If Alan Moore's Victorian Justice League seems like the obvious place to have started in this teaching endeavor, it is. Years ago, I taught a college literature class on *The League* and its key characters' respective novels (*King Solomon's Mines, Dracula, Sherlock Holmes,* and *Dr. Jekyll and Mr. Hyde*). Having encouraged my students to think of their own pop culture examples in response to Moore's satirical/critical look at the heroes and heroics of *The League,* when we actually read the comic, they disliked it. They felt Moore's depictions were inauthentic from their literary counterparts and didn't appreciate their more contemporary forms of heroics.

But Jekyll and Hyde are not only classic literary characters; their influences on pop culture (especially comics) are numerous—Moore demonstrates this through his Jekyll and Hyde as a Victorian Incredible Hulk who transforms into a raging monster to defend the Empire. But many students were not only unaware of the Jekyll and Hyde trope (which, granted, made for an interesting surprise ending for them), they couldn't understand why, if Jekyll's friends knew something was wrong with his strange friend Mr. Hyde, they did not do anything about it.

The story actually gives very few clues that the two men are actually the same man, and instead suggests that Hyde is blackmailing Jekyll (for either sexual incrimination, drug addiction, or both); Jekyll implores his friends to ignore the matter, which they dutifully do. In his introduction to Stevenson's work, Robert Mighall points out that "the 'ordinary' condition of his society is for individuals to sin in secret, but also to hold, hide or attempt to discover or reveal secrets" (xxvii). As such, these men embody the Victorian qualities of discretion and loyalty to the frustration of my students. This was so confounding to many of them that one of the only things they liked about the opening chapters of *The League of Extraordinary Gentlemen* was that they were again surrounded by heroes who took action. And much of their analysis of the comic turned into critiques of Victorian society regarding drugs, sexual orientation, and class. In a way, this supported what Rosenblatt suggests. Students took their understanding of what it means to be heroic and used it to critique elements of the novels we read as a class.

In a more recent version of this same course, many students went a step further and applied their criticism to Moore's work, too. Only twenty years old, they found it a problematic critique of the society it parodies, guilty too of an outdated form of heroism. They arrived at these conclusions through a series of fanfiction pieces I asked them to write (borrowing from Erick Gordon's "Occupying Spaces: The Mockingbird Monologues"), reimagining the stories and characters they were reading about for different times or circumstances, exploring secondary characters in ways that made sense to them.

In their work, I saw Mr. Hyde become someone not evil but in need of care, Dracula no longer an immigrant to be feared but a tragic hero. Offering them extra credit to go see Marvel's *Black Panther* film, some rewrote aspects of *King Solomon's Mines* as merely another story about colonialism, and with a little of my own prodding, we discussed the film as a kind of inverse of the novel, in which the colonizer doesn't come to save Africa from the Africans but in which Africans decide for themselves if and how to exist in the world. In short, creating space to not only analyze but reinterpret Victorian heroics with their own influences and by their own standards encouraged some students to trace their own lines from Victorian to contemporary heroics, critiquing them along the way.

Conclusion

This research is still theoretical and anecdotal (based on what I think I observed in these courses), and a more systematic study of how students make sense of canonical literature given prior experience with contemporary popular culture is the next step. But both my own research of the literature and reflecting on students' responses suggest ways of proceeding. Heroes evolve with time, and for all their similarities, classic heroes may be unrecognizable to students experiencing them for the first time. None of this is meant to suggest that students should stop reading comics or watching superhero films in favor of returning to "the classics." Instead, teachers need to create space for comic books and superheroes in the classroom because they're coming with students anyway. And while they may interfere with students' reading of noncontemporary literature, they also offer us ways of helping students understand those same texts, and perhaps give students ways of helping us understand them anew ourselves.

WORKS CITED

Bermejo, Lee. *Batman: Noel*. DC Comics, 2011.
Bettelheim, Bruno. *The Uses of Enchantment*. New York: Knopf, 1976.
Campbell, Joseph. *The Hero with a Thousand Faces*. New York: Princeton University Press, 1973.
Dickens, Charles. *The Annotated Christmas Carol: A Christmas Carol in Prose*. New York: Norton, 2004.
Dickens, Charles. *Great Expectations*. In *Five Novels*. New York: Barnes & Noble, 2010.
Dickens, Charles. *The Personal History of David Copperfield*. In *Five Novels*. New York: Barnes & Noble, 2010. 1179–481.
Gordon, Erick. "Occupying Spaces: The Mockingbird Monologues." *Becoming (Other)wise: Enhancing Critical Reading Perspectives*. Edited by Ruth Vinz, Erick Gordon, Greg Hamilton, Juliette LaMontagne, and Bill Lundgren. Calendar Islands, 2000.
Haggard, H. Rider. *King Solomon's Mines*. Oxford: Oxford University Press, 1989.
Hearn, Michael Patrick. Introduction. *The Annotated Christmas Carol: A Christmas Carol in Prose*, by Charles Dickens, New York: Norton, 2004. xiii–cxiii.
Herst, Beth F. *The Dickens Hero: Selfhood and Alienation in the Dickens World*. London: Weidenfel and Nicolson, 1990.
Mighall, Robert. Introduction. *The Strange Case of Dr. Jekyll and Mr. Hyde and Other Tales of Horror*, by Robert Louis Stevenson. London: Penguin, 2003. ix–xxxviii.
Moore, Alan. *The League of Extraordinary Gentlemen*. La Jolla, CA, America's Best Comics, 1999.
Newsom, Robert. "The Hero's Shame." *Dickens Studies Annual* 11 (1983): 1–24.
Rollin, Roger B. "Beowulf to Batman: The Epic Hero and Pop Culture." *College English* 31, no. 5 (1970): 431–49.
Rosenblatt, Louise M. *The Reader, the Text, the Poem: The Transactional Theory of the Literary Work*. Carbondale, IL: Southern Illinois University Press, 1978.
Schor, Hilary. "In the Shadow of Satis House: The Woman's Story in Great Expectations." *Dickens and the Daughters of the House*. Cambridge: Cambridge University Press, 1999.
Seger, Linda. "Creating the Myth." *Reading Pop Culture: A Portable Anthology*. Edited by Jeff Ousbourne. New York: Bedford/St. Martin's, 2013.
Stevenson, Robert Louis. *The Strange Case of Dr. Jekyll and Mr. Hyde and Other Tales of Horror*. London: Penguin, 2003.
Stoker, Bram. *Dracula*. London: Penguin, 1993.
Stone, Harry. *Dickens and the Invisible World: Fairy Tales, Fantasy, and Novel-Making*. Bloomington: Indiana University Press, 1979.

The Uncanny Power of Comic Books: Achieving Interdisciplinary Learning through Superhero Comic Books

—JAMES KELLEY, Colorado State University

When I think about Barry Allen becoming The Flash after lightning struck him and reacted with the chemicals in his lab to give him super-speed, Bruce Banner becoming The Hulk when exposed to a gamma radiation blast from a gamma bomb, or Peter Parker becoming Spider-Man when a radioactive spider bit him, I am always brought back to the second-grade. I've been a bona fide "comic nerd" ever since my second-grade teacher brought in his personal collection of superhero comic books for us to read. As I have grown older since then, my comic nerd-self blends into my educator-self when I think about the benefits that comic books, specifically superhero comic books, can bring to students in the classroom. Despite the long history of discrimination that has plagued comic books in American society as something that corrupts young minds (Hajdu; Hatfield, Heer, and Worcester; Wright), many advocates like myself champion comic books as an invaluable resource in the classroom (Bakis; Gresh and Weinberg; Guzzetti and Mardis; Hosler and Boomer; Monnin; Rourke; Tabachnick; Tatalovic; Witty, Smith, and Coomer). Comic books are more than a "mere gateway serving to introduce students to more 'serious' educational goals and subjects" (Sousanis 162), as they allow for individuals also to tap into their creativity and explore thoughts, concepts, and theories through inquiry. From helping students who struggle with reading and reading comprehension to teaching a gamut of other disciplines and themes, superhero comic books can adapt to almost any curriculum in any subject. Superhero comic books can help secondary-level educators create a unique learning environment in which they combine multiple subjects into their classrooms such as science and English Language Arts (ELA).

There is a lack of research that seeks to discover how superhero comic books can help educators to achieve interdisciplinary teaching in their classrooms, and how students master concepts using superhero comic books to learn multiple subjects such as science and ELA. Through my research of comic book use in interdisciplinary teaching, I used the following research questions to guide this study.

1. To what extent do students master using contemporary superhero comic books when developing their science literacy skills in a middle-school interdisciplinary-enrichment program?
2. To what extent do students appropriate comic book literacies when they are reading and comprehending scientific informational texts about genetics?
3. To what extent are students applying their acquired knowledge of genetics to *Spider-Man*, and in what ways, if any, are they relating *Spider-Man* to their learning of genetics?
4. To what extent do comic book literacies enable or limit students when developing their science literacies?

This chapter sets out to examine how superhero comic books can be used to teach students science literacies and concepts such as genetics along with ELA content such as creative-fiction writing in an after-school comic book club. I begin by presenting the literature that already exists on the subject of interdisciplinary teaching and Vygotsky's theory of mediated action, followed by the methodology that I used for this study. I then move into my findings and analysis of my results, as I end with a discussion answering my research questions and what questions remain for further study.

Theoretical Framework

Interdisciplinary Teaching

Advocates in education have promoted the need for interdisciplinary teaching for over two decades, as have many in recent years (Akerson and Flanigan; Baker and Saul; Pearson, Moje, and Greenleaf). Interdisciplinary teaching, as defined by Jacobs, is a "knowledge view and curriculum approach that consciously applies methodology and language from more than one discipline to examine a central theme, issue, problem, topic, or experience" (8). Interdisciplinarity goes further than one discipline, incorporating a few texts or facts from another discipline. In the union of superhero comic books and interdisciplinary teaching, educators can teach the reality of science concepts found in superhero comic books alongside teaching the craft of fiction writing. However, using superhero comic books to achieve interdisciplinary teaching is a pedagogical practice that many educators are unaware of or do not seek to implement in their classroom. Combining interdisciplinary teaching with students' outside literacies, such as superhero comic books (Alverman and Hinchman; Kittle; Hull and Schultz), creates the opportunity for an authentic learning situation.

Authentic learning occurs when "students actively [construct] meaning, grounded in students' experiences in contrast with the student simply absorbing and producing knowledge transmitted from subject matter fields" (Newman 1). In other words, authentic learning is when the student has the opportunity to engage with more real-world problems and subject matters that occur outside of the classroom or extend past the rote learning that has occurred in traditional schooling in the past. Students work collaboratively to examine a problem or idea and use information, materials, or technology along with their personal experiences to solve the problem or gain a better understanding of the subject matter instead of sitting in the classroom completing "drill-and-kill" worksheets.

Tchudi and Lafer argue that interdisciplinary teaching that incorporates such outside literacies creates an authentic learning situation for students and provides a real purpose for students to engage in learning. Gee and Kixmiller further the argument for authentic learning in the classroom when they argue in their individual research that educators provide students with "real-world" settings and audiences to apply the knowledge and skills that they have learned. However, before exploring how superhero comic books and interdisciplinary teaching can achieve an authentic learning situation for students, it is important to understand interdisciplinary teaching through superhero comic books as a mediated action in which comic books serve as a mediational means to master various skills such as science literacies.

Vygotsky and Mediated Action

Vygotsky defined mediated action as an action that one does with the assistance of a cultural tool—either external physical tools (a hammer), internal psychological tools (language), or both (a multiplication table that is memorized)—to complete a specific task (55). The tool to be used is constructed and implemented by the culture that uses it, and the tool helps the user (agent) to master a particular skill. Once the agent becomes proficient in the task, the tool becomes less relied on as the tool becomes internalized. Wertsch argues that some tools do not become internalized (such as hammers). Instead he argues that cultural tools allow the agent to master a skill or task, or at the very least, "know how" to perform the task proficiently regardless of whether internalization occurs (50). The tool functions as a mediational mean that helps the user to achieve an objective during a mediated action. The example that Wertsch provides is the pole used during the athletic event of pole vaulting. The pole (external tool) is mastered but never internalized. It allows the agent (athlete) to be successful at completing the task (pole vaulting).

To better understand the tool within the context of mediated action, one cannot analyze the tool or the agent in isolation as there is an "irreducible [tension] between tool and agent" (Wertsch 25–30); instead, both agent and tool must be analyzed together as one unit. Wertsch also speaks to other characteristics of mediated action and cultural tools: materiality of cultural tools, "multiple simultaneous goals," paths of development, affordances and constraints, ways in which mediational means will transform established mediated action, mastery, appropriation, functions of mediational means other than the intended purpose, and power and authority associated with mediational means (25). Wertsch demonstrates how these ten characteristics are applied to analyze mediated action and how mediational means function within the historical or social context of the action. He also speaks at length on the (non)materiality of cultural tools such as "the narrative," as well as mediational means used in social spaces, and how agents appropriate and resist such mediational means and mediated actions. Both Vygotsky and Wertsch stress the importance of understanding that the tools, the agent using the tools, and the mediated action do not exist in isolation but all are constructed and understood based on social, historical, and institutional contexts.

Methods

The following section describes the site, structure of the afterschool club, the participants, and the methods used for data collection and analysis. As a participant observer in this study, I utilized multiple methods (interviews, participant observations, artifacts, and field notes) when examining the use of superhero comic books in an interdisciplinary learning environment. The data for this project came from a qualitative study conducted during an afterschool comic book club that I created and facilitated at a local a suburban middle school nestled in the western part of the US called Midway Middle School. All names and locations are pseudonyms.

Site

The student body of Midway Middle School is predominantly white and come from middle- and working-class socioeconomic backgrounds. Almost half of the student body is eligible for free and reduced lunch, and state test scores have been steadily rising each year. I attribute this increase to the willingness of a very supportive and progressive administration, faculty, and staff. Recently, Midway has embraced more nontraditional approaches to their curricula such as having a class period in all grade levels learn life skills like time management, conflict resolution, and community service and outreach. Midway's progressive attitude in education made it an ideal location for this study, as I knew that the research that involved using superhero comic books in a classroom-like situation would be well received. Two weeks before the study began, I implemented a recruitment phase that consisted of displaying flyers around the school that announced the start of the comic book club (figure 1), as well as having a blurb in the daily morning announcements that briefly described the club. Any individual who was a student at Midway was eligible to join, and I encouraged any and all students to participate in the comic book club.

Participants

Tim is a sixth-grade white male, who self-identifies as a "newbie" to comic books. He expressed that he mostly read his *Lego* comics that came bimonthly and that he wanted to know and read more superhero comic books. Most of his background knowledge about superheroes came from television shows and the recent explosion of superhero movies such as Marvel's *Avengers* or *Batman Versus Superman: Dawn of Justice*. Raymond is a sixth-grade biracial male who aspires to be a comic creator one day. He stated that he has been reading various genres of comic books since he was seven-years-old, and he is constantly sketching out characters in his personal sketchbook. Erin, an eighth-grade white female who also aspires to be a comic creator, said that she had "grown up with comics all [her] life," as her father was an avid comic book fan and passed his love of comics onto Erin. She also kept a personal journal filled with character sketches and notes for potential comic storylines.

Cat is a sixth-grade white female, and she identifies as a "comic nerd," stating that she loves all genres and styles of comics such as manga (Japanese comics) and popular comic-based movies and televisions shows. Cat has expressed that she only reads comics and doesn't try to create her own or write about comics. Samantha, an introverted seventh-grade white female, stated that she is a casual comic book reader in that she doesn't consistently read comic books or follows any one series. She said that when she does read comic books, she mainly reads comics that feature the villainess Harley Quinn, a main character in the comic series *Suicide Squad* and the Joker's love interest in the *Batman* comic series. Samantha finds that when she does

Figure 1: Recruitment flyer

write about comics, she is usually creating Harley Quinn fan fiction with her friends. Lastly, Stanly is a sixth-grade white male and a devoted *Doctor Who* fan. His knowledge of comics is limited to a few select titles such as *Batman*, as his expertise is focused on everything *Doctor Who*-related. He indicated that he doesn't create his comic books, but that he has ideas for humorous comic storylines. When tasked with coming up with a group name like that of other superhero groups, these students decided on the name "The Core."

Structure of the Afterschool Club

On the start of the first day, sixteen students showed up in Midway's library, where famous celebrities on posters encouraged students to read. We congregated at a group of tables in the far corner of the library, and I explained to them my research on how superhero comic books are used in the classroom to teach and learn, and that this was a fourteen-week study. The club meetings convened every Tuesday and Thursday for one hour after school. Those that wished to be included in the study were required to have their parents sign a consent form; however, students who declined to participate in the study could still attend the club meetings. I outlined how the meetings would proceed, with one day being dedicated to reading and watching scientific informational texts and videos found on popular websites like YouTube and the *Huffington Post*, and discussing science concepts such as genetics. For this study, I follow the definition of Duke and Bennett-Armistead in which they categorize informational texts as being a part of nonfiction writing that uses specialized language attached to the field that the writing is situated in and makes use of other nonfiction devices such as graphs, charts, and images. The main designator for informational texts is the lack of characters and a linear narrative typically found in fictional texts. The reading of a fictional text was dedicated to the other day of the week when we would be reading the comic series *Ultimate Comics All-New Spider-Man* by Bendis and Pichelli, discussing genetics in the comic book, or learning fiction writing.

When structuring interdisciplinary units, it is important to construct the curriculum around the exploration of larger themes, issues, questions, and topics (Jacobs). For this study, I settled on the subject of genetics, a concept found commonly throughout the larger body of superhero comic book titles. Also, I chose the essential question of "what does it mean to be human," a complex question not easily answered without further exploring and contemplation. Both genetics and the essential question allowed for lively conversations and group discussions that led to data that helped me to begin to answer my research questions.

I provided journals for students to freely write down their thoughts about what we were discussing either about genetics, *Spider-Man*, what it means to be human, or anything else that they were pondering at the time. At times, I would also have students write in their journals during times of discussions about the previously mentioned topics. As a final project, I instructed students to create a comic book in which they were to incorporate a scientific concept that they learned about in science class or our comic book club. Students were guided through the comic-book-creation process, beginning with many brainstorming in the journal character and story ideas along with storyboarding and sketching out panels, to drawing and inking their comics. Students created their comics using various printed generic blank-panel layouts that I provided.

Data Collection and Analysis

As a participant-observer, I collected data from the students' journal writings and comic books for analysis, along with transcriptions of class discussions, conversations with individual students and small groups of two to three students, and a whole-class focus group interview at the end of the fourteen weeks. In analyzing the collected data, I open-coded the data (Merriam and Tisdell) to determine instances of mediated action according to Wertsch's model for analyzing mediated action. His method recognizes multiple characteristics associated with mediated action, as noted earlier, and he acknowledges that not every characteristic is present in every instance of mediated action. I examined four characteristics of mediated action: spin-off, transformations of mediated action, internalization as mastery and appropriation, and constraints and affordances, as these were the strongest four characteristics that emerged from my analysis that helped me in answering my research questions. What follows is a presentation of my findings, along with explanations of each characteristic of mediated action, and a discussion of how each of the four characteristics of mediated action demonstrate the students' mastery of superhero comic books to develop their science literacies and knowledge of genetics and to assist in interdisciplinary teaching and learning.

Comics in Mediated Action

Spin-off and Transformation of Mediated Action

Spin-off in mediated action occurs as an unintentional use of a cultural tool (Wertsch). One might not use cultural tools for what they were originally designed to accomplish. Sometimes these tools are used and manipulated for other intents and purposes. Comic books were originally created for entertainment purposes and were not intended to be used as a tool to assist in learning; however, some students were utilizing comic books as a reference guide when learning and reading about genetics and genetic engineering. Additionally, this spin-off of how comic books were used by the students created a transformation of mediated action. Transformation of mediated action occurs when a new form of a cultural tool is introduced into the mediated action in a way that the new tool changes how the mediated action occurs (Wertsch). Below are two examples of how Stanly and Samantha used a spin-off of comic books to transform their learning of genetics and creative writing.

Stanly created a comic book that featured anthropomorphic pieces of fast food that were genetically engineered by scientists. As he finished his comic, I asked him where he came up with the idea for his characters. He related to me that he remembered an article that we read about scientists creating genetically modified food to be drought-resistant. Stanly wanted to create his comic book with genetically engineered food as characters, and he wanted their creation to be logical. "In the comic [*Ultimate Comics All-New Spider-Man*] Miles was bitten by the spider that the scientist created, and I wanted to do the same thing. I wanted Burger and Butter [Stanly's characters] to also be created in a lab by scientists." The origin story of the Miles Morales Spider-Man served as a guide for Stanly to combine his knowledge of genetically modified food and his characters' creation. Hosler and K. B. Boomer highlight in their article "Are Comic Books an Effective Way to Engage Nonmajors in Learning and Appreciating Science?" the ability of comics to move beyond a form of entertainment and become repurposed as a tool to be used when teaching science literacies. They state, "Comics can make use of situational narratives to provide context for material and thus a mechanism for improving student learning [and] comic book stories lose nothing to traditional textbooks while having the added potential benefit of improving attitudes about biology" (316). Mimicking popular origin stories found in various superhero comic books allows for students to have a reference guide on how to combine scientific information into a compelling story. Students begin to master not only their science literacy skills through comics, but they also become better at "knowing how" to incorporate narrative elements into their comic story much like Stanly incorporated into his story the narrative element of "the flashback" to explain his characters' origins (figures 2a and 2b). The function of comic books not only changed through the spin-off, but the use of superhero comic books as a cultural tool transformed for Stanly and other students the mediated action of learning science literacies in an ELA setting into an engaging activity.

A similar transformation occurred in Samantha, as superhero comics allowed her to go from a resistant writer to seeing writing as a purposeful and

Figures 2a and 2b: Stanly's comic

enjoyable action. Samantha vented her frustration about writing for school purposes such as essays and reports and even creative writing assignments like poems and short stories. When I asked her why she did not like to write in school, Samantha stated, "I don't like the topics that I have to write about. They just don't interest me, and I'd rather write about stuff that I want to write about." I asked her what she writes outside of school. She shyly shrugged and said, "I don't know, just stuff about my friends and me doing things in comics that we like to read." Samantha related to me that she would create her comic books at home that featured characters modeled after Harley Quinn, and they would incorporate each other's characters and storylines into their comics. Once Samantha discovered that she could continue writing her comics in our club, with the only stipulation that she incorporate a science concept we learned or that she learned in her science class, she was the only student to produce a full-length comic, at twenty-two pages. Writing for Samantha became an activity that she once resisted but through comic book creating she found an interest and purpose for writing as well as an authentic audience (Tchudi and Lafer). She created comic books for her friends and found the

process of writing to be "more fun" and engaging. Comic books have transformed learning from an activity that students found arbitrary and burdensome into something purposeful and pleasurable. The transformation and spin-off that occured allowed for students to master and appropriate superhero comic books for the purpose of learning creative fiction writing as well as the scientific concepts of genetics.

Internalization as Mastery

Internalization occurs in the form of mastery and appropriation. Mastery is the individual's ability to use a cultural tool in mediated action with a level of natural aptitude, and appropriation is the level at which one finds a connection and acceptance with the cultural tool they use in mediated action. Mastery is not needed for appropriation, as one can master a cultural tool but still not come to accept the tool (Wertsch). Students' mastery of comic books, in general, was evident as we read the *Spider-Man* comics aloud. Most of the students internalized the skills needed to read comics through their years of

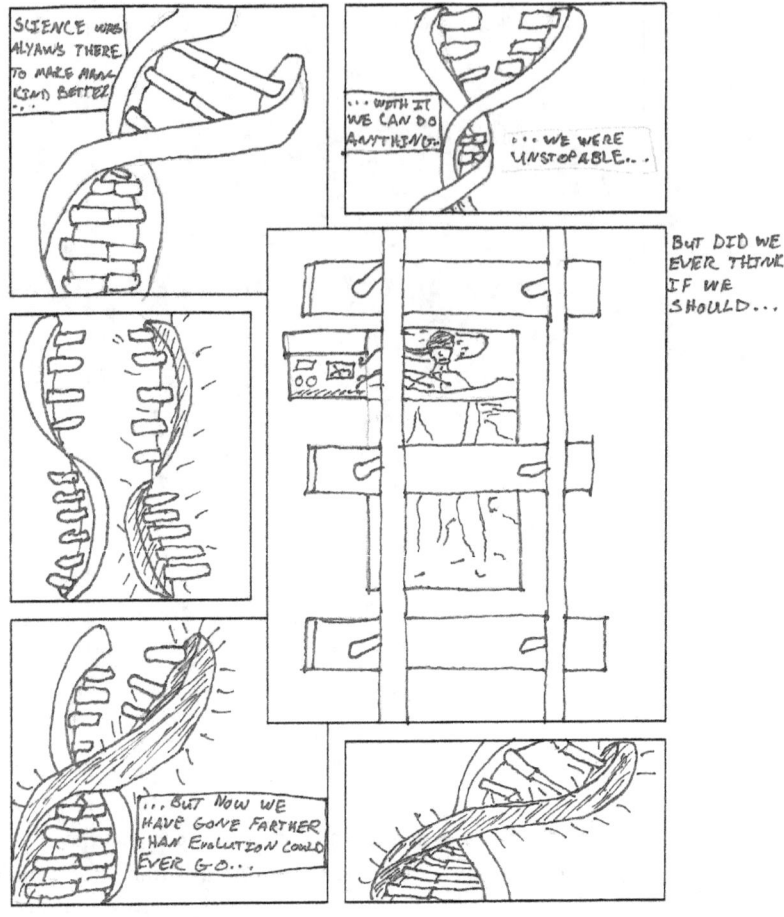

Figure 3: Raymond's comic

reading comics. On the reading days for comic book club, the digital issue of *Spider-Man* was projected on a large screen, and each student was assigned a character that appears in the issue. Each student reads aloud the dialogue that their character said and the whole process turned into something that resembled an impromptu play production. Each student demonstrated ease in reading each panel and the genre-specific elements found within it. Students knew to read bold words with emphasis, to read tiny printed words as the character whispering, or follow the correct sequence of panels and read the order of word bubbles. Their mastery of reading comic books demonstrated the degree to which each student internalized how to read comic books. Students found a level of comfort with the comics that we read and did not require further instruction on how to read comic books. When Tim and Raymond utilized the *Spider-Man* comics as a cultural tool to learn about genetics, it was the origin story of Spider-Man that they mastered and internalized.

Tim strongly demonstrated this half-mastery of comic books to assist in learning genetics. Tim expressed during a one-on-one conversation we had while he created his comic that science had always been an attractive subject that he struggled with at times. When I asked him how comic books might help him in understanding the informational texts about genetics that we read in the comic club, he related:

> Sometimes when we talk about genetics, and how it might be real in *Spider-Man*, that helps me to understand what the articles we read, or the videos we watched, were all about. I thought about when Miles got bitten by the [genetically altered] spider and turned him into Spider-Man when we watched the video about Spider-Man's powers being real, and when we read about GMO foods.

Tim's ability to read, write, and understand genetics and genetic engineering was assisted using the *Spider-Man* comics alongside the informational texts. He took a cultural tool such as superhero comic books and began to internalize different aspects like the origin story, which he then used to help him in his learning of genetics and genetic engineering.

The internalization of a cultural tool was first discovered by Vygotsky when he noticed how the child participants in his study used colored cards to assist them in completing a task. The children varied from as young as six years old to high-school age, and each age group was tasked with answering various questions that required a color to be the answer, such as "what is the color of the grass?" Their answers could be any color unless the examiner stipulated otherwise (such as that the color green could not be used for a particular question) or unless they had already used a color as their answer to a previous question. He gave the children a set of colored cards that they could lay out in front of them to assist them in answering the questions. If a color were already used or not allowed, the child would turn that colored card over as a reminder not to use it. As the children repeated the game multiple times, Vygotsky noticed that the children had internalized the cards to the point where they no longer needed the physical presence of the cards to successfully play the game. For Tim, he didn't necessarily internalize the entire comic book but had internalized the narrative (Wertsch) of Spider-Man's origin to allow him the ability to contextualize the concepts of genetics and genetic engineering. The physical comic book began as an external cultural tool that Tim and the other students used to learn, read, and write about genetics, and the immaterial origin story found within the comic book is what students internalized.

Internalization of this kind is evident in the first page of a comic that Raymond made for comic book club. The first page of Raymond's comic shows a sequence in which part of the protagonist's DNA is being removed and then replaced with some other creature's DNA (figure 3). The details show a double-helix strand being deconstructed and reconstructed with another partial strand that has something emanating from it, with a birds-eye view of an unidentified male (later to be determined as the main hero) lying in bed attached to machines like those found in a hospital. Raymond explained that he wanted his character's creation to be like Spider-Man's in that his character's DNA changes in some way. He explained, "I wanted to show DNA being changed because they didn't show Miles' DNA changing. So, I decided to show my hero's DNA changing." He continued to explain that his inspiration for illustrating the DNA sequence came from a web page we read about a genome-editing tool currently being used in the science world called CRISPR-Cas9.

The comic book functions as the external cultural tool that allows the user to extract different narratives that can become internalized and later applied by the same user in various mediated actions. One can argue that almost any narrative can assist students in the same way as the origin story narrative found in comics, but it is the level of appropriation of superhero comic books by students that leads to various affordances and constraints that superhero comic books provide.

Appropriation, Constraints, and Affordances

Wertsch derives his definition of appropriation in mediated action from Bakhtin's use of the term to mean the process of "taking something that belongs to others and making it one's own" (53). Appropriation of cultural tools in specific contexts correlates to the agent's mastery of the tool for a particular purpose, and the agent may or may not accept the cultural tool willingly. According to Wertsch, there are times when agents resist such tools despite their mastery of them: "Cultural tools are often not easily and smoothly appropriated by agents. Instead, there is often resistance, and there is minimally something that might be called 'friction' between mediational means and unique use in mediated action" (54). Wertsch provides an example of students in a college-level class appropriating the dominant narrative of America's discovery to explain its founding (Columbus's discovery and the Pilgrim's escape from religious persecution), while at the same time resisting the dominant narrative (e.g., focusing on the treatment of Native Americans in the building of the US) (141–76). All the students in my study already had a level of comfort with and acceptance of comic books as they have had many years reading various kinds. Even Tim, as a newcomer to comics, used comic books as a tool to learn about genetics and fiction writing. Most appropriated superhero comic books as tools to learn with little resistance.

Cat was the exception, as she was the only individual to use superhero comic books for their original purpose of entertainment. When learning about genetics and creative fiction writing, Cat stated in the focus group interview that she didn't think that comic books helped her to learn; instead, she simply saw comic books as something that she "reads for fun [and] didn't really learn much from it [*Spider-Man*]." Cat found reading only comics as the main purpose of the comic book club and attended only on our "reading days," or did not wish to participate on the "science days" when she was in attendance. Cat mostly sat with her tablet in front of her, listening to music with her earbuds in, or she created side conversations with other students close by when we had full group discussions about genetics or different narrative elements in the comic such as conflict, setting, and character development. It was evident that Cat did not care to use comics for anything other than to read for fun and occasionally talk about what was occurring in the story. When it came time to create their comic books with the requirement of incorporating a science concept into their story, again Cat resisted using superhero comic books as a tool for learning. Cat's resistance was evident in the comic that she created, which consisted of a nonsequitur plot that involved an anthropomorphic fox named Bink. The few panels she did create have no apparent logical connection, and it is hard to say where the story might have progressed since she did not finish the comic at the time of this writing.

But comic books afforded Cat a level of interest and fun in learning, as she stated that "comics make learning about stuff kind of fun." In the end, superhero comic books constrained any real opportunities for Cat to master them as a tool to learn about genetics or creative writing or to answer our essential question. For Cat, this tool is simply for entertainment purposes whenever the desire suits her, and the capacity of using comics for learning purposes remains a separate affair. Cat's separation of how she used superhero comic books in mediated action was a unique case among the rest of the students. Superhero comic books provided many affordances for students when learning about genetics and creative fiction writing.

Most students expressed that *Spider-Man* helped them visualize what they were reading in the informational texts. For Erin, comic books put these concepts into a context that seemed "more real," as these concepts were not "something I learned in class and then forget later. I like to look in my other comics to see if I can find science in them too and try to learn about it." Comic books began as a starting point that generated interest for Erin and then transformed into a tool that she used to compare real science against science fiction in other comic books. Erin's mastery of superhero comic books provided her the affordance of a more authentic learning situation (Gee), where she could take the depicted science in the comics she read and place it into a "real-world" context. This contextualization allowed for Erin to understand the real-world application of the portrayed fictionalized science and sparked a stronger desire to learn on her own. At least for Erin, and for most of the students in the comic book club, superhero comic books functioned as a cultural tool that allowed them the opportunity to understand and learn complex science concepts such as genetics better than from informational texts alone.

Conclusion

Superhero comic books possess the ability to assist students in developing science literacies, learning about complex concepts, and answering essential questions. When incorporating a superhero comic book curriculum in an interdisciplinary learning setting, or any learning setting, it is important to be aware of how students are using comics when learning and how the introduction of comics is changing the learning that is occurring. In answering my main research question—from the perspective of the students, to what extent do students master using contemporary superhero comic books when developing their science-literacy skills in a middle school interdisciplinary enrichment program?—I discovered that most of the students transformed superhero comic books from their original purpose of being a form of entertainment into a tool to learn about genetics and creative fiction writing. Raymond's comic book creation showed that internalizing the origin story narrative (Wertsch), a narrative element found in many superhero comic book stories, demonstrated his understanding of genetic engineering and modifications. Stanly used the narrative elements found within superhero comic books like *Spider-Man* not only to help incorporate the scientific concepts of genetics, but he was also able to incorporate narrative elements such as "flashbacks" and pacing into his comic book. Together, both students' comic books visually related complex scientific concepts in a way that was creative and accessible to a general audience.

To answer my sub-question—to what extent are students applying their acquired knowledge of genetics to *Spider-Man*, and how do they relate *Spider-Man* to what they are learning of genetics?—I looked to Tim for the answer. For Tim, superhero comic books became a reference guide that he used to contextualize his learning and understanding of genetics and genetic modification. When Tim read the *Spider-Man* comic that focused on the genetically modified spider that created the new Spider-Man, he referred back to the informational texts about genetic-modification research being conducted on food by scientists to help him understand what process the scientists in the story might have gone through to create such a creature. The comic book brought an added level of fascination and engagement for Tim when reading these informational texts and watching informational videos about genetics and genetic modification. In answering my sub-question, to what extent do students appropriate comic book literacies when they are reading and comprehending scientific informational texts about genetics, Erin demonstrated that she appropriated comic books as a gateway into exploring other scientific concepts. For Erin, comic books are a starting point in her inquiry process about other scientific concepts featured in the other titles that she consistently reads. Other titles such as *Iron Man* and *The Flash* led her to want to know more about the laws of physics, as well as other aspects of genetics. Superhero comic books transformed from an activity that she did for fun to a vehicle for exploration and learning.

Lastly, in answering my third sub-question—how do comic book literacies enable or limit students when developing their science literacies?—Samantha demonstrated how superhero comic books enabled her to have an authentic learning situation and an authentic audience (Gee; Kixmiller; Tchudi and Lafer). Samantha's self-created comic became a way for her to showcase her artwork and story for others such as her friends. She found a purpose for writing and discovered a level of enthusiasm for an activity that, before comic book club, was frustrating and unappealing. As with Samantha, the opportunity for an authentic learning situation generated in most students an interest and investment in learning science and ELA together through superhero comic books. Superhero comic books put old topics into new perspectives for students, as many began to see the act of learning as something more than rote memorization. Learning becomes an engaging act, students want to be a part of the learning process, and interdisciplinary teaching can occur successfully. Although superhero comic books furthered Samantha's learning, they also limited Cat's ability to learn about genetics alongside creative fiction writing.

As Cat demonstrated in this study, comic books are not always mastered and appropriated as a tool to assist in learning. This is not to say that she did not learn anything about genetics and story writing. She still demonstrated a level of expertise on the two subjects, but it was not evident that comic books assisted her in achieving this level of knowing. Educators wanting to incorporate outside literacies such as superhero comic books must remember that not every student in the classroom will find comic books to be a viable resource to use during times of learning. Resistance to comic books, especially superhero comic books, is still present in some students, and other cultural tools may be needed instead to help students to be successful in achieving specific tasks and objectives in interdisciplinary teaching.

For this study, I did not focus much attention on how teachers use superhero comic books as a cultural tool to achieve interdisciplinarity in their classroom. How educators are using superhero comic books in this capacity needs to be explored further to understand better how individuals, on both sides of the desk, use superhero comic books. Interdisciplinary teaching is a daunting task on its own, and to struggle to find a connection between two subjects amplifies this fight. Superhero comic books function as a tool for students to make the links between the two subjects and to achieve the learning objectives for the class, lesson, or unit. Multiple subjects can find common ground in superhero comic books as many titles provide an endless number of topics and themes that cross over multiple disciplines and subjects. Students can connect with the stories and the obstacles that many superheroes their age are facing, aside from developing powers and fighting supervillains, and they will be able to relate the topic they are learning about to the story they are reading. For educators looking to create an interdisciplinary classroom, superhero comic books are an invaluable resource to utilize.

WORKS CITED

Akerson, Valarie, and Julie Flanigan. "Preparing Preservice Teachers to Use an Interdisciplinary Approach to Science and Language Arts Instruction." *Journal of Science Teacher Education* 11, no. 4 (2000): 345–62.

Alvermann, Donna, and Kathleen Hinchman. *(Re)conceptualizing the Literacies in Adolescents' Lives: Bridging the Everyday/Academic Divide.* 3rd ed., New York: Routledge, 2012.

Baker, Linda, and Wendy Saul. "Considering Science and Language Arts Connections: A Study of Teacher Cognition." *Journal of Research in Science Teaching* 31, no. 9 (1994): 1023–37.

Bakis, Maureen. *The Graphic Novel Classroom: Powerful Teaching and Learning with Images.* Thousand Oaks: Corwin Press, 2012.

Bendis, Brian, and Sara Pichelli. *Ultimate Comics: Spider-Man.* New York: Marvel Worldwide, 2012.

Duke, Nell, and V. Susan Bennett-Armistead. *Reading and Writing Informational Text in the Primary Grades: Research-Based Practices.* New York: Scholastic, 2003.

Gee, James P. *Situated Language and Learning: A Critique of Traditional Schooling.* New York: Routledge, 2004.

Gresh, Lois H., and Robert Weinberg. *The Science of Supervillains.* Hoboken: J. Wiley, 2005.

Guzzetti, Barbara, and Marcia Mardis. "Thinking with Forensic Science: A Content Analysis of Forensic Comic Books and Graphic Novels." *Reconceptualizing the Literacies in*

Adolescents' Lives: Bridging the Everyday/Academic Divide. 3rd ed., New York: Taylor and Francis, 2012.

Hajdu, David. *The Ten-Cent Plague: The Great Comic Book Scare and How It Changed America*. New York: Farrar, Straus and Giroux, 2008.

Hatfield, Charles, Jeet Heer, and Kent Worcester, editors. *The Superhero Reader*. Jackson: University Press of Mississippi, 2013.

Hull, Glynda A., and Katherine Schultz. *School's Out! Bridging Out-of-School Literacies with Classroom Practice*. New York: Teachers College Press, 2002.

Jacobs, Heidi H. *Interdisciplinary Curriculum: Design and Implementation*. Alexandria: Association for Supervision and Curriculum Development, 1989.

Kittle, Penny. *Book Love: Developing Depth, Stamina, and Passion in Adolescent Readers*. Portsmouth: Heinemann, 2013.

Kixmiller, Lori A. S. "Standards without Sacrifice: The Case for Authentic Writing." *English Journal* 94, no. 1 (2004): 29–33.

Merriam, Sharan B., and Elizabeth J. Tisdell. *Qualitative Research: A Guide to Design and Implementation*. San Francisco: John Wiley and Sons, 2013.

Moje, Elizabeth B., Kathryn Mcintosh Ciechanowski, Katherine M. Kramer, Lindsay Ellis, Rosario Carrillo, and Tehani Collazo. "Working Toward Third Space in Content Area Literacy: An Examination of Everyday Funds of Knowledge and Discourse." *Reading Research Quarterly* 39, no. 11 (2004): 38–70.

Monnin, Katie. *Teaching Graphic Novels: Practical Strategies for the Secondary ELA Classroom*. Gainesville: Maupin House, 2010.

Newmann, Fed, Helen M. Marks, and Adam Gamoran. "Authentic Pedagogy and Student Performance." Annual Meeting of the American Educational Research Association, San Francisco, CA.

Pearson, David, Elizabeth Moje, and Cynthia Greenleaf. "Literacy and Science: Each in the Service of the Other." *Science* 328, no. 5977 (2010): 459–63.

Rourke, James. *The Comic Book Curriculum: Using Comics to Enhance Learning and Life*. Santa Barbara: Libraries Unlimited, 2010.

Sousanis, Nick. "Comics as a Tool for Inquiry." *Juniata Voices* 12 (2012): 162–72.

Tabachnick, Stephen E., ed. *Teaching the Graphic Novel*. New York: Modern Language Association of America, 2009.

Tatalović, M. "Science Comics as Tools for Science Education and Communication: A Brief, Exploratory Study." *Journal of Science Communication* 8, no. 4 (2009): 1–17.

Tchudi, Stephen, and Stephen Lafer. *The Interdisciplinary Teacher's Handbook: Integrated Teaching across the Curriculum*. Portsmouth: Boynton/Cook Publishers, 1996.

Vygotsky, Lev S., and Michael Cole. *Mind in Society: The Development of Higher Psychological Processes*. Cambridge, MA: Harvard University Press, 1978.

Wertsch, James V. *Mind as Action*. New York: Oxford University Press, 1998.

Witty, Paul, Ethel Smith, and Anne Coomer. "Reading Comics in Grades VII and VIII." *Journal of Educational Psychology* 33, no. 3 (1942): 173–82.

Wright, Brad W. *Comic Book Nation: The Transformation of Youth Culture in America*. Baltimore: The Johns Hopkins University Press, 2001.

Teaching the Unthinkable Image: An Interview with Lynda Barry

—LEAH MISEMER

On a cold, rainy February day in Madison, Wisconsin, I was delighted to interview Lynda Barry, a cartoonist who made her name in the days of alternative comics with *Ernie Pook's Comeek* and has since gained a following based on her genre-bending works *What It Is*, *Picture This*, and most recently *Syllabus*. While taking the "What It Is" class with Barry when she was a visiting artist at UW-Madison in 2012, I was struck by how much I learned about studying comics by making comics and by the often counterintuitive but always effective nature of Barry's pedagogical choices. After seeing what I—a self-described terrible artist—was able to produce given the right tools and armed with some simple techniques, I became, like so many others around the world who have heard her speak or taken her "Drawing the Unthinkable" workshop, a Lynda Barry disciple, spreading her message that everyone can and should draw. We met in her Image Lab in the Wisconsin Institute for Discovery, where she is now an associate professor of interdisciplinary creativity, surrounded by her students' work taped to windows and walls on all sides.

Misemer: You've talked a lot in the past about your experience as a student of Marilyn Frasca at Evergreen State. For example, you talk about being in her class in *What It Is*. Can you tell me a bit about how Marilyn's approach to teaching influenced your own approach to teaching comics?

Barry: Probably the most important thing was the way she did critique. In Marilyn's class, the artwork was never separated from the experience of viewing it or reading it. That is to say, it was never separated out as an object that we looked at critically and dispassionately. You know how people do, when they're doing criticism. Instead, she used people's work to help the rest of us see. So a critique would mainly consist of putting up five images, and then the class would just stare at them, sometimes for up to an hour. Afterwards, we'd do drawings from them or we'd respond to them in some way. But Marilyn made it clear that when you're looking at a piece of art, there is no way to take yourself out of that experience, to talk about it objectively. You're always, in a funny way, talking about yourself. When I began to teach workshops in my early twenties, that's what I would do. I would emphasize the experience of the work and looking at other people's work and copying other people's work, but not speaking about it directly. And certainly not speaking about it in a critical way where you would give suggestions about what would improve a piece. Marilyn would just say, "See what's there." That's something I do in my classes. That's how I look at work, too. That's how I move through the world. And I was nineteen when I started that practice. I'm sixty-one now.

Misemer: What about that uncritical eye helped you learn? How have you seen it help your students learn?

Barry: I think there are multiple parts of us, and that one part has speech, but another part doesn't have speech. It has language, but it doesn't have speech. So I think this approach gets my students to start to use, understand, and communicate in this other language. The only way to become versed in this other language is through total immersion. You have to stop the chatting or talking part of speech and pay attention to the thing I always call the "top of the mind" for this other thing to come forward. It was difficult enough to learn to do this when I was in school. Now we have all these devices that are always calling us back to this other state of mind. I call it the hamster wheel sometimes, you know, with the same fifteen problems that you just keep running through. Because we have so many things bringing us out of the top of the mind, it's harder to show people how to do this. People also don't have as long of a history with their hands, particularly writing by hand. Sometimes that can be hard. But I always say that it's a very difficult thing to explain and very easy to demonstrate.

Misemer: Moving on from Marilyn to some of your other learning experiences, how have your past experiences with school shaped how and why you teach? I'm thinking about teachers in your early life. For example, you talk about some of your early teachers in *One! Hundred! Demons!* How did their pedagogy influence you, or how did your experience as a student in their classroom influence you?

Barry: Elementary school, from the very first day, had a profound influence on me. I came from an immigrant family. My dad left early on, but I grew up in a Filipino family without a lot of money and no books. Nothing that would be at school. So for me, when I got to school, it was this remarkable place that was stable, that had materials, that had a desk that was just mine, a coat hook that was just mine, all these things that kids in stable homes may take for granted. And they should take them for granted. Everybody should feel like they have something that belongs to them. I also happened to have the same teacher for first and second grade, who understood that I had emotional problems, that I had a lot of trouble. You know, I flipped out. And she took an approach to helping me manage my issues that meant everything to me. She had an easel set up in the back of the room, and when I started to flip out, I could go to the easel. And it was without shame; it was without punishment. There was some part of her that understood that another part of me was trying to get out and couldn't do it with words, and so she thought that I could do it with pictures and stories. Those things would come together for me.

Right now, I go every Tuesday to a pre-K classroom here on campus at Eagle's Wing, and I know my time there is directly related to what happened to me in first and second grade. I'm really interested in seeing when kids become hesitant about drawing and storytelling. I used to believe, before I started working directly with little kids, that that hesitation, when it shows up, becomes more and more intractable until, by about the age of eight or nine, kids will decide they can draw or they can't draw. But what I'm finding is that it's more like a spiral, and there are opportunities over and over again for this kind of language to be learned and spoken. The most important thing is having somebody around who's doing it. Not teaching it necessarily. I don't go to my pre-K classroom to teach those kids anything. But I'm there drawing, and I have materials, and they know that I'm going to come there on Tuesday and lay on the floor, and they can come and draw with me and tell me stories. And I'm starting to see that practice moving away from where I am in the room to other parts of the room.

I do believe that drawing is our earliest language, in a certain way. It's attached to the movement of the hands. No matter what it is you're studying, it's invaluable moving into the future to have facility in this other language, which is drawing. And I don't mean representational drawing. I'm speaking specifically about comics. Today, there was a four-year-old who wanted me to draw a rock-and-roll baby in a diaper. They come over and tell me to draw stuff. And we have a tradition in that classroom where they'll be drawing, and I'll draw with them in real time, moving their hands like a

Ouija board. So I copy them in real time. They also copy me. So I start drawing this rock-and-roll baby and the kid put his hands on mine to copy in real time. This rock-and-roll baby had his eyes closed and squinted down because he was rocking out really hard, so instead of just being circles with dots in them, I made a different shape for the eyes. And the kid really liked learning the traditional anime way of using a V with a line in it. Then, I gave the rock-and-roll baby a turned up nose, and the kid said, "It looks like a pig nose," and I said, "Yeah, it does." But we drew it together.

Their brains and bodies are developing so rapidly, along with their ability to learn language. With the language of drawing specifically, the only limitation is whether their teachers are afraid of drawing or not. Most teachers are afraid of drawing. Most people are. So that really inhibits. If adults are scared of that language, the kids will pick up on that. There's also this really weird idea that you're not supposed to draw for kids. You can show them how to make an A, you can show them how to make a 5, but you're not supposed to draw a giraffe. I asked about the theory of that, and someone said that it's because kids will get so intimidated by what you're doing that they won't try themselves. But that's a wish! That's not what's going to happen. Kids aren't going to go, "Oh, you just drew a perfect giraffe, so I'm just never going to do it." I mean, they're really not that interested. That comes way later. So the other thing I'm working on is trying to get teachers to start drawing, too.

Misemer: You've taught all kinds of populations since you started teaching at twenty-five. From the pre-K kids that you're talking about to prisoners, business people, elderly people, everybody. I have met so many people who have taken workshops with you all over the world. How does your teaching approach change based on who you're working with? How do you adapt what you're teaching?

Barry: That's one of the most wonderful things about this job. Somehow, in the course of forty-eight hours I work with everyone, from people who are four years old to people who are getting their doctorates. And I do adapt what I'm teaching. Mainly I teach to where I think the person is kind of scared, to an ability the person or group doesn't realize they have. I always try to create surprise. That's what I was doing when I brought in that little tin box for you that you made *Made in Atlanta* [the project I made for her class] out of. The way you looked when you put everything in that box... I'm getting teary eyed thinking about it, because you were so surprised that you had done this. And that's the thing I always try to teach. Where can I add this element of surprise?

For adults who are completely sure they can't draw, one of the most important things is to have other people drawing at the same time, so they can show each other their drawings. I like to have people draw with their eyes closed. In fact, a giraffe drawn with your eyes closed almost always looks fantastic. It looks like a cave painting, you know, because people will lift their hands and they don't know quite where the dots are supposed to be, so the giraffe will be on one side of the page and the dots will be over about four inches away from it. But they always look good. [Laughter] And the way you're laughing right now, that happiness? That's what happens in the classroom. If they're just looking at their own giraffe, they look all concerned, but if you say, "Now hold up your drawing and show your neighbors," this joy happens in the classroom. This kind of drawing can bring this immense and immediate joy.

I was giving a university roundtable talk, and I wanted people to draw, but I didn't understand they would be eating lunch while I talked. All of a sudden, I realized there was no way that I was going to be able to get them to draw. Then I realized they were eating. So I said, "Whatever you're doing with your meal right now, I want you to make a face on your plate." Nobody moved. They were all looking at me like I was crazy. I said, "Just arrange stuff on your plate so that you're making a face that's showing some kind of emotion." What was so funny is that it was quiet for a moment, and then you heard this mad clinking, as they started making the faces. And then people started to laugh. Then I said, "Show your neighbor." Everybody turned their plate around and showed their neighbor, and the place erupted in laughter. They were having such a good time laughing at each other's food faces that it was hard for me to get them back. That kind of big physical change is possible just by moving your lettuce around or by drawing with your eyes closed. What the hell is that?! The cool thing about comics is they can just leap right over all the problems representational drawing caused. It jumps right over all that fear immediately. Especially if you give people just the most basic tools: that Ivan Brunetti means of drawing. You start there and you'll always end up somewhere.

Misemer: I drew an Ivan Brunetti drawing in a job interview recently, and I taught the method to my students. It's such a good way of helping people create simple, expressive figures interacting with their environments. And it takes seconds to teach. The formula helps scaffold the experience, so people can get beyond thinking about their lack of technique and focus on drawing to communicate or to think.

Barry: I do Ivan Brunetti drawings all the time. That style has such a long human tradition. I found a drawing that was made I think in the thirteenth century in Russia by a little kid, and it looked just like an Ivan Brunetti drawing. It was scraped onto a piece of birch bark, but it was definitely the same style. So I think it's a common language that all people have, this use of images. And following the basic idea of evolution, the characteristics that contribute to our survival tend to persist. Drawing persists. And not only does it persist. Even when people quit drawing, they wish they could draw. One of the things I love to say to people is, "If I was a genie, and I could give you the power to draw to your satisfaction, but the rule was you could never make a dime off of it, would you accept that power?" Most people say yes. And I say, "Wish granted."

Misemer: You're making this distinction between representational drawing and comics, and I just want to clarify that distinction. I'm familiar with the distinction McCloud makes in *Understanding Comics* about how reader interaction is related to the level of detail in the drawing. How do you see the two as different from one another?

Barry: It's easy to explain. Most people quit drawing, or they become sure that they can't draw, at about the age of eight or nine. Around that age there will come a time when they'll draw everything else on the page, but suddenly they'll realize the nose doesn't look right. Or hands. Those are the two things that trip people up, noses and hands. And unless they develop a symbol for that nose or hand, they'll quit drawing. Most people who think they can't draw are living with a decision they made about themselves when they were eight. Then I'll say to them, "Okay, so imagine Charlie Brown. Now imagine Charlie Brown with a hyperrealistic nose and realistic hands." It'd be horrible, right? In fact, a cartoon really needs to have just symbols, little symbolic marks, for the hands and the face. Part of that is because we're born being able to recognize faces. Also, anything in the hand position is going to read as a hand. Anything in the nose position is going to read as a nose.

    I love to prove this to my students when we do drawing jams. I'll tell students to draw an object in the nose area. I had one student draw a can of beer. Then I'll tell them to draw a letter of the alphabet where the nose would be. Then an exclamation mark. Then a scribble. And once we get all the other features in, you can see that, yes, it's the letter Q somebody wrote for a nose, but it totally reads as a nose. Again, that's the surprise element I love to show people. You can also see this ability to recognize faces from symbols when you do a drawing jam, where you draw and then pass me the paper, and then I draw and pass it back and so on. Say we each drew a head shape, then we passed it, then we each drew eyes and passed it. Maybe we'd do four of these heads. And we lay them out, and I ask you, "Which one's drunk?" and you'll know. No one intended to make a drunk person, but it's really easy to tell which one is drunk. So where's the comic? The comic is somewhere between the person who made it and the person who's looking at it.

It's a relationship. And it's one that stutters through time, because somebody might have made that comic in 1954, and then here in 2017, I may activate something from it. Or it may activate some part of me. And that's the thing that's so great about comics. Once you realize that sweating over the tiny details isn't going to get you close to what you're trying to do, it's freeing. There are cartoonists who leave you more and more to find, and that's heavenly. But comics can also be very, very simple, because the tiny details aren't visible.

Misemer: For me as a comics reader, the digital has changed that a little bit. I don't know if you read comics digitally, but with guided view your whole iPad screen can become one panel. I'm currently super fascinated with the cartoonist who's doing *The Fade Out*. Ed Brubaker's writing it. Sean Phillips is drawing it. He uses a different brushstroke style depending on the character he's writing. [Gesturing] The noir detective guy, his brushstrokes are all scratchy. And then, the femme fatale, hers are all sinuous. But even being able to see those details, I can see what you're saying in terms of that relationship created by the drawing. That it can be detail oriented, but sometimes it's elements of the image that we don't even think about.

Barry: You just demonstrated the universal language of drawing to me. [Gestures] You did this to show the noir guy and this to show the femme fatale. So you were drawing. When people are gesturing, one of the things they're doing is drawing. It's just that they're drawing in the air without leaving any kind of evidence. Another thing I've been trying to study is the tendency of people who haven't drawn something in a while to want to cover up their drawings. They have this look of distress, and the only thing I can compare it to is if you had suddenly lost control of a bodily fluid. It's the same kind of shame you'd have if you just started drooling while you were talking to somebody. It's intense shame and embarrassment.

Misemer: I'm interested in the role of shame and the forbidden and the idea of permission in your work and teaching. In your own history, you talk about how drawing was forbidden, how you had to scrounge scraps of paper and things like that. And then you talk about giving your students permission to draw in your classes in a way that is not representational or giving them permission to draw even though they haven't drawn in twenty years. Do you feel like one informs the other? Do you feel like your idea of giving students permission comes from your own history of drawing being forbidden or difficult?

Barry: It wasn't just drawing that was forbidden. It was pretty much engaging with anything. Drawing, a book, anything. But I do think that for me, the permission is more about permission to speak in this other language, to try to use this other language that's there. To be able to make pictures in real time in class. You know from working with me that we move rapidly. Often, you make a drawing and it's out of your hands before you even have a chance to look at it. Like when we're doing drawing jams. It's more like total immersion in learning a language versus studying verbs and conjugation. Conjugation and sentence structure, all that stuff can come later, but you have to have the language first.

Also, I just love drawings made by people who quit drawing at about the age of eight or nine, because there's so much that's intact from that time. Like your drawings just drove me wild, as you know. I was a huge fan. Because I'd just see these drawings that I'm not capable of doing anymore. A lot of people who are trained artists can't draw like that anymore unless they're around people who draw in a very natural way, who are mostly untrained. That's the big advantage of having a really mixed class. I feel like when people are taught to draw well, they basically just learn how not to draw badly, which means there's so much they can't say. It's like they're trying to write everything with one vowel. And it's not bad drawing, but the untrained students have a very fresh approach. I think everybody benefits from the class when I can get the people who feel like they can't draw to not be scared.

Misemer: It's interesting that you describe this as a language immersion program, because that's what I felt like when I was in your class. I was sort of swept up in the flow, and I never really knew what was happening, and you wouldn't really tell us what we were going to do. I didn't even have time to think about the fact that, before coming to your class, I was a self-classified "bad drawer." I just kept doing what I was told. As someone who has students in my writing classroom reflect on their writing all the time, which is a research-supported method for helping someone become a better writer, it was really strange for me. But it worked. What other techniques do you have for getting people over the idea that they are bad writers or bad drawers?

Barry: Exhaustion is one of my main techniques. So that you get to the point where you just can't care anymore. That's where the timer comes in. I work really hard to get people to understand what three minutes feels like without having to keep a timer. If you have to do a drawing in three minutes, you can't really think about it. I also frontload the class. Now the most difficult part of the class is the first six weeks. I just make them draw nonstop. Make comics. Observe people. I lessen that frantic pace as we go toward the end of the semester, so that in the last four weeks, they just have one comic strip due, which is way more than most teachers ask people to do. My "Comics I" class had to do ten comic strips last semester. And each strip had to have a silent moment, so that they'd start to understand what that silent beat is. There's this point where you just can't freak out because there's just too much due. You're not going to stress over how to draw that eye, because you have too much to do. You're just going to go, "Okay, that's how I'm going to draw an eye."

Also, we copy each other's work a lot. And we copy work from books. I think copying is probably the best way to learn how to draw. Boy do I see that in the pre-K classes. They do not have this concept of intellectual property. One draws a princess, and the princess happens to have this long blue nose. Suddenly, you'll see that blue nose appearing all over the classroom. Or an element will be in a story, and then it appears in all these other stories. They borrow each other's stuff constantly. And that's how they're growing. They're picking up stuff from all over. I often go to those kids to help me figure out what's going on in my classroom with my grown students. One of the things I always say is that the class is open source. When you see someone try something, you have the absolute right to copy it and try it. So far, everybody's been cool about it. That's the kind of thing in fine art that you're not allowed to do at all. And I'm like, "Why?" I don't get it.

Misemer: If you think about how art, or really any skill, was taught in the guild system, people learned by copying their masters, by imitating what they did with whatever tools that they were learning to work with. So learning from copying makes sense. And having interviewed a number of women cartoonists because of my interest in *Wimmen's Comix,* so many people learn to make comics by copying comics.

Barry: How else would you do it? How else do you learn to speak any language? You copy what people are saying. You don't have to invent an entirely new language to be able to speak. The only kind of comics instruction you used to get was in the backs of magazines, you know, where you could take a comics course. There are people who taught caricature. But this idea that comics are being taught now is really interesting to me. And the idea that they're being taught without drawing is fascinating to me. How do people study comics, but not draw them? It's sort of like studying the Portuguese language without ever speaking it. I think that, if you're studying comics, even if you feel like you can't draw, just trying to copy one panel will teach you way more than anything that can be spoken.

Misemer: There's a small, but growing, movement within scholarship that emphasizes the importance of comics creation. Nick Sousanis's work springs to mind, and Aaron Kashtan had a piece in *Digital Humanities Quarterly* entitled "Materiality Comics" published a few years ago that argued for a similar practice-based approach to scholarship. He was talking about the importance of materiality in comics and used BitStrips and Comic Life to create his own comic, basically theorizing the comic as he was creating it.

Barry: That's so much nicer than writing out the script and then finding pictures that go with it.

Misemer: This actually brings me to another question about the relationship between art and literature and drawing and writing in your class. So often, in school, we separate the two. We have separate classes in literature and art. And in college, at least here at UW-Madison, they're on opposite ends of the campus. I imagine that your students bring this artificial distinction with them sometimes. What kinds of challenges have you faced in trying to get students to both create art and write?

Barry: If they have to do it with the intention of creating art or creating a piece of writing, they are already not going to be very happy. So again, what I try to do is walk them into it in a surprising way. For example, somebody might read in our class, and then everybody in our class has three minutes to draw a picture based on that reading. What we've done is take a piece of text that somebody's read, and then suddenly, there are twenty visual images of that text. We can do the same thing with a visual image, which your class often did, where we write from a photo. And then there'd be twenty text versions. What I try to show is that everything that we call "the arts" is image-based.

Whether it's an image that's in a sound form, like in music, or whether it's in some other form, the image is there, but the formula for that experience differs whether it's a painting or a comic strip or an opera or a novel. It's the language of that experience. But what I'm able to show in a classroom is that you can have the same image—so it can be like a picnic somewhere—and you can put the formula for that experience in the alphabet or written language. Or the formula for that experience can be a drawing. But either way, the person has to experience it while they are using that formula. I don't think images transfer very well if you're just thinking logically about what it should look like and then handing it to somebody. That's really different than having an experience while you're making something. Then, I think the image transfers a lot better.

One of the problems I have about comics that are trying to teach is that rather than doing the amazing thing comics can do, they are infomercials. It's mainly a head looking directly out of the frame and talking to me with text that oftentimes feels that it was written before this little head and was just popped into the panel. Those things don't do what comics do. I look at them and I think they're not comics. They look like comics, but they're not in this other world that I'm sort of looking into. In comics, there aren't imperatives for me like, "Hey you, now make comics!" Nobody's talking out at me. I think it would be really weird to try to read a novel where the person was trying to talk to me the whole time I was reading it.

The thing I feel like hasn't been done in comics yet, and I think it will be, is that when people are trying to do scholarly comics, they have not yet found a good solution for giving information to people. And I think the solution is pretty damn simple, but nobody believes it. If you're giving a citation or some scholarly observation, to just have a person telling you that, that doesn't do anything. If you had instead a picture of a plate of spaghetti or a mountain range or a dog pissed off at another dog or a cigarette smoking or anything, suddenly, whatever text I'm reading and the image are going to try to communicate with each other in the back of my mind. That's where all the associative thoughts happen. That's also where comprehension happens. So the thing that comics can do is put text together with an image that is not quite exactly right and suddenly open up a way of thinking through that juxtaposition. And that's the thing I hope people will start to realize when they're doing educational and scholarly comics.

Because I know that comics and scholarship are intertwined now. Ebony [Flowers's] dissertation is almost done and it is gorgeous. It's this beautiful, drawn piece of art. But even she had to use some of these talking faces. She had to figure out how to write a whole dissertation in comics. Can you actually write a whole dissertation in comics? She couldn't do the whole thing, but she did part of it. And she also talks a little bit out, but mainly, she has conversations with people in her comics. So in a funny way, I still get to be the reader, instead of someone who's being directly addressed and bored, by the way, by that direct address. They might just as well say, "Eat sausage. Eat sausage, eat sausage." That's what it seems like to me. It's like an infomercial for sausage.

Misemer: I think Nick's [Sousanis] work takes advantage of this juxtaposition you're discussing. And *Unflattening* came from his dissertation, so it is possible to write a dissertation in comics. Having a willing committee is the tricky part. It's interesting that you bring up these comics that teach you how to make comics, because I was recently reading *Everything Volume 1*, and I found one of those that you did from 1979.

Barry: I was already critical about the whole thing then. How old was I? Like twenty-three, and I was already critical about the idea that this is how you do it.

Misemer: When I was reading through your oeuvre, I noticed that elements of teaching start to emerge at a certain point. It seems to start happening at the end of *One! Hundred! Demons!* but maybe it happened before that. *What It Is, Picture This,* and *Syllabus* are all very much about teaching. Was writing about teaching something you always wanted to do? Or did it happen organically? What was that process like?

Barry: For a lot of people, what's published has to do with what a publisher is willing to publish. The publisher Sasquatch didn't care for *One! Hundred! Demons!* and really didn't care for that instruction stuff at the back. The next book that I had planned was *What It Is*, and they didn't want any part of it. I met with my publisher to talk about my next book and he said, "Is it going to have comics in it?" And I said, "Yeah, I'm a cartoonist." And he said, "We're not interested." So that was in 2002, I believe. Then all the way to 2008 or 9 I couldn't find a publisher who would touch anything. I had this career that was going really well, and then it just crashed, and at the same time, these alternative newspapers started to fold up. Interestingly enough, I got to the point where I really had nothing to lose. Nobody wanted to publish *What It Is*. There was something wonderful about that, because I thought, "I'm not going to try to make these comics in a way that people think of comics."

I've been interested in the nature of images since I worked with Marilyn, and teaching is one of the ways that I get to know more about the image. It's really weird. If you think about that little watercolor set that you had with all those colors that you could mix and make all this stuff with. That's what students are like for me. You're like this palette with these amazing colors. Things I cannot figure out on my own, in my own practice, I can for some reason figure out when students are working. I was just going through my computer. I have to find some images that I have to send to New York for this event that I'm going to. And I was just laughing because I have hardly any pictures of my own stuff. It's like baby pictures of you all. Just every little thing that you did. The main memory of my computer is just pictures of your stuff. When I look at it, I'm just like wrecked and wowed, you know. It'd be so much better if I wasn't. Because then I could just go home and make comics. But I feel this strong need to show people what my students are making.

Misemer: So is that where *Syllabus* comes from, then? The idea that the work you are doing right now is made up of what your students are making?

Barry: Being in love? Yeah. Actually, when I was hanging some stuff up in the hallway of the sixth floor in the art building, one of my colleagues walked by and he looked at me and he went, "Show off." I said, "I totally am. I'm showing off their work." One time, when I was hanging something up, somebody said, "How do you get them to make so much work? What do you do with them?" Because my students make more work than anybody. But I believe in it, and I believe it has a biological function. And I believe comics are the oldest form of art. If you watch the little kids I work with, they'll say, "I'm going to write a story and read it to you." So they'll write the story by drawing it, and then they hold it like a book and they read it to you. Today, a girl came up to me who has been telling me the same story about this snake every time I visit. She'll tell it to me and I'll write it down. So she drew the same snake today and she says, "This time, I'm going to write it." So I said, "Alright." She took an index card and imitated handwriting and said, "Now I'll read it to you." And she went, "Blah blahblah blahblah blahblah blahblah." And then we started laughing really hard. And then other people would pick up this card with her scribbles and they'd read it and they'd go, "Blahblah blahblah blahblah blahblah blah." They're really funny.

Misemer: I see this idea of using student work as your materials in *Syllabus*. But in *What It Is* and *Picture This*, it's the teaching without the student work. Where does that impulse come from?

Barry: I think it's teaching myself. That's the way that I sort stuff out. I sit down and I try to write about it. And always try to include some visual element, whether it's collage or just any kind of drawing. Ebony [Flowers] came up with something that blew my mind. She figured out to take a double-paged spread in a comp book and actually draw the places where the pictures are going to go, even though you don't know what in the hell it is that you're going to write about. She's also a person that really started to play with frame shapes and sizes. It's as if I was able to show her something that made her able to teach me. That's happened over and over again, where from working with students, particularly students who are teachers themselves, I end up learning so many things and getting so many ideas. Things that become an integral part of my practice. For example, one of my students, Chef Boyardee, he teaches, and he started doing the attendance thing where you draw a self-portrait, but he started directing the students. He'd say, "I'd like you guys to draw yourselves getting shot out of a cannon." So that's what I do now. Everyday as I drive into school, I think about what I'm going to have them draw. I had them draw themselves leaving their bodies yesterday. And I gave them these little tiny red rhinestones that are adhesive on the back. I said, "Start by putting two of those on your index cards. Those are your eyes." They were just fantastic.

[We are interrupted by one of Lynda's students] Joe's an ag student. That's the part that's wild. Comics allow me to talk to anybody. Everyone wants to do them.

Misemer: They allow you to go to NASA.

Barry: They wanted me there. I got to do the monster exercise with them at NASA. And some other things. I got them to draw self-portraits. It was really cool. I just got back from the medical school at Penn State Hershey. It's one of the only medical schools in the country that has a medical humanities program, so the fourth-year medical students are required to take humanities classes. I was there teaching comics to fourth-year med students. Just teaching them how to do all this stuff. And then afterwards we sat around and had a drink, and I talked to them about the crazy shit they did, like having to take apart cadavers. Or having to solve the problem of how are you going to get twelve legs from one place to another place, because you're going to have to go through the hospital? The way they do it is they line them all up on a bed and cover that up so no one knows there are twelve human legs just rolling down the hallway. So it's really wild knowing that I'm showing somebody how to draw a nose, but that person also knows how to take a leg off. That's the part that's really humbling. They're freaked to draw a nose; they're not freaked to take a leg off.

Misemer: I want to go back to the flow of the class, the surprise of the class, which in *What It Is* you describe as being between knowing and not knowing. Or you might call it "the unthinkable," after your "Drawing the Unthinkable" class. The educational environment, right now in particular, is very objective driven. You have standards and testing and all that drives instructional practice. I think that leads students to form expectations based on stated learning goals. Have you seen this attitude reflected in your classroom? How do you respond?

Barry: I see it in the initial three weeks' terror of the students if they get one thing wrong. I do ask people to work to capacity and beyond, so they'll often be missing a couple drawings or something, and they just flip. Then I get to tell them it's not that kind of class. But it is a very serious class, and we're going to work until we fall over. But when they fall over, I believe them. When they say they just couldn't get those other three drawings done, I'll believe them. Especially because I'll look at how they did the first six, and they were supposed to spend three minutes, and on that first one they probably spent an hour. It's all about learning how they work. I think the critical thing is for people to not know what they are about to do. Also, taking a different name is important. You guys went by cards.

Misemer: Seven of spades forever.

Barry: Yeah. Right? And when you see the seven of spades, it's you, right? It's like an avatar. For instance, I had a student named Frida $flow and the "cash" was spelled with a dollar sign. Her real name is Gretchen, and Gretchen will say, "I can't do this. I'm not good at drawing. I don't like to do this," and I'd say, "Yeah, you can't, but Frida $flow loves doing this." And then she'd start laughing. When people start to identify themselves with their avatar, they get over some of the fear. I'll say, "Lynda Barry can't keep a class like this together, but Professor Mandrake is all about it." It's about identifying this different part of yourself as a different name. Also in the classroom, it keeps people so that they stay classmates rather than saying, "That's a PhD student." Or, "That person's just a sophomore." That's one thing I do.

I also control where my students sit. They have nametags that they leave with me, and I arrange them so when they come in, they're always sitting in a different part of the room and next to someone else. Everybody seems to really like that, because whatever hierarchy is usually created by space in the classroom just can't happen. That's also why I don't have them put their names on the front of their drawings. Ever. We start to recognize the drawings. They'll start to recognize someone's style, but they don't know who it is. And then, after a while you connect who it is. Yesterday in "Comics I," I was able to hold up stuff and people were able to tell who did it. And how that happens, I will never know. It's a very mysterious thing. What is it? How are we able to recognize someone's style of handwriting? It's interesting. It's a very complex thing, and yet we can do it. And what's weird is I can recognize who did what when I find just pieces of drawings from our class.

Misemer: It seems like such a counterintuitive way of creating a classroom community. Usually, the way you're taught to do that as a teacher is to do endless icebreakers and group work and things like that. And it's very important that everybody know everyone else's name. That's been my approach to teaching. But I was part of a community when I was in that class, despite the fact that I knew nobody's real name. I knew their card number. How does that work? Is it just because you're sharing such an intimate part of yourself?

Barry: Without ever taking the work and putting it somewhere that we would talk about it as if it could exist outside of that living space. That relationship is so strong. I'm spending Spring Break with Marilyn. That's the thing that's wild. These are lifelong relationships. I'll always feel that way about my students. It's a kind of love that I didn't expect, and I didn't see coming. When I think about all the things comics have brought me, it's amazing that they brought me an entire life. A very rich, good life.

Misemer: In *What It Is* you say that your experiences working as a painter, cartoonist, writer, illustrator, playwright, editor, commentator, and teacher are very much alike. Can you explain that comment? How is teaching like cartooning, for instance?

Barry: Because it has to be responsive, and it has to have an element of being alive. The logical way that people might think you do a cartoon is to think of a story first, then figure out the text, then figure out how to get an illustrator ... [Laughs]. But that's not how a good conversation goes. There has to be an element of being prepared for all of those things at the same time. You have to be prepared to respond to what's going on, alive, right in front of you. Say I'm making a comic, and I'm thinking, "Okay this is going to be a comic about Marlys telling a story about going to buy a goldfish," and I call it "Goldfish." And I draw her holding something in her hand that's supposed to be a bag with a goldfish in it, but somehow I've drawn it so that it looks like cotton candy. I've really learned that when I'm trying to draw a goldfish in a bag and it looks like cotton candy, the story is about cotton candy. So I respond to what the drawing's doing, and I try always to see where the drawing takes me. My characters very rarely talk out to the reader. They have a few times, and I never like it when I do it. I think Marlys is the only one that's ever talked outside of the panel. Sometimes she's having a show, so she can talk out at you. I always just try to watch and listen. All of those things that I mentioned. You watch and listen and it's all image based. You've got to be prepared, but you have to be completely willing to improvise, to see what's there. Otherwise, it's like trying to have a relationship with someone where they're not even there, you're just kind of planning the whole thing.

Misemer: Do you have any last advice for people who want to teach courses where students create comics?

Barry: They have to draw. The teacher also has to draw comics. And copying is a really good way to do it. I think one of the best books to get started is that Ivan Brunetti book. It's just brilliant. I keep going back to it and finding more stuff.

BIBLIOGRAPHY

Barry, Lynda. *One! Hundred! Demons!* Seattle: Sasquatch Books, 2005.
Barry, Lynda . *Picture This*. Montreal: Drawn & Quarterly, 2010.
Barry, Lynda. *Syllabus: Notes From an Accidental Professor*. Montreal: Drawn & Quarterly, 2014.
Barry, Lynda. *What It Is*. Montreal: Drawn & Quarterly, 2008.
Brunetti, Ivan. *Cartooning: Philosophy and Practice*. New Haven, CT: Yale University Press, 2011.
Kashtan, Aaron. "Materiality Comics." *Digital Humanities Quarterly* 9, no. 4 (2015). http://www.digitalhumanities.org/dhq/vol/9/4/000212/000212.html.
Sousanis, Nick. *Unflattening*. Cambridge, MA: Harvard University Press, 2015.

PART III

FUTURE DIRECTIONS IN COMICS PEDAGOGY

In educational contexts, the idea of "best practice" is one that frequently shapes teacher professional development. Recognizing that educators have myriad instructional choices, offering specific pathways for meeting students is an enticing proposition. And yet, one reason we resist "best practices" is that they are often described without offering the contexts of the cultural, economic, social, political, or temporal milieus in which instruction takes place. Simply put, practice is *always* tied to when, where, who, and under what circumstances. Best practices live and die within the blink of an eye and—as demonstrated by the chapters in Part II—depend on the expertise of teachers and their relationships with their students.

Comics pedagogy too is in a moment that must resist the simple naming of "best practices." Instead, we center the chapters in this concluding section around recognizing that ours is a field in wild development and rapid growth. What comics and pedagogy mean—as both separate and intertwined terms—can continually be reimagined, contested, and built anew. This is an exciting moment, and while this volume offers some principles, ideas, and vocabulary to guide our collective work, these are neither cemented nor definitive.

In his review of the burgeoning comics studies field, John Lent reminds us that there are tremendous areas of scholarship still waiting to be excavated. His is a vision of further growth through interdisciplinary scholarship. In particular, we emphasize the need to understand political economy and intellectual property as tied to comics production and labor. These are *big* areas of comics studies that fundamentally shape what is taught, under what conditions, and for what purposes. Related to this framing, Johnathan Flowers offers an important critique of some of the foundational tenets of comics studies and questions the epistemological grounding on which our pedagogies stand. By exploring how Scott McCloud's work has shaped our field, Flowers deftly illustrates that this field is constantly moving and calls for new voices and pedagogies. He does this by interlinking power and visibility with politics and race within the field of comics studies. Linking theory and practice, Frederik Byrn Køhlert and Nick Sousanis offer multiple examples of what their co-teaching approach with and through comics looks like. Sharing prompts, students' work, and their pedagogical decisions, Køhlert and Sousanis give readers a peek under the hood of what their comics pedagogy looks like within traditional English settings. Finally, in conversation with Jenny Blenk, comic creator Kelly Sue DeConnick discusses the possibilities of learning and pushing against patriarchal assumptions that ground comics; embracing an ethos of "noncompliance" as referenced within her series *Bitch Planet*, DeConnick highlights how comics serve as pedagogical mediums as well as tools for scrutiny.

Taken together, these chapters offer powerful new directions for where teachers, researchers, creators, and fans may be taking comics pedagogy as a growing field. And yet these chapters are by no means the final statement. Rather, we see these as contributions that invite readers into conversation with each other and with the broader world of educators using comics in intentional and powerful ways. Considering the future of the field of comics pedagogy, each of these chapters offers encouragement for new conversations, new inquiry, and new teaching practices to emerge.

Comic Art Research: Achievements, Shortcomings, and Remedies

—JOHN A. LENT, Temple University

Signifying a new field of study's "arrival" are factors such as the dwindling justifications and defenses for its right to be part of academia and the generation of historical and critical overviews of its research portfolio. Comic art studies satisfy both of these criteria. Until recently, it was not uncommon for articles and conference presentations to find it necessary to start off with reasons that comics/cartoons must be taken seriously (e.g., political cartoons help form public opinion, or comics and animation are significant cultural and economic parts of the entertainment world) and why they were not (academic snobbery, lack of funding, or links to popular culture and "low culture").

As comics scholarship blossomed, especially since the early 2000s, enough research was completed to merit analytical overviews of these bodies of work. Among these were articles by Steirer and Lent ("Winding"; "Comics Scholarship"). In Steirer's critical appraisal, he calls for disciplinarity, claiming that comics scholarship remains in an "academic no-place," having "ghettoized" itself within the academy (Steirer 263), and he calls for "greater theoretical sophistication and a more coherent disciplinary reflection" (Steirer 264). Reviewing comics studies publications, Steirer identified six major approaches regularly used by researchers: factual (often leaning towards reiterative), sociocultural, ideological, auteur, industrial, and formalist. He was surprised by how minimally the industrial approach figures into comics scholarship, blaming this deficiency on the "anticommercial prejudice" of most humanities departments and the "stubbornness" of mature scholars who stick with "familiar methodologies" of literary studies (Steirer 274). As editor of *International Journal of Comic Art* (which in forty huge issues has included more than a thousand articles), I can attest to this lack of scholarship on the comics' industrial sector. Despite numerous calls for more research using an industrial-commercial approach, very little has been forthcoming.

Two of my own articles attempted to survey the status of comics studies. In the initial issue of *Studies in Comics*, I characterized the initial route of comics research as "pot-holed" and "winding," consisting of isolated individual and short-term efforts, carried out by fans, collectors, aficionados, and cartoonists, often using their own collections as resources (Lent, "Winding"). The road began to take the shape of a paved highway in the mid- to late 1990s, with an attitude change towards comics scholarship in the academy, the reinvention of comics more suitable for an adult readership, the cross-fertilization of research partly because of globalization, the emergence of theoretical frameworks as young researchers from the full spectrum of academia entered comics studies, and the acceptance of comics scholarship by many graduate students who felt safe approaching professors with ideas about comics for their dissertations (Lent, "Winding").

The second article (Lent, "Comics Scholarship") identified the issues of definition and disciplinarity as devourers of considerable chunks of academic comics discourse, with no consensus reached on either. With definition, the difficulty results because different labels are used, and their meanings vary country to country; the terms "comic art" and "narrative art" are not always applicable because comics are not exclusively humorous or sequential. Characterizing comics through the lexicons of cinema, literature, or graphics also does not solve the problem, as forms and formats differ. My contention has been that both definition and disciplinarity, seen by some as earmarks of legitimatization, should not evoke so much concern. Ever-changing forms of comics demand different definitions and categorizations, and the delimiting function of definition can be accomplished by keeping readers' interest in mind when organizing and presenting research (Lent, "Defining"). Retaining an interdisciplinary approach makes sense; it allows for borrowing from, linking with, and reaching across other disciplines (Lent, "Comics Scholarship" 19).

From my vantage point as the author or editor of books, articles, and a journal, and organizer of many academic panels, I have observed trends, problems, and gaps in comics scholarship, many of which are elaborated on in the following pages. Perhaps as a means to summarize these tendencies, the communication paradigm (communicator, message, channel, and audience) is useful. It is fairly safe to say that comics studies falls short at every stage of the continuum except for the message (text), which dominates much of the literature. Though biographies, profiles, and interviews of comics creators have proliferated since the 1990s, very little is known about publishers and owners and their ideologies and the extent of the control they exercise over content and labor. Channels (the comics distributors and comics retailers) and audiences continue to receive sparse research attention, resulting in insufficient information on how comics are distributed, the controllers of these channels, or the impact of digitalization on comics delivery. The scant research on comics readers is based on very narrow samples (a handful of fans interviewed online or at a comic-book store or convention or through letters to comic-book editors), which are not systematically constructed nor representative of more meaningful universes.

Encouraging, and pleasing at the same time, among my observations of trends are the hugely augmented community of comics researchers worldwide, hailing from a plethora of disciplines in addition to literature (e.g., medicine, disability, many of the social sciences and humanities); the expansion of links and collaborations of comics researchers through the availability of more conferences and the internet; and personally most satisfying, the move away (especially in the United States) from the insular, myopic, and occasionally arrogant notion that only American comics were worthy of studying. There have been gigantic strides made to study comics from international, transnational, intercultural, and multicultural perspectives in this century.

These successes aside, deep gaps remain in comic art studies, most prominent being the lack of the following.

1. A political-economy approach to answering: Who owns the industry? What are their vested interests? Who benefits/who pays in the current financial arrangement? What are the implications of conglomerate ownership of comics industries?
2. Legal studies on censorship, other restrictions on the "right to cartoon," copyright, and intellectual property; morality and ethics.
3. Labor studies: how comics companies, print media, and feature and comics syndicates treat cartoonists in terms of wages, benefits, gender equality, job security, and work load.
4. Historical method and archival usage, digging into the increasingly plentiful comics and media archives (not only online) to rediscover the evolution of comic art, perhaps pushing its beginnings further back; to make connections between early cartooning and that of today.

Political Economy

Comics studies need to be grounded more deeply in political economy theory. With roots in the Frankfurt School and the criticism of capitalism, political economy encompasses patterns of ownership, production and distribution, labor-management arrangements, the commodification of comics hardware and software, the remaining impacts of colonialism, modernity, westernization, and other dependency relationships, and other topics. Because of its connection to Marxist thought and some disciplines' strong allegiance to the market (e.g., mass communication), political economy scholarship for decades was not welcomed in academia. Such exclusion is not as prevalent today; yet, topics such as the ownership of comics enterprises has received scant attention.

Today, transnational conglomerates own a substantial portion of the comics and animation industries. Two of the world's top ten media conglomerates own the largest US comics firms—Time Warner owns DC Comics, and the Walt Disney Company owns Marvel Comics Group. In mid-2018, the way was cleared for the big to become bigger as AT&T's bid to acquire Time Warner was court approved, clearing the way for a proposed Comcast acquisition of Fox. Already, children's cartoons and much of the overall US animation industry are dominated by Disney with Pixar in its fold, Time Warner through its Cartoon Network, and Viacom owning Nickelodeon (Westcott 254). Some of these are giants tied to other comics-related companies. For example, Marvel Comics is affiliated with the French-originated book publishing giant Hachette through a distribution arrangement. Hachette's parent company Hachette Livre is the sixth largest trade and educational publisher in the world. With the prospect of digitalization drastically changing comics, Amazon in 2014 purchased ComiXology, the dominant digital comics marketplace, and by 2018 ComiXology Originals added the creative dimension when launching four new titles. Other large comics publishers such as France's Delcourt have also seriously entered the digital comics fold.

Others of the world's biggest mass media conglomerates are or have been major comics owners. Bertelsmann has comics through its Random House subsidiary; the once-powerful Robert Maxwell media conglomerate owned Fleetway Editions, representing 60 to 70 percent of the UK's comics market, before the Danish Gutenberghus Group took it over, and Mexico's Televisa Group has in its fold at least one-half of the small companies responsible for the hundreds of comic book titles on the Mexican market.

In Europe, the centuries-old Casterman, a publisher later of Franco-Belgian comics (including *The Adventures of Tintin*), recently became part of Groupe Flammarion, which in turn was bought by RCS Media Group of Italy; DC Thomson of Scotland, owner of television, book publishing, newspaper, and website interests, brings out important comic books such as *The Dandy, The Beano, Jackie, The Broons, Commando,* and *Oor Wullie*; and in India, Virgin

Comics LLC, which later became Liquid Comics, was founded in 2006 by Sir Richard Branson and his Virgin Group of transnational companies.

A 2017 *Publishers Weekly* list of the largest revenue-producing book publishers worldwide found at least nine of the first twenty-five heavily involved with comics production. Four of them were located in Japan—Shueisha (sixteenth), Kodansha (seventeenth), Kadokawa Publishing (nineteenth), and Shogakukan (twenty-second). Shueisha and Shogakukan are affiliated with the mammoth Hitotsubashi Group. Each of these conglomerates has many holdings in other media and entertainment properties, such as broadcasting, newspapers, records, a theme park, software (websites and mobile sites), video games, and film. As an indicator of their size, Kadokawa Group Holdings owns forty-three companies; Shogakukan publishes sixty-four magazines (eighteen of which are comics) and about 760 new book titles yearly; and Shueisha, the largest manga publisher in the world, also owns Hakusensha Publishers and (jointly with Shogakukan) Viz Media to produce manga in the United States and ShoPro to distribute, license, and merchandise popular magazines and comic books in Japan.

Other transnational publishers with significant comics holdings listed by *Publishers Weekly* are Holtzbrinck (fifteenth) of Germany, Bonnier (twenty-first) of Sweden, and Egmont Group (twenty-fifth) of Denmark and Norway. Bonnier is composed of 175 decentralized companies in five divisions (books, magazine group, business press, newspapers, and broadcasting and entertainment) operating in more than twenty countries. Bonnier, which owned comics publisher Carlsen in Germany before its sale to Egmont, consists of book publishers and book clubs throughout Scandinavia and is the major publisher of fiction in Finland, Norway, and Sweden; the leading publisher of children's books in Germany; and the owner of the online book retailer Adlibris. The Egmont Group includes magazines, books, films, cineplexes, television, comic books, textbooks, online communities, games, and game consoles. Egmont's one hundred plus companies are active in more than thirty countries (see Milliot). The synergistic holdings of these companies lend themselves well to spin-offs of comics on multiple platforms.

Other large US book publishers produce comic books and graphic novels, such as Scholastic Corporation, Simon & Schuster, Penguin Random House, IDW Publishing, Harper Collins Publishers, Macmillan Publishers, Boom! Studios, Houghton Mifflin Harcourt, Hyperion Books, Little Brown & Co., St. Martin's Press, and more (Woo 33–36).

The concentration of comics industries in fewer conglomerates is a justifiable concern worthy of research attention. A number of possible research questions come to mind:

- How much of the world's comics industry is controlled by these behemoths?
- How real are trends towards monopolization of the industry?
- How are the companies interlocked, and how do these interlocking directorships play out in terms of influence?
- What are the vested interests of these conglomerates with comics appendages?
- Are the interests a threat to artists' freedom and autonomy and to the quality and diversity of comics titles and content, and do they relate to considerations other than those of marketing?
- To what extent are the conglomerates enclosing culture and intellectual property, making sure, in media critic Herbert Schiller's words, that these rights are "strengthened and extended [for the sole benefit of the conglomerates], and new means devised to ensure that these rights cannot be breached"? (see Schiller).
- Finally, would comics publishing survive without these large-scale companies?

Close public document analyses and, in the rare cases where they are open, corporate records can reveal the breadth of conglomerate ownership of comic art. Yet data and analyses about the concentration of comic-art ownership are rare everywhere. Using Asia as an example, the Philippines *komiks* industry, for most of its ninety-year existence, was nearly totally in the hands of media magnate Ramon Roces; a large proportion of Indonesian-produced comic books come off Kompas Gramedia Group presses; in Hong Kong, Jademan controlled the industry for years, its books garnering 70 to 90 percent of the market; in South Korea, Dai Won Publishing and Seoul Cultural Publishers brought out fifteen of the country's twenty comics magazines for years; and Art Square Group controls much of the comics and graphic novels titles in Malaysia (see Lent *Asian Comics* 162–63).

Remembering that comic art also encompasses political cartoons and comic strips, the possible ramifications of conglomerate ownership and control become even more serious. Corporations of the magnitude of those that operate newspaper chains in North America, Europe, and Australia especially wield enormous control over their appendages and their journalists and artists. These corporate giants have many vested interests that are tied to government and big business with the potential to interfere with truthful reporting by writers and cartoonists. It is vital to know the operational mode of these corporations, the entities they own and control, and their links to potential influence peddlers.

Once this information is determined (a published study of its own), research by content or textual analyses, supplemented with interviewing, can yield findings on threats by corporate interests to the "right to cartoon" (author's term). It is difficult research, for corporations are extremely protective of their ledger books, and cartoonists and other editorial staff are sometimes reluctant to address such issues for fear of losing their jobs. Examples of corporate vested interests figuring in cartoonists' autonomy abound. In the US in 2018, a veteran cartoonist for a family-owned newspaper was fired because his anti-Trump drawings were disliked by the publisher, a Trump supporter. In the Philippines a few years back, the publisher of the country's largest daily *Bulletin*, shipping mogul Emilio Yap, often humiliated his veteran cartoonist, showing him with rudimentary stick figures how he wanted a cartoon drawn.

Commodification of comics has also been given short shrift in studies. The notion of "creative industries," at one time probably thought of as an oxymoron, has led to high levels of commercialization and the treatment of comic art as a commodity. This is not a new trend; the "Yellow Kid" strip of the nineteenth century spun off all sorts of products, including tobacco, as did "Buster Brown" and others. Different now is that in many cases, merchandising has become the end-all of cartooning, cranking out thousands of toys, games, posters, cards, and what I have called "cartoonized junk." Seemingly, in some instances, this has made the by-product more important than the work of art, resulting in what American cartoonist Bill Watterson said was a "cheapening" of the comics (23, 26). Research into the commodification of comics is called for in an attempt to find out the extent of this phenomenon, its largest benefactors, and the positive and negative effects on comics business and artistry.

Legal Studies

It is indeed puzzling that legal studies associated with comic art are just now emerging from an embryonic state. There has been more than enough evidence that cartoonists' freedom to work has been increasingly thwarted by legal and nonlegal governmental moves and terroristic actions by fundamentalist religious groups, and that cartoonists' rights to use and own their cartoons are still in doubt in many countries, and that they are hampered by nonexistent or poorly enforced copyright legislation and by piracy. Add to that the dilemma of political cartoonists who, employing satire, must determine the boundaries of the red line not to be crossed, or whether there is a red line in satire, and you have a full plate of research topics.

In an interview with British comics researcher Paul Gravett, law lecturer Thomas Giddens termed the field of study "graphic justice," placing a range of topics under this rubric. Giddens granted that comics have much potential for legal studies and emphasized that the field relates "mostly to criminal law and justice, with a large helping of moral philosophy" (Gravett, "Graphic Justice").

In such a borderless field, some possible research projects are the rights of comic art workers, relative to contracts, trademarks, and copyright; the "right to cartoon," to be free to graphically express opinions; the legal regulations that shaped the comic art industry; the ethical and moral considerations of using humor to mock institutions and individuals; sexual harassment or other gender issues in comic art; the moral/immoral dimensions of vigilantism in superhero and some crime comics; the libel and obscenity legislation pertinent to comics and cartoons, and criminal justice portrayals in comics featuring legal professionals (e.g., "Judge Parker," Matt Murdock [Daredevil]). A possible base for legal studies and comic art is law and humor studies (see the journal *Humor*; Little 1235–92).

The concentration here is on the currently seriously challenged "right to cartoon," which I have assigned to categories of the perpetrators of infringements on this right, their means of victimization, and the mechanisms cartoonists use to offset or cope with the infringements. Each sub-category of this three-pronged structure merits the attention of comics researchers worldwide, using a myriad of research techniques—historical method, archival searches, interviewing, content or textual analysis, and interpretation of law cases.

Perpetration of infringements is more likely to be committed by government suppression through legislative means, such as the use and misuse of libel and sedition laws, copyright and intellectual property violations and piracy, vague and nonuniform obscenity and child pornography laws, and unwritten restrictions and national guidance policies (respect for royalty, sensitive topics, national ideologies, such as Rukunegara in Malaysia and Pancasila in Indonesia, and policies during war, martial law, or states of emergency).

In recent years, incidences of religious intolerance of cartooning have risen in number and world attention—the Danish cartoons of the Prophet Muhammad, the *Charlie Hebdo* humor magazine massacre in Paris, and the murders of bloggers in Bangladesh, among them. Intolerance by hate groups (such as fascist, neo-Nazi, racist, or anti-LGBTQ) has also attempted to negatively affect cartooning.

A third means to infringe on the "right to cartoon" is through the already-discussed corporate/conglomerate control, with possible implications of the homogenization of content, the drying up of the watchdog function of political cartoons, and the downsizing of cartoon staffs.

There are also infringements brought about by organized publics, such as Parent Teacher Associations, schools, ethnic groups, and churches, sometimes because of political correctness going afar and turning into censorship, and by the most dangerous form of censorship, that by editors and cartoonists themselves.

As for the means of victimization, cartoonists have been killed or "disappeared," arrested, imprisoned, fined, fired, terroristically threatened, pressured economically, and exiled; their publications have been suspended or boycotted by printers and distributors, and their premises burned or otherwise ransacked. For centuries, cartoonists have used a whole array of means to cope with infringements, including subtlety, stealth, insinuation, double meanings, and innuendo. Hidden meanings have appeared in the titles of cartoons (e.g., a very popular South Korean political strip is called "Kobau," meaning high, firm rock), symbols used (a South African cartoonist during apartheid included splattered ink in his cartoons, symbolizing blood), by plots and language (proverbs, rhymed sentences, and bon mots), and by characters (an Iranian cartoonist's use of a crocodile, representing treachery, to depict a hardline cleric). In other cases, cartoonists have coped by going underground, working in exile, or participating in campaigns (see Lent, "Global Infringements" 4–70).

Closely tied to legal studies and comics and cartoons are issues of ethics and morality. Globally, there have been numerous occasions when the ethics of using certain cartoons took (or should have taken) precedence over all else, most notably, the Danish newspaper and *Charlie Hebdo* cartoons mocking the Prophet Muhammad. On the heels of these monumental events, systematic surveys of the opinions of the public, and of the cartoonists, would have gone a long way in determining where the red line is drawn, or even if there should be a red line.

A number of questions concerning the publishing of the Prophet Muhammad cartoons might be suitable for inclusion on a comics/legal studies research agenda: as a magazine, should *Charlie Hebdo* be held to the same values and ethics of other print media? Should there be an ethical code for satire? If there were, would it still be satire? Discussed in terms of freedom of expression, should satire be expected to work within the norm of freedom of expression? Further, should there be a freedom of expression norm? Is freedom of expression an absolute right, or is it relative to where it is exercised and by whom? If provocation is the goal of a cartoon, what purpose does it serve and is the provoked person a public figure meriting attack? Should provocation cartoons be published, knowing a result is likely to be death and injury to others? Answering these questions through surveys of newspaper or magazine editors or juridical scholars and scrutinous readings of relevant legal decisions would benefit both the academic and practicing journalism communities.

Labor Studies

Common worldwide are the travails of comic art laborers, often ill-treated and marginalized by media managements who focus merely on their bottom lines and treat cartoonists as expendable subjects, unworthy of reasonable payment, job security, and manageable workloads.

The history of United States comic art is full of sad stories concerning labor and management—the payment of a mere US $125 to the creators of the Superman character by National Publications (now DC Comics), which later battled them in court as they sought a small pension; the denial until the 1980s of US newspaper comic strip creators' rights of ownership to their characters; more recently, the stranding of political cartoonists, left jobless as conglomerates close newspapers or abandon posts to cut costs or avoid possible litigation; the maintaining of very stressful and demanding workplaces by major comics publishers such as Marvel Comics, whose editors, artists, and writers called it a place of stressful and broken lives, premature deaths, legal entanglements, firings, rude and disrespectful behavior, sabotage, betrayal, and shady deals (Howe); and the movement of about 90 percent of American animation production offshore as companies seek low wages and strike-free environments (see Lent, "Animation" 239–54).

Since at least the 1970s, American comics publishers also "farmed out" work to less-expensive artists in Asia, Latin America, and Australia. To the question of whether such labor treatment is exploitation, solely a means of survival, or a transfer of skills, the answer is probably all three. Non-American artists working for US comics and animation companies are paid at a lower scale for sure, but they still make more money than they can from their home countries' comic art industries. Offshore comic art employment has provided some training and career opportunities for non-American artists and writers, but it also has damaged some cartoonists' and animators' styles. New Zealand cartoonist and graphic novelist Dylan Horrocks told how writing for DC Comics became a nightmare he had to escape: "It almost killed me as a cartoonist. I was writing in a voice that wasn't mine and felt trapped in other people's wish-fulfillment fantasies. Eventually, I lost my cartooning voice entirely, and my lifelong faith in stories and art" (Gravett, "Dylan Horrocks").

Conglomeratization of comic art has also led to brain drains as Asian, European, and Central and South American artists and writers left their homelands for the glitter and money offered by DC, Marvel, or Disney. One cannot in true conscience blame them for leaving; cartoonists throughout the world face precarious existences. Among the hundreds of cartoonists I have interviewed on every continent, a majority had to keep "day jobs"—as an architect, farmer, clerk, tattoo artist, psychiatrist, ferry-boat operator, graphic artist, betel-leaf merchant, military colonel, teacher, long-distance truck driver, hair stylist, French-horn musician, engineer, electrician, medical doctor, boxer, and orchestral soprano. In Asia and Africa particularly, to survive, cartoonists must draw for multiple outlets and regularly produce many drawings, a number of which are not used, thus wasting the cartoonists' time. That (the economic factor) and political reasons are why we see in the US and Western Europe considerable pockets of West African, Philippine, Cuban, Mexican, Brazilian, and other nations' cartoonists. Unfortunately, a number of them do not realize their dreams in their new countries and end up doing freelance cartooning and working non–comic art jobs. In Paris and Brussels, there exist organizations of West and Central African cartoonists-in-exile (for political and economic reasons), providing a variety of services, such as finding accommodations for newly arrived artists and publication and exhibition venues (Lent, "Out of Africa")

Other transnational comics-labor problems hound cartoonists. In much of Africa, Asia, and the world generally, newspaper and magazine editors continue to use less-expensive American and sometimes British syndicated gag and political cartoons and comic strips rather than indigenous ones, thus depriving local cartoonists of employment opportunities and readers of content more in tune with their own culture, traditions, and issues. For example in Asia, local newspaper comic strips are almost nonexistent in important English-language dailies in India, Malaysia, Singapore, and Thailand. Because international intellectual property regulations are either vaguely interpreted or not enforced, cartoonists' rights are not normally respected. Widespread piracy endemic to these regions has added to cartoonists' woes. (see Lent, "Unfunny": 180–89).

Many unanswered or partially answered questions concerning transnational comics labor need researchers' attention.

- What is the operational mode of US and Western Europe comics and features syndicates relative to their newspaper clients abroad?
- How have non-Western comics syndicates succeeded or failed?
- How have immigrant cartoonists fared in their new countries of residence?
- How do cartoonists doing offshore comics work feel about their creative integrity and their situations more generally?
- What are the policies of conglomerate-affiliated comics corporations relative to their offshore artists and writers?
- Is (or has) any part of transnational or national comics industries unionized?

- In any given country, are cartoonists' rights spelled out and effectively enforced?
- If they are, how—by established law, medium protocol, codes of ethics?
- What are the implications of comics that are collaboratively created by artists of different national origins—their experiences, problems?
- How do comics that are joint labor productions handle different cultural, religious, and political norms? The example that comes to mind is a comics firm in an Arab Muslim country that sent stories to Brazil to be drawn by artists accustomed to explicitly depicting women's bodies.

Though animation labor history has merited some academic attention, studies about cartoons and comics labor are rare. Needed at a beginning stage are, first, to determine the meanings of terms such as "union," "movement," and "collective" in each case (are the groups' goals to help cartoon labor or to simply offer a socializing place?), and second, to find out how many organizations really function as bargaining and arbitration units protecting and advancing cartoonists' rights to their creative work, payments and other benefits, and job security. Specific studies stimulated by the above and other questions would at a preliminary stage demand historical and descriptive research. Identifying archives rich in labor materials, especially newspapers and magazines, is a first step, for too little research has been completed on the history of comic art labor (see Sito). Other sorts of studies can follow—on specific labor cartoonists and their works, such as Fred Wright, Mike Konopacki, and Gary Huck (Borrelli) in the United States; cartoon content during major labor strikes; strikes affecting cartoonists and animators, or nonmedia, labor- or union-related comic art (advertisements, posters, leaflets, and so on).

The subject of digitalization and comic art labor and creativity also needs more study. How much do cartoonists and animators depend on computers and the internet? And for what purposes? Has the internet attracted (and, if yes, to what extent) women creators to cartooning, especially those who are homebound caring for families or restricted in their social movement by religious and social norms? In many parts of the world, digitalization has been lauded as a savior of comic art traditions as print comics dwindled in sales. In China, for a while, the internet allowed *xinmanhua* (new comics) to survive through *oekaki* bulletin board systems that helped anyone desiring to draw comics use computer graphics and post their works (Chew and Chen 186). The internet rebirthed Korean *manhwa* as well, opening new avenues for established cartoonists and for amateur ones who would have found it nearly impossible to have their work printed conventionally. Korea's leading role in adoption of high-speed broadband internet in the early 2000s spearheaded the surge in online comics, also called essay comics (see Kwon 320–50).

Though not as supercharged as the cases of South Korea or Japan, digitalization has opened up creative avenues in many parts of the globe and allowed previously isolated cartoonists to network through online groups and forums, websites, and blogs; and enabled cartoonists (especially political ones) to dispense alternative views and stories in highly restricted countries or to divulge the circumstances when governmental, religious, or other public entities threaten their "right to cartoon." Research topics can be siphoned out of any of these and other related subjects. Overall, systematic research is called for in determining the strengths and weaknesses of digitalized comics labor, similar to work done by Liu Chang De in Taiwan. Using survey methods, Liu found that the "introduction of ICTS (information and communication technologies) has negatively influenced the artists' works, as well as their labor process" (459–62).

Historical Method and Archival Research

Much of the comics history has been written from an antiquarian approach, taking a very small part of what will become the history and writing about it in a descriptive, nonanalytical manner. Some purists among historians would scoff at this as nonhistorical method. However, contrary to their notions, antiquarianism plays an important role leading up to historical method, filling small holes in the larger story and, in the case of a new field of studies such as comic art, helping to create a chronology. Sometimes this type of researching and recording of past events has been snidely referred to as "journalistic," but again, this is shortsighted thinking. Good (and I emphasize *good*) journalism is based on thorough research, using interviewing, public documents, and observation, backed up with corroborative sources, and written in an accessible style. The significant difference between historical method/historiography and journalism practice is that the latter is written with a shorter deadline.

Journalism's traditional home (newspapers) offers historians a vital source in tracking down information, providing important leads, and setting a chronology, but newspaper content should always be corroborated with other sources. In comics studies, newspapers and magazines can also be the research item itself. Undoubtedly, much more research is needed about comic strips, gag cartoons, editorial and political cartoons, and advertising graphic humor, all of which are in abundance in newspapers of the past. Searching for newspapers and magazines has been made much easier in the past quarter century with the establishment of repositories in many libraries. The best places to start in the United States are the Billy Ireland Cartoon Library and Museum at the Ohio State University, the Library of Congress, and the Michigan State University comics collection. The Billy Ireland Cartoon Library houses the huge collection of newspaper comic strips donated by Bill Blackbeard. Comics researchers owe a huge debt to Blackbeard, who, upon learning that libraries were dumping old newspapers in favor of microfilmed copies, hired five trucks and drivers to bring them to his California home (Blackbeard 205–15). Many libraries worldwide have, over the years, made spaces for historical newspapers, most of them containing comic art; more recently, libraries have increasingly sought out private collections of individual creators' papers, correspondence, and drawings.

Though more entrenched in Europe and North America, the practice of preserving comic art–related material for public use is just catching on in much of Asia and Latin America, and to a lesser degree in Africa. As in the past nearly everywhere, comics materials in these regions often are taken out of the reach of the public and researchers as they are thrown away upon cartoonists' retirement or death, shredded for packing purposes, or bought up by collectors and, as in the case of China, by the new upper class to decorate their homes as a sign of "arrival." Other impediments to the comics researcher's hunt for materials are their destruction during wartime, restrictive government campaigns (such as China's Cultural Revolution), and natural disasters, and sometimes by the very nature of a culture. For example, Mongolia has not maintained many files on comics (and most other things) because of the society's nomadic nature that requires traveling lightly with only necessities.

In recent years, many parts of the Global South have stridently engaged in projects to preserve and publicly display original comic art, with the establishment of museums, libraries, centers, and other facilities beneficial to researchers. Some are online, such a Gerry Alanguilan's Komikero museum of Philippine komiks and a loosely structured group of family members of deceased, mainland Chinese cartoonists, who regularly post among themselves materials related to their cartoonist relatives' life, work, and career.

Proper usage of the increasingly available archival materials will enrich comic art history immensely, supplementing or contradicting information passed down from one historian to another, offsetting the "over familiar pantheon of 'greats'" (Gravett, "Rewriting"), bringing up from footnotes important cartoonists slighted by the subjectivity that is intrinsically endemic to historical research and "backplacing" the history of comic art.

The concentration of much of the comics history on twentieth-century United States comic books and strips has valorized certain American creators and works and tended to all but ignore or obscure other significant pioneers, such as *kibyoshi* artists of eighteenth-century Japan, the comics magazine *The*

Glasgow Looking Glass of 1825, a nineteenth-century Wilhelm Busch strip in Germany, work by Apeles Mestres in Spain, Mary Darly in eighteenth-century and Marie Duval in nineteenth-century England, an Angelo Agostini strip in Brazil in 1869, and prints by Gustave Doré and Nadar in France. Others requiring elevation from footnotes or needing first-time discovery in comics scholarship are the numerous women artists who undoubtedly satirized society or told narratives often in image-text combinations.

Other Research Gaps

Other areas of comics scholarship needing a jumpstart are:

1. Theoretical studies using creative models or approaches poached from other disciplines besides literature (such as mass communications, aesthetics, social sciences). Additionally, fitting or fashioning theory and methodology for regions of the world that operate on noncapitalist economies, non-Judeo-Christian religions, nonalphabet languages, and non-Euro-American cultures, in the process recognizing comic scholarship of the Global South as equal in importance as that of the North and rethinking North scholarship, which is the norm for the South, because of its dominance in books and journals and its impacts on students who study in the North and then impart those ideas and theories in their home countries (see Lent, "Imperialism":14–17; Lent, "Western": 33, 35–38).

2. Analyses of alternative (to mainstream) models of creating, producing, distributing, and exhibiting comic art, such as comics collectives, underground and alternative comics, and nonprint comics.

3. Broadening of comics scholarship through more translations, especially of the whole trove of research written in Japanese (such as articles in the twenty-four volumes of *Manga Studies*), Chinese, Korean (such as articles in *Cartoon and Animation Studies*), and European languages.

4. More emphasis on slighted forms of comic art, such as the already-mentioned newspaper and magazine comic strips and one-panel gag cartoons; printed, animated, and televised editorial cartoons; humor/cartoon magazines; advertising graphic humor and narrative; and various comics images on posters, leaflets, record covers, postcards, and other paraphernalia. Similarly, other genres (Western, horror, sports, romance, adventure, religion, education) need to be studied.

5. Studies, set in a socio-cultural context, of publishers, distributors, and comic shops that played important roles in the development of comic books. This suggestion aligns well with Sydney Kobre's 1940s notion of a sociological

perspective to journalism history and Casey Brienza's recent call for a "sociological methodology" for comics study, bringing in "the larger social and organizational context of [comics] production and dissemination" (106, 115).

Conclusion

Much of this chapter discusses shortcomings in the field, but this is not to imply that comics scholarship is in poor shape. Far from that, advances made in the setting up of an infrastructure (journals, publishers, organizations, conferences), the attracting of researchers from many branches of the humanities and social sciences, the establishing of theoretical bases, and the spreading of the field internationally have been phenomenal.

It must be remembered that relatively, comics and cartoons are a new study area, and as such, will require settling-in time, during which ideas and notions will be tossed about, some accepted, some rejected, and others adapted, but all done in an open-minded atmosphere. It is in this spirit that I make these suggestions as to how comics studies are likely to develop (or as I wish them to develop).

Already it is apparent that social scientists are increasingly entering and enriching comic studies and are likely to introduce more research based on political economy and cultural studies. As a result, important information will be yielded about the industrial and commercial aspects of comics, the socio-cultural contexts in which they are created, produced, and consumed, and possibly their effects and uses and gratifications derived from them.

Though the optimal goal for a new field of study is to develop its own theory (or more accurately, its own "educated guesses," "notions," "hunches," and even hypotheses), for the most part, the conceptualization takes its strengths from other disciplines. The condition should be that the "poaching" not be confined solely to one discipline. The comics study field should be both interdisciplinary and multidisciplinary.

As an example, recently a comics study or two used David Manning White's late-1940s "gatekeeper theory," a mainstay of mass communications study that attempts to locate the "gates" that, for example, a comic book or political cartoon must pass to reach the consumer. Sticking with the mass communication discipline as an example, other of its theories can be applied, with modifications of course, to comics and cartoons: media-cultural imperialism, active audience (readers and viewers do not passively consume others' cultures or media), uses and gratifications (how comics are used by readers and what satisfactions they derive from them), agenda setting (such as political cartoons setting the agenda for discourse), or even the very old "cloze procedure" test, where readability is determined by gauging the number of omitted words a reader can fill in because of familiarity, a bit akin to the notion of the comic-book gutter. Other disciplines have lent concepts to comics studies, going back to psychology and psychiatry with the Wertham-inspired comics effects on children in the 1940s and 1950s, and the application of language and semiotics to comics studies by Western European researchers in the 1960s and 1970s.

As the borrowing continues in the future, the hope is that it be a process of adaptation and not total adoption, and that it be applied with the knowledge that most of these concepts were fashioned in the West, and the feasibility of their use in some cultures and languages may be problematic. On the horizon also is a proliferation of original historical research that will be dug out of troves of newspapers, magazines, and journals, much of which has not found its way into comics scholarship previously, the greatly augmented collections of drawings, correspondence, and other materials made available by cartoonists and others closely affiliated with the profession, and the preserved audio and video recordings of interviews with comics and cartoons personnel. From this research, the history of comic art will be pushed back, factual holes will be plugged, myths will be obliterated or corrected, and trends will be made discernible, thus satisfying the principles of historical method and historiography.

The recent spate of transnational and multicountry anthologies and surveys will spawn even more collaborative research, produced by scholars highly knowledgeable of their subjects and the languages in which they originated, in the process pushing to the sidelines very short-time "safari" researchers.

Granted that this essay has concentrated on the accomplishments and shortcomings of comics studies, a number of the approaches used to find answers to the many questions raised have major implications for comics pedagogy. Because comics studies is an inexact and flexible discipline (compared to physical sciences), it opens up a wide range of ways in which knowledge and skills can be exchanged while teaching comics and teaching with comics.

Teaching comics effectively requires abandoning or downplaying some of the methods and practices traditionally used. First of all, comics need to be taught by drawing from multidisciplinary and international perspectives—such as by showing how comics and cartoons generally or individual titles specifically enhance, blend in, or defy social norms; acknowledging that a world of comics exists besides those of American or Japanese origins; taking into consideration the wealth of genres open for study besides superheroes; and paying more attention to the industrial components of comic-art production, distribution, and consumption.

Second, comics pedagogy needs to include more critical approaches and contents—to look at comic art through other lenses (political economy, cultural studies, etc.), and to discuss more often topics such as comics and their relevance to censorship and control, ownership, transnationalism, and labor. The imparting of knowledge about these subjects can still be accomplished somewhat objectively (if that is a concern) through analysis of the strengths and weaknesses of the discussed theories, practices, and systems related to comic art.

Perhaps too much energy is spent in the pursuit of objectivity, considering that teaching itself is not neutral, but rather political, and never completely balanced, favoring some perspectives and marginalizing others (such as through types of assignments, exercises, and textbooks). Students, if prepared properly through a variety of readings and assignments, can be expected to add to the discourse, challenging some notions and sharing their experiences, observations, and readings of and about comics, oftentimes as avid fans. This teaching method aligns with the Freirean pedagogy, where the passing of knowledge functions as a two-way street, with teachers and students learning from each other.

In upper-division undergraduate and graduate courses in comic art that I taught from the late 1980s onwards, I used a quasi-Freirean approach that worked well, intersplicing my lectures and discussions with student-occupied panel discussions on assigned comic art topics and, later in the semester, with student reports on their primary-research term projects.

Hopefully, the study and teaching of comics and cartoons will remain flexible, employing a wide swath of topics, theories, approaches, and contents endemic to multidisciplinarity, at the same time moving into new dimensions through experimentation with new concepts, forms, and perspectives and reinterpretations of those that came before.

WORKS CITED

Blackbeard, Bill. "The Four Color Paper Trail: A Look Back." *International Journal of Comic Art* 5, no. 2 (2003): 205–15.

Borrelli, Christopher. "For Labor Union Cartoonist, These Are Lonely but Busy Days." *Chicago Tribune*, March 3, 2015.

Brienza, Casey. "Producing Comics Culture: A Sociological Approach to the Study of Comics." *Journal of Graphic Novels and Comics* 1, no. 2 (2010): 105–19.

Chew, Matthew M., and Lu Chen. "Media Institutional Contexts of the Emergence and Development of Xinmanhua in China." *International Journal of Comic Art* 12, no. 2/3 (2010): 171–91.

Gravett, Paul. "Rewriting Comics History: Changing Perspectives." *Paul Gravett: Comics, Graphic Novels, Manga.* July 29, 2012. http://www.paulgravett.com/articles/article/rewriting_history

Gravett, Paul. "Graphic Justice: The Emerging Field of Comics & Legal Studies." *Paul Gravett: Comics, Graphic Novels.* August 27. 2013. http://www.paulgravett.com/articles/article/graphic_justice

Gravett, Paul. "Dylan Horrocks: All Pens Are Magic." *Paul Gravett: Comics, Graphic Novels, Manga.* January 9, 2015. http://www.paulgravett.com/articles/article/dylan_horrocks

Howe, Sean. *Marvel Comics: The Untold Story.* New York: Harper, 2012.

Kwon, Jae-Woong. "New Type of Popular Culture in the Internet Age." *International Journal of Comic Art* 7, no. 1 (2005): 320–50.

Lent, John A. "Imperialism by Q Sorts." *Democratic Journalist* 9 (1974): 14–17.

Lent, John A. "Western Type Communications Research in the Third World: A Critical Appraisal." *Vidura*, February 1983: 33, 35–38.

Lent, John A. "The Animation Industry and Its Offshore Factories." *Global Productions: Labor in the Making of the "Information Society."* Edited by Gerald Sussman and John A. Lent. Cresskill, NJ: Hampton Press, 1998. 239–54.

Lent, John A. "Defining Comic Art: An Onerous Task." *Journal of Communication Studies* April–June (2004): 1–11.

Lent, John A. "Out of Africa: The Saga of Exiled Cartoonists in Europe." *Scan: Journal of Media Arts Culture* 5, no. 2 (2008).

Lent, John A. "The Winding, Pot-Holed Road of Comic Art Scholarship." *Studies in Comics* 1, no. 1 (2010): 7–33.

Lent, John A. "Comics Scholarship: Its Delayed Birth, Stunted Growth, and Drive to Maturity." *International Journal of Comic Art* 16, no. 1 (2014): 9–28.

Lent, John A. *Asian Comics.* Jackson: University Press of Mississippi, 2015.

Lent, John A. "The Unfunny Tale of Labor and Cartooning in the United States and Around the World." *The Routledge Companion to Labor and Media.* Edited by Richard Maxwell. New York: Routledge, 2016. 180–89.

Lent, John A. "Global Infringements on the 'Right to Cartoon': A Research Guide." *International Journal of Comic Art* 19, no. 1 (2017):4–70.

Little, Laura E. "Regulating Funny: Humor and the Law." *Cornell Law Review* 94, no. 5 (2009):1235–92.

Liu, Chang-de. "Negative Impact of Digital Technologies on Artists: A Case Study of Taiwanese Cartoonists and Illustrators." *International Journal of Comic Art* 8, no. 1 (2006): 456–65.

Milliot, Jim. "The World's 54 Largest Publishers, 2017." *Publishers Weekly*, August 25, 2017.

Schiller, Herbert I. *Culture, Inc. The Corporate Takeover of Public Expression.* New York: Oxford University Press, 1989.

Sito, Tom. *Drawing the Line: The Untold Story of the Labor Unions from Bosko to Bart Simpson.* Lexington: University Press of Kentucky, 2006.

Steirer, Gregory. "The State of Comics Scholarship." *International Journal of Comic Art* 13, no. 2 (2011): 263–85.

Watterson, Bill. "The Cheapening of the Comics." *WittyWorld* 8 (1989): 23–26.
Westcott, Tim. "An Overview of the Global Animation Industry." *Creative Industries Journal* 3, no. 3 (2010): 253–59.
Woo, Benjamin. "Is There a Comic Book Industry?" *Media Industries* 5, no. 1 (2018): 27–46.

Misunderstanding Comics

—JOHNATHAN FLOWERS, Worcester State University

Scott McCloud's *Understanding Comics: The Invisible Art* has been essential in developing the vocabulary in use by the field of comics studies while providing students with a fundamental understanding of comics not only as an art form, but also as a medium of communication. As noted by Henry Jenkins, *Understanding Comics,* together with Will Eisner's *Comics and Sequential Art,* served as the basis for a formalist approach to the field of comics studies, wherein comics are studied critically through the lens of the "visual language" (Cohn, "Visual Language Manifesto" 5) of comics structured around a "vocabulary" connected to other historical forms of sequential art ranging from Egyptian hieroglyphs, to medieval tapestries, to the culturally specific uses of space and transition in Japanese manga. Consequently, McCloud's approach, like Eisner's that precedes him, has been a driving force in the development of linguistic understandings of comics (Cohn, "Comics, Linguistics, and Visual Language" 4), which has subsequently served to organize the pedagogy of teaching readers not only to read comics but understand them.

Although McCloud attempts to connect his work to a global history of sequential art, and therefore the diversity of approaches to developing a visual language of comics, this connection is surface level: the "language" developed in McCloud's work is grounded on an assumption of cultural neutrality. That is, the language, and the reader constructed by McCloud's work, seems to presume an uninterrupted capacity to be embodied in the work absent cultural or social barriers. Thus a central problem of McCloud's work is the assumption of a "default" or "unmarked" reader as the subject taught to "understand" comics, as well as an "unmarked" or "default" object that is created through the mastery of the language of comics. Put another way, by assuming the comic itself is a "vacuum into which our identity and awareness is pulled . . . an empty shell that we inhabit which enables us to travel to another realm" (McCloud 36), McCloud presumes that each reader has an unmediated experience of embodiment in the reading of the comic.

Thus, through *Understanding Comics*, McCloud seeks to offer a perceptual framework, a phenomenology, of how a comic coheres to enable a reader to be fully embodied in a comic through the experience of reading. In this experience, for McCloud, the embodiment of the reader is not an impediment to their embodiment in the narrative constructed by the comic. To this end, while McCloud's *Understanding Comics* starts, as all works of phenomenology do, with the body in the world, it only attends to what is before the reader, the comic, and not what is *behind* the reader, the embodied experience of the reader. Put simply, the reader brings with them the totality of their lived experience in the act of reading, an experience that informs not only *what* is being read, but *how* it is read. Thus, in this chapter I suggest that for some readers, their embodied experiences deny them the capacity to be fully embodied through the language of comics. Because McCloud's proposed reader proceeds from an extension of his own experiences as a white male, his hypothetical reader shares in this orientation towards the world. As a result, a nonwhite or nonmale reader would not have the same orientation towards the comic: because of the way that McCloud has organized "understanding" in line with the dominant organization of culture around the experience of whiteness, their bodies fail to trail behind the action of "understanding" comics, and their experiences are not fully accounted for in the act of "understanding" comics as described by McCloud.

This chapter will explore the way in which the language of comics developed by McCloud, and taken up by the field of comics studies, participates in what George Yancy calls a "social ontology of whiteness," or the social organization that produces whiteness as a privileged identity (Yancy 24). For Yancy, the "social ontology of whiteness" is what allows for the cultural and social products of white individuals to maintain their cultural and social dominance through the ways in which whiteness is treated as an invisible and universal standpoint to approach the world (Yancy 24). DiAngelo refers to this as "the discourse of universalism," which makes it possible to view the "white" experience as the "human" and "universal" experience (DiAngelo 59). As a result, McCloud, like many other white people, does not view himself as white or positioned as a result of his whiteness: he is simply human. As a consequence of McCloud's failure to recognize his experience as a "white" experience, the way of understanding comics outlined in *Understanding Comics* is one that seeks to understand comics through the frame of *whiteness*. McCloud's vocabulary of comics is not a neutral or an "unmediated" language that, despite the historical trajectory he traces, is accessible to all potential speakers: it is a language structured, organized, and grounded in a social organization that constructs the "neutral" standpoint as equivalent to the white standpoint. This neutral standpoint allows McCloud's project to assume the function of reinscribing the colonial project of the West through its assimilation of the historical "languages" of the other.

Further, this chapter takes up the argument that an experience of unmediated embodiment in comics is only possible for bodies who feel "at home" in the space created from McCloud's language of comics. This concept of being "at home" is described by Sara Ahmed as a consequence of the way that spaces are organized by the repeated actions of some bodies and not others. The language of comics, because of its predication on an experience of whiteness, is familiar to white bodies because it participates in the repeated actions of white bodies. As white comics fans, scholars, and educators who bring with them the histories and cultural practices that give rise to whiteness as a mode of organizing the world, white bodies are better able to "understand" the language developed in *Understanding Comics*. In contrast, nonwhite bodies who seek to learn the "language" set forth by McCloud must be "disciplined" or "straightened" into an "understanding" that does not align with their lived experience of the world, rather than allowing their experience to inform their way of understanding.

Thus, to conclude, this chapter will suggest a "misunderstanding" of comics through the critical pedagogy of Paulo Freire and its emphasis on collaborative, dialogic understanding to address the way that queer comic fans, nonwhite comic fans, female-identified or genderqueer comics fans, and all other fans whose identities do not align with McCloud's own identity "understand" comics in the context of comics pedagogy, and how "understanding comics" through whiteness serves to reproduce inequalities in comics scholarship and pedagogy.

The Hidden Orientation behind McCloud's *Understanding Comics*

McCloud's universal or neutral standpoint for understanding comics begins in the second chapter of *Understanding Comics*. In describing his choice in stylistic representation of his narrative avatar, McCloud states:

> Apart from what little I told you in chapter one, I'm practically a blank slate. It would never occur to you to wonder what my politics are, or what I had for lunch, or where I got this silly outfit.... You give me life by reading this book and "filling up" this very iconic (cartoony) form. Who I am is irrelevant. I'm just a little piece of you. But if who I am matters less, maybe what I say will matter more. (McCloud 37)

Here is where we must look "behind" the neutral orientation presumed by McCloud, which allows him to presume that the reader who engages with his text through his comic avatar will not question his politics, his eating habits, his outfit, or those social relations that constitute the meaning of his avatar. In doing so, McCloud privileges the interiority of the reader while simultaneously treating the interiority of the creator as irrelevant through what he terms the "amplification through simplification" of the comic character. For McCloud, "by stripping down an image to its essential "meaning," an artist can amplify that meaning in a way that realistic art can't" (McCloud 30). However, McCloud warns us that this "stripping down" is, paradoxically, a means to focus on specific details of the comic image. The "stripped down" image serves to focus our attention on the details that remain: in this context, "cartooning isn't a way of drawing, it is a way of seeing" (McCloud 31). As a "way of seeing," amplification through simplification in comic art serves to orient our perception of the image, the action, on the page in such a way as to make present those elements the author has selected as our focus.

Using his own avatar as an example, McCloud argues that a consequence of the "amplification through simplification" of his avatar is our ability to treat the avatar as a "blank slate." Amplification through simplification is what removes any preexisting social meaning of the avatar by distancing it from the "sensory world" through the simplification of its features, which, McCloud argues, also distances it from cultural presuppositions about the avatar. As a result, the reader is able to "fill" his avatar with their own inner thoughts and experiences without being distracted by the form of the avatar. In describing his own comic avatar as a "blank slate," McCloud puts forth the argument that his avatar is not raced, it is not gendered, it does not call attention to its representation in the comic medium because of its simplification of the form, which fails to arouse our socially organized perceptions. McCloud, however, fails to recognize that it is his own whiteness that is amplified through simplification of his avatar. It is only because whiteness goes unnoticed as a consequence of what George Yancy calls "the social ontology of whiteness" that McCloud can present his avatar as a blank slate.

To understand the "social ontology of whiteness," we must understand what "whiteness" is. For Yancy, "Whiteness constitutes an ensemble of power relations that places whites in positions of advantage and power (that is, puts them in potential and actual positions of power in virtue of their whiteness) vis-à-vis nonwhites" (*What White Looks Like* 4), which includes the power to define the ways that we engage with the world. As an "ontology," or a structure that provides the conditions for existence, individuals who are identified as white emerge from within power structures that constitute the social ontology and are participants in maintenance of white supremacy regardless of their intentions: their power to organize the world around themselves is a consequence of a colonial structure of the world. Further, the *social* ontology of whiteness is "the intersubjective and interpersonal matrix in terms of which whites perform a shared mode of being-raced-in-the-world, a form of being-in-the-world that is marked as 'benign' and 'natural,' but is nefariously oppressive and cunningly deceptive" (*White Self-Criticality* xii). As both "benign" and "natural," the white self that emerges through the social ontology is naturalized into the world as unremarkable, unnoticed, and unseen. Whiteness, therefore, is not known or understood *as* a social project that grants specific social, economic, and cultural privileges to those identified as white. Moreover, the above actively prevents whiteness from being viewed as constructed, nor are those identified as white being *raced* in any meaningful way. So thoroughly does the social ontology of whiteness perform this function that it conceals itself from the very white people it privileges. It is in this way that the social ontology of whiteness renders whiteness and the white body as unremarkable, unnoticed: it is what enables McCloud's comic avatar to be represented as a "blank slate" onto which a reader may project their understandings.

Here we can turn back to *Understanding Comics* as a phenomenology of experiencing comics. On this view, McCloud's "blank slate" concept, his assertion that his avatar goes unmarked save for what we bring to it, and his argument that we would not think to consider his politics both position those who *do* stop to consider the social ramifications of his white avatar as bringing something (problematic) to the avatar rather than addressing what is present. Put another way, when we question the whiteness of McCloud's avatar, its universality, we begin to question the fundamental nature of a world that is organized by whiteness and treats whiteness as universal. Because the white form of McCloud's avatar is both simplified and abstracted, it becomes more universal through its distancing from any visual markers of race: the whiteness of the avatar does not invite us to bring in assumptions about it because of its "default" organization. Thus, while we give McCloud life, this life is not raced, its politics are not questioned, its social relations are "natural": were McCloud's avatar that of a black man, the life we brought to it would be different by virtue of the social ontology of whiteness.

Moreover, within the social ontology of whiteness, it does not occur to us to view McCloud's avatar *as* white: McCloud's avatar is simply a blank slate onto which we may project everything *except* whiteness. If we turn back to the "missing syllable" in McCloud's phenomenological approach to understanding comics, the orientation of the body towards the comic character, it becomes clear that McCloud is taking his own body as the starting point for *all other bodies* that encounter the visual language of comics. Because of his emergence as white from the social ontology of whiteness that, again, renders whiteness natural and benign, or a "default" position from which to approach the world, it would not occur to McCloud, or any other reader positioned by the social ontology of whiteness, to question the extension of his starting point across all bodies who seek to understand comics. Moreover, it would not occur to a reader who occupies the "default" position to view McCloud's assumptions as cementing the position of the white body as the default body. This, in turn, is connected to the function of the ontology of whiteness as enabling white bodies *not* to recognize themselves as invested in white supremacy, or whiteness itself, as a consequence of the generation of knowledge that fails to render whiteness visible in any meaningful way.

Following the above, the identity of McCloud's avatar is only made "irrelevant" insofar as it participates in an ongoing social structure that renders whiteness invisible in comparison to the social construction of nonwhite bodies, which enables us to fill McCloud's avatar with ourselves. Put another way, the implied whiteness of McCloud's avatar is what enables him to put forth his avatar as a "blank slate," the "thesis" through which all other bodies can interact with a world that unfolds from an "invisible" white subjectivity, which would be an impossibility were McCloud's avatar black. According to Yancy, "The black body ... is ontologically mapped; its coordinates lead to that which is immediately visible: the black surface. There is only the visible, the concrete, the seen, all there all at once" (*Black Bodies, White Gazes* 38), which is to say that the social ontology of whiteness is that which simultaneously enables McCloud's avatar to be a "blank slate," yet the ontology of whiteness is also that which denies a similarly positioned black avatar the capacity to be a "blank slate," for it is always perceived as *being black*. Put simply, the capacity for McCloud's avatar to remain invisible in the action of narrating the "language" of comics, and therefore to make his words "matter" more than the representation of his avatar, is itself a function of the social ontology of whiteness, without which his avatar would call attention to itself in the execution of its narration.

To fully understand the above point, specifically the argument that a black avatar could not function in the same way, we must turn to the ways in which a black body moves through a space organized by whiteness. Sara Ahmed, drawing upon Frantz Fanon, argues that bodies are never neutral: they are shaped by the activities of colonialism, which serve to make the world "white" (Ahmed 153). A world made white is a world that is "prepared" for some bodies and not others prior to their arrival in it. In so doing, the world made white serves to place some "objects," by which she means the objects within

McCloud's conceptual and sensory worlds, in reach. A white body is therefore "at home" in a world already prepared for it in a way that a black body is not: bodies that are at home are those bodies that do not stand out in the execution of their actions, that do not call attention to themselves through the ways in which they move through space. These bodies are "habitual."

Ahmed, drawing on Merleau-Ponty, describes the "habitual" body in the following:

> The body is 'habitual' not only in the sense that it performs actions repeatedly, but in the sense that when it performs such actions, it does not command attention, apart from at the "surface" where it "encounters" an external object (such as the hands that lean on the desk or table, which feel the "stress" of the action). In other words, the body is habitual insofar as it "trails behind" in the performing of action, insofar as it does not pose "a problem" or an obstacle to the action, or is not 'stressed' by 'what' the action encounters. (Ahmed 156)

For Ahmed, white bodies are habitual bodies: because of their whiteness, they do not impede the actions taken in the world; they "trail behind" the action in such a way as to enable the action executed to stand at the forefront, rather than the body that acts. Here, we may see similarities with the white bodies defined through Yancy's social ontology of whiteness that enable white bodies to be "natural" and "benign" through a shared mode of being predicated on asymmetrical power structures: the habits of this shared mode of being in the world are such that white bodies never have to confront their whiteness in the execution of their actions. For Ahmed, this means that "white bodies do not have to face their whiteness, they are not oriented 'towards' it" (Ahmed 156), which is what allows whiteness as a shared mode of being to come together *as* whiteness, or the background against which all other modes of being in the world are projected.

The inverse, however, is true for nonwhite bodies. Because nonwhite bodies never trail behind their actions, because they are always present in their action, a nonwhite body is not "at home" in the world as made white by colonialism. That is, because they are not at home in a world made white, they are unable to "extend" themselves through the world: they are stopped in the extension of their bodies towards "objects" in the world by virtue of their lack of whiteness, which is that which draws attention to the action in the world. Thus, for Ahmed, "To be black in 'the white world' is to turn back towards itself, to become an object, which means not only not being extended by the contours of the world, but being diminished as an effect of the bodily extensions of others" (Ahmed 161), which is to say that as whiteness extends through the world, other bodies are diminished as a consequence of that extension. More specifically, Ahmed treats this failure to be extended by a world made white as manifested in being "stopped."

Stopping, for Ahmed, is embodied in questions asked. For example: "Who are you? Why are you here? What are you doing? Each question, when asked, is a kind of stopping device: you are stopped by being asked the question, just as asking the question requires that you be stopped" (Ahmed 161). Not being stopped, on this argument, is manifested in the way in which some bodies are not questioned upon their arrival in the world. To turn back to McCloud and his avatar, that we would not stop to think to ask about his politics, his clothes, or his food indicates the way in which the simplified version of his white body can amplify the narrative by not calling attention to itself. On the other hand, because the black body is immediately visible in its historical and social construction, it would be unable to extend fully into the space of a narrative that was predicated on articulating *how* to understand comics. The black avatar would, consequently, be "stopped" by questions about the political objectives of a black avatar teaching an understanding of comics, of the legitimacy of the understanding presented, of the sources used. Not only would the black avatar be unable to be a "blank space" into which identities are poured, the very structure that denies the black avatar this capacity would also serve to stop the avatar from communicating its message *despite* any simplification. Put simply, no amount of simplification can enable a black avatar to amplify anything but the politicization of the narrative.

To be stopped by whiteness, for Ahmed, is to be oriented by whiteness in the action of moving through the world. Insofar as white bodies do not encounter whiteness in their movement through the world, in the execution of their actions, by being "at home" in the world, white bodies are not oriented by whiteness: whiteness orients other bodies. Moreover, whiteness, through colonialism, serves to organize and orient spaces. Spaces, phenomenologically, emerge because of the repeated actions of the bodies that dwell within them. Put another way, spaces become "white" as they take on the contours of the repeated actions of the bodies within them. To draw upon Yancy, the coherence of a space around the shared whiteness of the participants in the space is what makes this space white. Insofar as this space forms around whiteness, within a social structure that naturalizes whiteness, the space itself will appear *naturally* white, and this whiteness will not be taken as a problem for white bodies that seek to move through it. As a consequence, white bodies are not oriented by spaces made white, whereas nonwhite bodies are *disoriented* by those spaces, made uncomfortable by their inability to fit in.

For Ahmed, "Whiteness may function as a form of public comfort by allowing bodies to extend into spaces that have already taken their shape. Those spaces are lived as comfortable as they allow bodies to fit in" (Ahmed 158). Insofar as nonwhite bodies do not fit in by virtue of not participating in the shared being-in-the-world that gives rise to whiteness, nonwhite bodies are not comfortable. Here we may critique McCloud's identification thesis: as McCloud's imagined reader is a projection of himself, a white projection, it assumes an innate capacity to fit in. "Fitting in" in this context is the ability for the reader to "fill" the abstracted and simplified comic character with what they bring to the work. In contrast, a nonwhite reader would have difficulty "fitting in," or filling McCloud's avatar with their lived experience, given the way in which the world, and *Understanding Comics*'s vocabulary as an extension of that world, is not "comfortable" for them. To this end, McCloud's identity thesis, as it draws upon a "conceptual world" for the source of the power of identification, draws upon a conceptual world already made white wherein the reader need not face their whiteness: because McCloud's white body as simplified trails behind the action of narrating *Understanding Comics*, he may claim an objective position from which to articulate a language of comics without "distracting" from the message. The invisibility of his white body, therefore, allows the narrative to take center-stage. A black body, which is always visible in its actions, would be unable to "trail behind." This, then, places into question the universality of McCloud's thesis.

If whiteness is comfortable because the space of the world has already taken the shape of whiteness, identification with McCloud's avatar is easy depending on one's proximity to whiteness. However, the inverse is possible as well: a black avatar created through simplification is not a space that takes the shape of whiteness. Because blackness cannot be simplified away from its social history, the black avatar stands out in its actions: it is "stopped" in the action of narrating. Further, because the black avatar is not a space that has taken on the shape of whiteness, a white body, and its experience, would consequently be "uncomfortable" filling it. This discomfort, drawing upon both Yancy and Ahmed, would be experienced as an inability to "fit in" within the narrative, resulting in a narrative that is an "uncomfortable" fit. The attempt to "fill" the simplified black body with white experience would consequently interrupt the construction of whiteness by displacing the white body from a site of privilege and power: it would, in essence, deny the white self the capacity for mastery of its definition as a consequence of the history of blackness. To this end, the white body would be "stopped" by the black avatar because the world it seeks to inhabit is not one that is perceived as made for it, and therefore not one that the white reader could sink comfortably into.

The preceding description of McCloud's understanding of comics, and the vocabulary of comics that proceeds from it, as grounded in a social ontology of whiteness, is not to attribute a nefarious intent to McCloud's work. Rather, the above serves to indicate the ways in which the social context from which McCloud's work proceeds results in its adoption of implicit assumptions about the nature of comics creators, readers, and how to read comics. Moreover, as *Understanding Comics* represents an early attempt at articulating a language of comics and defining the form of comics in a comprehensive way, it is unsurprising that McCloud's initial entry into the field would reproduce social inequalities common to other attempts at creating an objective definition of a form. Specifically as *Understanding Comics* was developed in the absence of the conceptual language provided by recent entries into the field of comics studies, the above demonstration of the implicit assumptions within the text becomes more necessary given the prominence of the work within the field.

Put another way, McCloud's articulation of how to "understand" comics does not proceed from a neutral ground as implied by his articulation of the conceptual world or the sensory world, nor is it free of the social ontology that conditions McCloud's understanding of comics through the experience of whiteness as neutral. Moreover, the widespread adoption of McCloud's text as an introduction to a phenomenology, a method of reading, serves to institutionalize the implicit assumptions made within the work. As such, *Understanding Comics* serves as an "orienting device," in the words of Sara Ahmed, that directs the appropriate engagement with the language of comics and, given its dominance in the discourse of comics studies, the field of comics studies itself.

Understanding Comics as an Orienting Device

To understand *Understanding Comics* as an "orienting device," we need to understand *Understanding Comics* as providing a way to organize our perceptions of comics through providing a language to *understand* comics. In doing so, *Understanding Comics* serves to structure our perception of the way comics unfold, or to provide instruction for how they *should* unfold before a reader. This unfolding is established through a history of sequential art, albeit one that serves to draw the traditions of other cultures under the ambit of McCloud's own definition and thereby legitimate diverse comics traditions as something worth understanding. However, insofar as McCloud is attempting to provide an orientation towards comics through the "straightening" of our perceptions of comics, he does so from within the sedimented power structures of the social ontology of whiteness, which informs the ways of understanding comics presented within *Understanding Comics*. Put another way, *Understanding Comics* seeks to place "ready to hand" the appropriate "tools" for understanding comics: it predicts a line along which the "world" of a comic unfolds, a line that has been taken up within comics studies without reference to the way in which *Understanding Comics* is itself an extension of McCloud's orientation towards the world itself.

For Ahmed, "orienting devices" provide our initial orientation towards or away from an object: in her description of whiteness as orienting nonwhite bodies, Ahmed treats whiteness as directing nonwhite bodies towards or away from things in the world. As an orienting device, *Understanding Comics* functions similarly: the text shapes the understanding of the reader through its provision of a language that gives meaning to comics beyond bare perception. Further, *Understanding Comics* serves to shape comics by the ways in which the text directs the perception of the reader towards comics to enable the "world" of comics to unfold along the "lines" inscribed by McCloud throughout the text in the form of a "vocabulary" of comics. The orientations produced by McCloud's specific language of comics, as indicated through the structure of his amplification through simplification, are shaped by a history that is hidden from McCloud by the social ontology of whiteness. *Understanding Comics* participates in this history through the totalizing effect of its "vocabulary," which subsumes the uniqueness of non-Western traditions of sequential art into a Western vocabulary of comics, which thereby serves to orient the presumed reader towards non-Western comics in ways that serve as an extension of an understanding of comics grounded in whiteness.

Here we can turn to McCloud's historical exegesis and repeated references to Japanese manga throughout *Understanding Comics*, and limitedly within the rest of his corpus, as an example of the way in which McCloud's vocabulary serves to render the nonwhite other, and their cultural traditions, as an instantiation of the "sameness" of whiteness. Put another way, McCloud, like Eisner before him, redefines comics through the language of the "white understanding," which proceeds from the "sameness that issues from whiteness's proclivity towards totalization" (Yancy, *What White Looks Like* 14). Insofar as the objectivity of McCloud's definition relies implicitly on "white understanding" as a default position from which comics unfold, it is necessary to interrogate the ways that *Understanding Comics* structures our perceptions of what it is to be a comic within the world defined by McCloud's text. That is, we must consider that the very definition of comics derived from McCloud's encounter is rearticulated through the "white understanding," which renders the nonwhite experience "civilized" or intelligible to whiteness.

Briefly, McCloud presents comics as "juxtaposed pictorial and other images in deliberate sequence" (McCloud 9) as the definition necessary for "most cases" where we seek to understand comics. Consequently, McCloud moves to impose this definition on a pre-Columbian picture manuscript by reorganizing the work so that it becomes intelligible in his understanding and definition of comics. McCloud describes this process in the following: "First, we separate words from pictures, then reverse it and straighten it (the original read right-to-left and zigzagged) and begin" (McCloud 11), where "begin" indicates the initiation of reading the reordered picture manuscript. Here McCloud's process of dismembering and reordering the pre-Columbian scroll serves to maintain, rather than deny, "the imperial epistemological and ontological base from which it sees what it wants (or has been shaped historically) to see" (Yancy, *What White Looks Like* 13). In so doing, McCloud enables the assimilation of the nonwhite experience, embodied in the work of art, into the totalizing form of whiteness by dismembering the work and rearticulating it through the "white understanding," thereby enabling its inclusion within the development of a history of sequential art as a colonial project.

This colonial project is limited in its scope within *Understanding Comics*, as McCloud subsequently presents the totality of an Egyptian work with the appropriate reading order as an example of the historical construction of comic art; however, the preservation of the appropriate order of reading is not, as we might be quick to assume, an attempt at what Yancy might call "genuine inclusion," or the "opportunity for the development of a porous horizon, one that responds positively to the other in his or her difference, learns from the other, and changes based upon an encounter with the other" (*What White Looks Like* 14); rather, the work serves as a means whereby the culture of the Other can serve to establish and confirm a preexisting colonial narrative of "juxtaposed pictorial and other images in deliberate sequence," a mode it shares with McCloud's representation of Japanese manga later in the text. That is, while McCloud does not disparage the two traditions and their distinctions from the established Western canon, and indeed recognizes them as "comics," it is their difference that McCloud is concerned with: they serve to establish the dominance of the language already developed rather than expand on it. James Banks speaks to this project by reminding us that our failure to "recognize the ways in which social location produces subjectivity and influences the construction of knowledge" allows us to continue to maintain the marginalization of underrepresented groups through our reproduction and failure to interrogate established ways of knowing that are grounded in the subjugation of marginalized individuals (Banks 65).

The case of Japanese manga is particularly interesting, as McCloud notes with regard to aspect-to-aspect transitions in manga that "through these and other storytelling techniques, the Japanese offer a vision of comics very different from our own" (McCloud 83), a vision that on the following page is presented as valuable for the way in which the elements from Japanese culture have been taken up in the Western milieu. That is, while McCloud emphasizes the difference between manga and the Western tradition, he does so only to make clear existing elements within the Western tradition, as well as the way in which the West has *benefitted* from the assimilation of the Japanese elements of culture. Here it might be argued that the "vocabulary" developed draws upon nonwhite and non-Western works in order to make clear the ways in which the Western, white imagination has anticipated the works generated by nonwhite cultures within its own totalizing vocabulary, and not to emphasize the cultural and social distinctiveness of those works. Put simply, while McCloud makes overtures to the development of a language of comics that is "porous" and as such open to expansion, the way in which these overtures are framed as an invitation for the Other to confirm a language present within "white understanding" precludes a genuine contact with the Other in the development of McCloud's language. This function of *Understanding Comics* is crucial given the prestige that it has enjoyed within the field of comic studies. As presented by Cohn:

> McCloud's approach has permeated nearly all linguistically driven studies since its publication. Both Saraceni (2000) and Stainbrook (2003) focused their dissertations on adapting McCloud's panel transitions to theories of verbal discourse, while Narayan (2001) compared them to cognitive theories about event structure. Similarly, Saraceni (2001), Bridgeman (2005), and Lim (2006) all invoke McCloud's ideas in their discussions of multimodal texts integrating images and words. (Cohn 95)

Taking the field of linguistics as our example, *Understanding Comics* has served to orient the ways in which we produce knowledge where comics is concerned. Through the repeated citation of *Understanding Comics* as crucial to developing an understanding of comics within the field of comics studies, the underlying assumptions of McCloud's works and the vocabulary generated within the text become sedimented into the field. To this end, the orientations adopted as a consequence of the repeated use of *Understanding Comics* as an authority within the field of comics studies, unless critically interrogated, will reproduce the "blind spots" of the ways of knowing that develop McCloud's orientation towards comics. Thus, for comics studies to become truly expansive, it may become necessary that we *misunderstand* comics through a critical reading of *Understanding Comics*.

Conclusion: Misunderstanding Comics as a Critical Reading of *Understanding Comics*

Even if *Understanding Comics* is implicated in the ways of knowing that have maintained the marginalization of underrepresented groups, it does not stand to reason that *Understanding Comics* should be discarded as a tool for understanding comics. Instead, we should seek to critically engage *Understanding Comics* because of its place of prestige within the field of comics studies and comics pedagogy as a guide to how we should understand comics. Doing so can enable the "democratization" of McCloud's "comic vocabulary" by validating the ways of knowing and experiences of comics brought to comics by marginalized comics fans, scholars, and educators. Critical, in this context, is grounded in the work of Paulo Freire (1970), who presented education as the means whereby the oppressed can develop the consciousness of their oppression and the social relations that maintain it.

To be critical, therefore, involves challenging the assumption of a text as an absolute authority on a subject from which "pure" knowledge is received. Instead, the text and the reader are collaborators in developing an understanding of the material within the text. This dialogic or collaborative engagement with the text subsequently empowers and validates the experiences that the reader brings to the text in order to transform the text into a site of resistance. In the case of *Understanding Comics*, it would be to challenge the authority of McCloud's treatment of the comics vocabulary and the process of reading comics as absolute, rather than an initial starting point for a dialogue between McCloud and the reader: it would open the possibility of using the concepts within *Understanding Comics* to generate a unique and situated way of understanding comics. It would be to use the concepts within *Understanding Comics* to ask readers how they understand comics *through* the vocabulary provided rather than assuming universal understanding through mastery of the vocabulary.

A critical reading of *Understanding Comics*, therefore, would seek to develop an *understanding of comics* through McCloud's that seeks to orient a reader in a direction taken towards comics that makes comics available to readers in new and unique ways through validating a reader's experience of a comic. For example, if we take McCloud's blank slate in *Understanding Comics* as a starting point to ask how different readers understand comics from within their social and cultural positions, McCloud's blank slate in *Understanding*

Comics takes on new meaning as an entry point into the experiences and ways of knowing of marginalized peoples. It is this power of *Understanding Comics* that opens up the possibility for understanding comics as a liberatory practice by incorporating critical or dialogic pedagogy. A dialogic, or critical, approach to *Understanding Comics* would not rest on McCloud's "blank slate" as the prototypical reader: instead, it would engage in a conversation among multiple readers to collaboratively develop an understanding of comics from multiple perspectives that serves to decenter the assumed "default" body.

As an example, insofar as McCloud assumes that all readers possess the same "starting point" when interacting with both the sensory world and the conceptual world, *Understanding Comics* seeks to institutionalize this universal starting point without attending to its social position. It is on this presumption that McCloud argues that readers are better able to identify with simpler comic characters by filling up their forms with material from the conceptual world when those characters are juxtaposed against realistic backgrounds. In so doing, McCloud presumes that the primary barrier to identifying with characters in comics is the degree to which they approximate objects in the "sensory world," which denies readers the capacity to identify with the character represented. Thus, a simplified form provides a means whereby readers can extend themselves into the comic character *because* they are abstracted from the sensory world and thus do not have a ground in it: the abstracted form of the comic character does not "orient" the reader in the same way that a photorealistic character would, and it thereby allows a reader to bring their own orientation to the comic character.

However, what McCloud misses is the ways in which readers possess an initial orientation, an initial starting point that places the simplified character "in reach" so that they may fill it with their identity. As indicated in the discussion of the black avatar, a simplification of the black avatar does not evacuate it of its social meaning: it functions to pull in the social meanings of the black body in the narrative. Here, the black avatar becomes not a "vacuum into which our identity and awareness is pulled . . . an empty shell that we inhabit which enables us to travel to another realm" (McCloud 36), but a vacuum into which social meanings are pulled and a site where those meanings can be interrogated. *Understanding Comics*, both as a text and an action, thereby can serve as an aid to understanding our specific orientation to the work such that we can be pulled into the work. A critical pedagogy could approach *Understanding Comics* as providing the language for readers to articulate their own orientation to comics by rephrasing its initial assumptions concerning the "work" that comics do.

For example, while Superman's origin is treated as a universal story, an "all-American" story that describes how the character comes to embody

American cultural ideals in a white body, a body which all readers are expected to "see themselves" in, a black reader would decode Superman's origin in light of the way that white bodies are able to become the embodiment of American virtues by virtue of their whiteness, while nonwhite or black bodies are denied this privilege. Conversely, a white reader would struggle to view the narrative of *Black AF: America's Sweetheart* as a universal narrative because of the racialized perception of the black female body as subjective, as only being able to represent the experience of black womanhood, and not as being able to represent a universal narrative. Thus different orientations of the body produce different unfoldings of the world, as some objects in the world are placed in and out of "reach" of our bodies, just as different orientations of readers produce different ways that the text unfolds.

Here we can turn back to the "missing piece" of McCloud's work elaborated through critical theory: as amplification through simplification creates a universal image only insofar as our perceptions are oriented to view the image as universal, *Understanding Comics*'s language of amplification through simplification can articulate the ways that some images are *not* universal because of the social meanings of the images, thereby opening a critical space for readers to explore what it is that they bring to the experience of reading, and how the critical space of comics makes present their orientation not only to the comic but to the world. Experiences of disidentification as a consequence of an avatar's social history can be explored by *misunderstanding* comics through McCloud's language, particularly in the mode of the reader's engagement with the comic as *subjective* rather than *objective*. Put simply, the ways in which McCloud's thesis fail are as informative as the ways in which it succeeds, specifically insofar as who the language fails for can open a space for critical engagement with the text.

Additionally, a critical pedagogy of *Understanding Comics* is not simply limited to exposing tensions within and between groups: it can be used to unpack the ways in which marginalized subjects have deployed comics within their own communities. As an example, applying the concepts of amplification through simplification to the cultural history of comics in the African American community can provide crucial insights to the ways that comics do "work" in a social sense. Using *Understanding Comics* to articulate how Orrin C. Evans used "juxtaposed pictorial and other images in deliberate sequence" (McCloud 9) to "give American Negros a reflection of their natural spirit of adventure and a finer appreciation of their African heritage" (Evans 1947) allows for an expanded use, and historical reinterpretation of the ways in which comics were used by the African American community, through McCloud's assertion of the universality of comics' ability to draw in the reader, to connect contemporary African Americans with a past that they had lost. Moreover, critical use in this way can indicate significant differences in the ways that languages are used across cultures.

Further, readers may critically reflect on how the simplification of some avatars serves to amplify some narratives and not others through the ways in which those narratives are "attached" to the social histories of the simplified bodies. Or, taking up Robin DiAngelo's assertion that the universality of whiteness is grounded in the assumption that "whites can represent humanity, while people of color, who are never just people but always most particularly black people, Asian people, etc., can only represent their own racialized experiences," *Understanding Comics*, interpreted through a recognition of the positionality of the reader *prior* to being provided with the language to "understand" comics, can allow readers to critically interrogate the habits of perception developed through the language provided by *Understanding Comics* (DiAngelo 59). It would be to interrogate how the "language" of the comics changes, or *what* narratives are amplified through *which* simplified bodies.

Drawing on Margaret Noori, this critical approach can be useful for understanding the nuances within the respective traditions of the visual narratives of indigenous Americans, specifically insofar as these narratives do not conform neatly to McCloud's comics language. For Noori, drawing upon McCloud's language of "juxtaposed pictorial and other images" serves as an expedient method of exploring the connections between early Anishinaabe visual culture and its modern representation. Specifically, Noori argues,

> if centuries of Anishinaabe were able to develop and deploy a complex agglutinative structure made mostly of verbs to communicate images, ideas, and relationships across time, there must then be a way of interpreting them based on more than printed and published texts. Furthermore, the layered construction of the sound and meaning is perfectly suited to the comic format, where text, line, and color combine to communicate action and relationships. (Noori 58)

In Noori's view, the visual form enables the preservation and articulation of multiple indigenous narratives because of its connection with indigenous visual culture. Comics, in her view, are the natural progression of indigenous oral and visual culture. Thus, it is this alignment of Anishinaabe cultural works with the modern form of comics, and the recognition that "not only are comics rich with potential in their own right, they are historically one of the original formats of native narrative" (Noori 59), that makes the language provided by *Understanding Comics* well suited to bridge the gap between the historical visual culture of the Anishinaabe people and its modern equivalent.

For Noori, the language of *Understanding Comics*, as a means whereby the visual image and the written word come together to make manifest a narrative, may be used by "the 1,681 sovereign nations in the United States, Canada, and Central and South America, so that they may understand themselves as connected in new ways to one another and to the nations that surround them" (Noori 71), and thereby recover a connection to a history nearly lost through colonialism.

Given *Understanding Comics*'s position of privilege where orienting understandings of comics is concerned, it is necessary to take seriously the critical use of *Understanding Comics* within a pedagogical space. Insofar as *Understanding Comics* not only orients the fields of comics studies and comics pedagogy through its repeated citation in publications, syllabi, and informal criticism of comics and its role in establishing the critical study of comics as an academic enterprise, *Understanding Comics* serves as a privileged orienting device, albeit one that suffers from the limitations of the time and space of its publication. While McCloud's subsequent works *Making Comics* and *Reinventing Comics* make great strides in developing and expanding the initial thesis advanced within *Understanding Comics*, McCloud's formalistic, objective approach does not lend itself to an engagement across subject positions.

It is for this reason that we must "queer" our understanding of comics through *Understanding Comics* by reappropriating and redeploying its language to make explicit the implicit assumptions about the organization of comics and our orientations towards comics. What has been sketched above is but one way of reorienting *Understanding Comics* to accomplish the aim of using its language to open up a critical space for the interrogation of our implicit assumptions about the ways in which we are oriented towards comics, how we should read comics, and the "uses" of comics. By engaging with *Understanding Comics* through the lens of critical pedagogy, we may decenter the "default" assumptions within the text and redeploy its language to make clear other ways of understanding, or misunderstanding comics. Put simply, as the field shows little sign of abandoning the language and orientation of *Understanding Comics*, it becomes our task to reorient *ourselves* towards *Understanding Comics*.

In this way, adjusting our own orientation towards *Understanding Comics* allows us to treat the development of comic literacy presented in *Understanding Comics* as a means to attain a critical understanding of a reader's social relation to a text and the society that produced it. *Understanding Comics*, therefore, would become a site for readers to engage in dialogue, ideological critique, and transformative action (Luke) to change the conditions that give rise to those relations rather than an authority on the *right* way to understand comics. Critically engaging *Understanding Comics* in this way would "democratize"

Understanding Comics by encouraging students, comics fans, and comics scholars alike to bring their own experiential knowledge into the process outlined in *Understanding Comics*, thereby limiting the privileging of one dominant "voice" (Cahan and Kocur) as the authority on understanding comics.

WORKS CITED

Ahmed, Sara. *Queer Phenomenology: Orientatios, Objects, Others*. Durham, NC: Duke University Press, 2006.
Ahmed, Sara. "A Phenomenology of Whiteness." *Feminist Theory* 8, no 2 (2007): 149–68
Banks, J. A. "The Historical Reconstruction of Knowledge About Race: Implications for Transformative Teaching." *Multicultural Education, Transformative Knowledge, and Action*. Edited by J. A. Banks. New York: Teachers College Press, 1996.
Cahan, Susan, and Zoya Kocur. *Contemporary Art and Multicultural Education*. New York: The New Museum of Contemporary Art, 1996.
Cohn, Neil. "The Visual Language Manifesto: Restructuring the 'Comics' Industry and Its Ideology." Emaki Productions, 2007.
Cohn, Neil. "Comics, Linguistics, and Visual Language: The Past and Future of a Field." In *Linguistics and the Study of Comics*. New York: Palgrave MacMillan, 2012.
DiAngelo, Robin. "White Fragility." *International Journal of Critical Pedagogy* 3, no. 3 (2011): 54–70.
Fanon, Frantz. *Black Skin, White Masks*. London: Pluto Press, 1986.
Freire, Paulo. *Pedagogy of the Oppressed*. New York: Continuum, 2007.
Luke, Allan. "Critical Approaches to Literacy." In *Encyclopedia of Language and Education Literacy Volume 2*. Springer, Dordrecht, 1997.
McCloud, Scott. *Understanding Comics: The Invisible Art*. New York: Harper Collins, 1993.
Noori, Margaret. "Native American Narratives from Early Art to Graphic Novels: How We See Stories / Ezhi-g'waabamaanaanig Aadizookaanag." *Multicultural Comics: From Zap to Blue Beetle*. Edited by Frederick Luis Aldama. Austin: University of Texas Press, 2010.
Yancy, George. *What White Looks Like*. New York: Routledge, 2004
Yancy, George, ed. *White Self-Criticality Beyond Anti-Racism: How Does It Feel to Be a White Problem?* Lanham, MD: Lexington Books, 2015.
Yancy, George, ed. *White on White, Black on Black*. Lanham, MD: Roman & Littlefield, 2005.

In the Cards: Collaboration and Comics-Making in the Traditional English Classroom

—FREDERIK BYRN KØHLERT, University of East Anglia
—NICK SOUSANIS, San Francisco State University

In the 2015–2016 academic year, we were both postdoctoral fellows at the University of Calgary's Department of English. Including Professor Bart Beaty, who served as our supervisor, this might have been the highest concentration of PhD-holding comics scholars in a single department worldwide, and the situation provided for a fertile and productive environment in which to conduct our postdoctoral research. When Bart's administrative responsibilities made him unavailable to teach his customary "Comics and Graphic Novels" course in the winter term, we hatched the idea of teaching it together in his place, welcoming the opportunity to make it a truly collaborative effort that would both take advantage of and bridge our different scholarly and teaching backgrounds.

We knew from the beginning that collaborating on the course would be both an exciting opportunity to learn from each other and require a certain amount of adjustment to our usual methods. Co-teaching requires a high degree of collaboration, or it swiftly becomes dysfunctional. Fortunately this was anything but the case for us, although it's important to note that we didn't know each other well before embarking on this joint venture, with Frederik having arrived in Calgary nine months after Nick and just a semester before we taught the course. Teaching with another person is almost always more work than teaching by yourself, requiring a great deal of coordination, compromise, and patience. But working with someone—if both parties are as open and willing to try new approaches as we were with each other—was in our case most definitely a gift that we feel greatly elevated both of our individual teaching practices. Our extended planning process and discussions before and after each class taught us a lot about one another and ourselves, and our conversations always came back to finding ways to improve engagement in the classroom. In addition, having the perspective of someone else proved to be energizing, extending even to the preparation of class slides (which we always did together), as we were continually finding new ways to improve and refine the flow of how we conducted class together.

Our collaborative dynamic began with the selection of our reading list and with both of us introducing new texts to each other (or at least texts we had not taught before). We then had a prolonged discussion about what to include and why, before settling on our texts. The final list included Chester Brown's *Louis Riel* (new to Nick, at least in terms of teaching), Alan Moore and Dave Gibbons's *Watchmen* (new to Frederik's teaching), Jim Woodring's *Fran*, G. Willow Wilson and Adrian Alphona's *Ms. Marvel*, and Mariko and Jillian Tamaki's *This One Summer* (all three of them new to both of us), as well as Alison Bechdel's *Fun Home*, David Mazzucchelli's *Asterios Polyp*, and Gene Luen Yang's *American Born Chinese* (all of which both of us had previous experience teaching). In addition to the planning process, we also made the co-teaching dynamic a formal part of the class, writing in the syllabus that "this is a co-taught class in which both professors will be contributing equally to the lectures, discussions, and grading. Each of us brings a different perspective to the study of comics (Nick is a maker-theorist-educator; Frederik focuses on the formal and cultural aspects of the form), and we are excited to combine our approaches to expand on the depth of the conversation." From the beginning, then, the course was intended to take advantage of our having been brought together in Calgary, and to offer the students an opportunity to learn about comics from two different perspectives, at the same time that we of course also intended to learn from each other and expand on our own established methods and classroom practice during the process.

Nick's previous comics courses—which included education-specific courses while a doctoral student at Teachers College, a readings-heavy course at Parsons, and "Comics as a Way of Thinking" in the previous semester at Calgary—all centered around the comics form and how it can be used for education and communication, especially in terms of its potential for scholarship, research, sharing ideas, and self-growth. Prominently, although each course was set in a typical academic space, all were strongly based in hands-on practice (as detailed elsewhere in this volume), and students made comics from the first day all the way through to their final projects. Frederik, on the other hand, had taught comics in both traditional literature courses in English departments and in comics-specific courses at OCAD University in Toronto. In his experience, the most striking difference between teaching comics to literature and art students is how each group tends to focus almost exclusively on either the textual or the visual elements. Literature students, in other words, tend to respond well to text-heavy and self-consciously "literary" comics like Alison Bechdel's *Fun Home*, which they can apply their customary arsenal of analytical skills to. Art students, conversely, who commonly have less training in traditional literary analysis but a greater ability to evaluate and discuss images, respond more strongly to comics driven by the visuals, such as for example David Mazzucchelli's *Asterios Polyp*.[1] Moving between the two, Frederik had previously designed assignments that took advantage of each student group's facilities while also including elements that would challenge each group to leave their comfort zone. For his part, Nick had developed exercises and prompts intended to quickly get students comfortable with thinking about themselves as comics makers (despite almost all of his students self-describing as nondrawers) and to understand how much about drawing they already knew. Through these experiences, students would be better able to analyze and get a handle on the affordances at play in comics.

Since the collaboration was taking place in a traditional English department, our backgrounds and previous teaching therefore led us to design a course that would include untraditional assignments meant to challenge students to pay more attention to the visuals. In much the same way that students learn a lot about the form and craft of literature by writing traditional essays, we believe that students working on comics gain a deeper appreciation of comics by producing work in the form itself, such as visual analyses or even minicomics. For the course, we therefore knew that we wanted to include a large element of analytically informed image- and comics-making, both as informal in-class exercises and as assignments to be evaluated as part of their final grade. With a large lecture course of approximately seventy students on our hands, however, the challenge became how to achieve this in a way that would both feel natural in the classroom and be manageable in terms of evaluating student work.

This situation led us to hatch two simple but surprisingly enriching and effective innovations: a daily notecard assignment and, of all things, a new approach to the midterm. The notecards exercise consisted of us giving students a brief in-class drawing or comics-making prompt to be undertaken on the spot and on a single index card, often at the end of every class. The assignments varied from attempts to recreate the visual styles of artists whose work we discussed in class to formal play with composition, and each exercise was intended to give students an actual taste for how comics creators do this work. This had the effect of making students try their hand at drawing in every class, although not in such a massively involved way that it would run up against the built-in constraints of class time and our ability to assess the work of this many students twice a week. In addition, the index card format also eliminated some of the fear and self-doubt around drawing that students might have, since anyone could fill one side of a three-by-five-inch card in five minutes. To reassure students, we also emphasized in the syllabus that "prior drawing experience is not necessary, and that every exercise can be done by anyone of any skill level or background in drawing." We used these assignments as learning tools corollary to our readings and discussion, employing them in ways intended to give additional insight into the process of making a comic, but in terms of grades they were purely about participation. There were twenty-six class meetings over the semester, and we had students do one in each class, twenty-five of which we counted at 1 percent each, for a combined 25 percent of their final grade. This meant that they could miss one class without it affecting their grade. We collected cards directly from students at the end of each class, standing at the exit and gathering them as they passed by, which meant they couldn't forget to hand them in while simultaneously providing us with a little ritual of closure at the end of each class. If students handed in their card, they received full credit, and if they didn't, they received none, although we did of course make accommodations for excused absences. Each card was to have the student's last name and first initial, along with the date, written in the lower right-hand corner, in order that we could organize them but also—most importantly—so we knew which card had been made by who in a class of seventy!

Sometimes the assignments for these "dailies" were conceived of in advance, with prompts that tied neatly into and were suggested by the day's class content. Other times the "just right" exercise wasn't forthcoming, and we were brainstorming and bouncing ideas off one another trying to find something that didn't feel random, that the students would learn something from, and that they'd enjoy. At times a final plan was only conceived on the long walk to our classroom through the various hallways and buildings at the university (all of them connected to avoid Alberta winters), and occasionally we made them up on the spot in class, based on where the discussion had been going. There were definitely times where we were concerned that maybe the students would not be able to come up with something when we offered them a particularly difficult prompt or a shorter than usual window to work on it, but they always did—and they always exceeded, at least collectively, our expectations. Besides everybody having fun with this, and students getting a good sense of comics-making even in these tiny chunks, what was perhaps most unexpected was that students came to *every* class. Our attendance was off the charts. From an administrative standpoint, this presented a bit of a problem for the grading curve. Considering how hard this level of attendance can be to achieve in a large lecture course, however, and keeping in mind that the exercises themselves made sure that students were engaging with course content in every single class, we decided to consider our above-average grades as simply a reflection of increased attendance and participation. We have both continued to do the same kind of exercises in our solo courses since, although Nick has opted to collect them online with students doing the drawings in their notebooks. This digital practice has been useful for organization and comparing student work, as well as for giving them the opportunity to have discussions with each other about their responses. One aspect where it falls short is that students don't have to be so attentive to attendance, as they can figure out what to do for the drawing exercises and turn them in online without coming to class, which sometimes is the case.

For those looking to try some of these, we thought we'd share the prompts we gave the students in class. Because we always had a great time going over the index cards together after class and seeing what everybody had come up with, we saved all of them and share a few select ones here as well. (See figures 1–4.) Although the following list naturally does not provide the context for each exercise, we hope it will at least give a sense of the varied nature of the assignments, and of how they can be adapted to fit most texts, themes, or classroom discussions.

Notecard Exercise Prompts:
1. Draw two self-portraits: one from memory, and another from a photo on your phone, and then compare the two
2. Draw a cartoon version of yourself/draw a series of "boids" (abstract loops turned into birds with just a dot for the eye and a triangle for the beak, via Colin Ware)
3. Make a short image-text essay on why you signed up for this course
4. Draw Batman multiple times, first in 3 mins and then progressively quicker: 2 mins, 1 min, 30 secs, 15 secs, 5 secs (via Lynda Barry)
5. Draw a series of self-portraits that are realistic, cartoony, and abstract (using Scott McCloud's triangle)
6. Draw your day in the Grids & Gestures format (Nick's nonrepresentational comics-making exercise, detailed elsewhere in this volume)
7. Do the Panel Lottery group exercise, making a collaborative comic from individual drawings (via Jessica Abel and Matt Madden)
8. Redraw a panel from today's comic, paying attention to composition and style
9. Make a comic that does something interesting with time
10. Make a comic with emphasis on interplay between image and text (like *Watchmen*)
11. Make a comic that makes use of the concept of simultaneity
12. Redraw a page from our reading and do a mini-analysis/annotation
13. Draw a self-portrait with pupil-less eyes (like *Louis Riel*)

Figure 1: Notecard example

Figure 2: Notecard example

Figure 3: Notecard example

14. Reflect visually on: what is art?
15. Give us suggestions for the midterm
16. Make a comic that emphasizes panel breaking
17. Draw a short comic about what you think Nick and Frederik are doing (Bart's fill-in for a class when we were both traveling)
18. Draw a cartoon self-portrait that reveals your character
19. Make a collaborative comic where one does layout and words, the other draws pictures
20. Draw a comic that makes use of sound effects and onomatopoeia
21. Make a wordless comic
22. Draw Jim Woodring's Frank (inspired by a YouTube video by Woodring)
23. Draft thumbnails for the page layout for a comic
24. Write or draw a draft of your final project proposal
25. Draw yourself as a superhero, listing abilities and motivation
26. Make a comic about what you learned in this course

In addition to the notecard exercises, we also wanted to design a midterm that involved an element of comics-making, and which would follow naturally from these daily engagements with form. We needed something that carried a little more weight in terms of assessing what students had taken from the course, but we also wanted to preserve that same spirit of play that was central to the notecards. Could we come up with a midterm that was both challenging and reflected their learning, while also being fun? We thought about it for some time before term and over the weeks leading up to it, and even requested suggestions from the class as part of our daily notecard exercises. What we came up with was a take-home test in three parts. The sections would be quite different regarding the types of skills required, in order to give each student at least one area in which to really shine.

The first section was a short essay of minimum three hundred words where they could either: a) write a letter to their parents or other authority figure (say a principal at a school, for example), explaining why comics are worthy of study at the university level; b) describe some essential ways in which comics are unique and distinct from other art forms such as literature, film, and poetry in terms of conveying narrative; or c) focus on a single aspect of one of our three readings thus far (which had been *Asterios Polyp*, *Fran*, and *Watchmen*), and discuss how it contributed to how meaning was made in the comic. Most students chose to write the letter, and often they combined elements from the other prompts into one. The midterm's second part was to visually analyze and annotate a single comics page selected from a set included at the end of the take-home exam, a skill we had already practiced regularly over the term, including for an earlier key assignment. As detailed

Figure 4: Notecard example

more extensively in Nick's solo chapter in this volume, the assignment asks students to engage directly with the chosen page by drawing directly on a sheet of tracing paper or mylar placed on top of it, redrawing the page while also providing annotations and diagrams to point out and explain the various stylistic choices and other elements they notice in the process. Similar in some ways to such techniques familiar from literary analysis as close reading of prose or the scanning of poetry, the idea was for students to offer analytical commentary about the creative decisions made by the artists, including how these affect the reader's understanding of the page.

Finally, the third part of the midterm, which in our view is the coolest innovation, gave students a chance to demonstrate their understanding of comics-making by creating a reverse-engineered comic. For the assignment, we provided students with a list of twelve comics features (see below) discussed in class, including one wildcard of their choice, and asked students to draw a one-page comic that incorporated at least eight of these. In addition, they had to briefly annotate their comic, pointing out where and why they incorporated those features. As with the notecards, we emphasized that their comic did not have to demonstrate strong artistic skill, but that it should be cohesive and well-planned, and should demonstrate an advanced understanding of the form.

Reverse-Engineered Comic Features:
1. Iconic variation (within McCloud's triangle)
2. Action-to-action transition
3. Aspect-to-aspect transition
4. Scene-to-scene transition
5. Interdependent word/picture combination
6. Wordlessness across at least three panels
7. Visual sound effects
8. Emanata
9. Negative space
10. Overlapping panels
11. Simultaneity (images that continue across multiple panels)
12. Wildcard of your choice (please note this in your comments)

The assignment gave the students license to experiment further with comics-making first-hand and to try things they would otherwise have not. As with the notecards, the results were terrific, and the concept of flipping creation on its head—of having form generate content—led to some surprisingly innovative and ambitiously conceptualized comics. The generative potential of limitations to the creative process is both well-documented and has a long history in most arts, and by providing students with a set of specific features to be deployed in any way imaginable—and with absolutely no guidelines regarding content—we encouraged them to not only pay attention to, but also to experiment with, how comics can tell stories in new and untraditional ways. The assignment thereby helped reinforce the importance of form to our students, as they learned that how stories are told is intrinsically bound up with their meaning. For students of literature, this lesson can sometimes be easier to learn with traditional prose than with comics, which are often approached as if the visuals were merely a transparent vehicle for the storytelling. What the midterm did, then, was to highlight the many formal features and authorial choices involved in comics-creation and to underscore both similarities and differences between comics and other artforms. This sort of reverse creative process is something Nick continues to do in his making-specific courses, with fascinating results, and both of us continue to regularly do the exercises dreamed up for the cards and the midterm in our current classes.

In the classroom, our different backgrounds and teaching styles led not only to new ways of collaboration, but also to reflections on the form and content of our own teaching. While Frederik's previous teaching had accustomed him to lecturing to large classes, Nick's background as a practice-oriented teacher meant that he had often worked with smaller groups. This difference often manifested itself in our physical presence in the lecture hall, where Frederik tended to be in front of the class at the podium while Nick roamed more freely among the students when he was not presenting. This dual focus typically had the advantage of keeping the students' attention to the front of the class at the same time that they benefited from individual attention. This setup was especially useful during in-class assignments, where Frederik could guide the class as a whole while Nick was providing real-time feedback and encouragement. Capitalizing in this way on our dual presence and different teaching styles in order to keep everyone on their toes made for a strikingly attentive and engaged class, especially considering the relatively large number of students and the size of the lecture hall itself.

Another difference that was highlighted by the collaborative situation, and one that speaks directly to a central feature of the comics form itself, was our different approaches to designing slides. While Nick tended to show a series of images and talk around them, Frederik usually included a few key words, terms, or phrases for the students to take note of. This discrepancy initially produced a few humorous exchanges about why Nick was so wary of words and why Frederik didn't just let the pictures speak for themselves, and when we first mixed our existing slides and used them in class, something interesting happened: when shown a slide with only images, the students looked at them attentively, but as soon as words were introduced, they all immediately took notes, presumably writing down the words from the slide. This difference was so pronounced that we soon came to expect it, and whenever we switched from a Nick slide to a Frederik one, we knew exactly what that would mean for the classroom dynamic—namely that all their heads would go down in unison as they began writing away. While both approaches to slide-making can be useful when done right, this discovery highlighted a few things for us.

Firstly, it would seem that even students in a comics course tend to think of text as information to be retained, and images as mere illustration. This division obviously goes directly against a central principle of the course, as mentioned above and inspired also by Nick's work in *Unflattening*, namely that comics are simultaneously visual and verbal, and that the images are as much a part of the information being conveyed as the text. How to get around this existing classroom bias in favor of text as being better suited to carry meaning and argument became a challenge throughout the course, and we continued to experiment with various word-image combinations on the slides in order to see if we could trigger different responses in our students. While we didn't entirely overcome the initial hardwired impulse to treat text as information and image as entertainment, we highlighted the behavior to the students themselves, and asked them to reflect on their own preconceptions about what text and images can do separately as well as in combination.

Our second observation was that while student note-taking is of course to be welcomed, the fact that we lost the immediate attention of almost the entire class for a moment whenever we showed a slide with text on it caused us to reflect on our teaching practices and the roles we play in the classroom. Are we, to put it in contrastingly extreme terms, entertainers who are there to inspire a room full of people by showing them cool images, or conveyors of information to be written down and retained? The ideal teacher is likely a combination to be found somewhere in between these two poles, and the discovery accidentally made from the slides meant that we continued to search for this middle ground.

Thirdly, the initial discrepancy in our slides also highlighted a related expectation built into the higher education system itself, namely that learning is often reduced to the ability to parrot certain bits of information at crucial moments, such as exams. While a university-level course will probably always contain a certain amount of information-dumping, a course concerned with the multimodal storytelling potential of comics, especially compared to traditional prose, as well as the form's ability to forge new and unexpected connections between various visual and textual elements, would be a failure if the students themselves didn't come away with new ways of thinking about both comics and the learning process itself.

Finally, making these observations throughout the term meant that we were constantly reflecting on both our own teaching practice and our students' learning. To begin with, we were always watching each other teach, which is something we rarely take the opportunity to do with our colleagues once we are left alone for extended periods. Throughout the term, we were watching each other closely, certainly to be ready for our cue, but also as fellow learners along with the students, always observing and evaluating: what is he doing that I want to try, or why didn't that go over well? The dynamic practically forced us to question our own teaching methods, and definitely to expand them. As we've noted throughout, the conversations we had prior to class was an incredibly generative and stimulating process, but class time itself had this as well, for us as well as for the students. We believe that the students seeing our different approaches to teaching along with our distinctive perspectives on class material provided a means to shake up more monolithic approaches, much like the comics form itself has the potential to forge new ways of thinking and communicating. For the students, to see their teachers have different expertise and opinions in real time—and to see them not always agreeing with one another, which was certainly also sometimes the case—shows them the limitations of their teachers as well as the possibilities for themselves as scholars.

From the initial impulse to collaborate, which was based on the idea that together we would be able to offer students something neither of us could do alone, we both knew that combining traditional analytical skills with hands-on comics-making practice had the potential to enrich our students' appreciation for what the comics form is capable of expressing. Offered, as it was, in a traditional English department, this was never going to be a studio course, and our students at first expressed a great deal of skepticism regarding the idea that they would have to—gasp!—actually draw in class, not to mention that they would be graded on their efforts. After a slightly anxious first few classes, however, the students soon relaxed into a comfortable groove, to the point where they started to anticipate and even look forward to the drawing exercise at the end of class. Through the opening of the course to play and experimentation with the daily notecards exercise and the untraditional midterm, moreover, our students soon became more sophisticated readers and sometimes even creators of comics narratives. This increased ability and confidence was evident also from the comics that many of them produced for their final, where they had the choice between writing a traditional essay, doing a presentation on the University of Calgary's comics archive, reviewing a comic in comics form, and an "invent your own project" category that we left as open as possible in order to encourage further creativity and experimentation. That balance of creation and analysis, hands-on and reflective, kept the class both lively and intellectually on its toes throughout the term, as did our own collaborative interaction. While our collaboration on this course began from the idea that our respective strengths would in some sense be analogous to how the textual and visual modes collaborate to create meaning in most comics, it was through the creative application of comics-making to literary analysis—and, conversely, of literary analysis to comics-making— that the course reached its highest potential. The experience combining the two has strongly convinced us that there's no reason any comics course, no matter how large or how untrained the teacher is in making comics, should not regularly incorporate some amount of hands-on practice with the form.

It's fun, it's engaging, and it has the potential to fundamentally transform how students approach and are able to analytically engage with the form.

NOTES

1. This preference for text-heavy and "literary" comics seems to have been reproduced in comics studies as well, where most scholars come to the form from a background in literary studies. Despite both *Fun Home* and *Asterios Polyp* being considered key works in the form (and having been published within a few years of each other), for example, the former has been the subject of roughly ten times as much scholarship as the latter, according to the Bonner Online-Bibliographie zur Comicforschung.

Educated Bitches: An Interview with Kelly Sue DeConnick

—JENNY BLENK, Dark Horse Comics

Kelly Sue DeConnick can be a difficult person to pin down, but only because she's constantly working on something amazing. Thanks to her award-winning comic series *Bitch Planet* and the rising popularity of her work on the series *Captain Marvel*, DeConnick is busier than ever with conferences, interviews, and—yes—writing more comics. Her name has become synonymous with a part of the contemporary feminist movement that recognizes the progress still lacking in areas of inclusivity, while refusing to accept them. DeConnick's work revels in reclaiming ownership of derogatory terms like "bitch" and in ideas of nonconformity as not only acceptable and worthy of acknowledgement, but in some ways normative. I spoke with DeConnick over the phone in June of 2017, about a year after the end of my internship with her at Milked Criminal Masterminds, to ask about the place and purpose of her unapologetically provocative and feminist comics in the classroom.

Blenk: I have a few questions here regarding comics and your experience of their usage in the classroom, particularly pertaining to one of your most popular series, *Bitch Planet*. So, I'll start out by asking, just for a little bit of background, what year did you graduate high school?

DeConnick: 1988.

Blenk: And at that point, did you see comics being used in classrooms at all?

DeConnick: No.

Blenk: Was there a general atmosphere regarding comics?

DeConnick: No, I don't recall ever using comics, or reading comics in school, even casually.

Blenk: So when you created *Bitch Planet* and saw it start taking off in popularity, did you think it might be appealing for classroom settings at all?

DeConnick: No. I mean, I never sat down and thought, "Perhaps someone will be able to use this in a classroom!" Nor did I think, "There's no way anyone will ever use this in a classroom," you know? Like, that's not a part of your thinking when you're making a book that's fiction.

Blenk: Were you surprised, then, when it started cropping up in people's syllabi?

DeConnick: Totally.

Blenk: In your opinion, what aspects of the comic—looking at it from this point—what aspects of *Bitch Planet* lend themselves best to that classroom discussion?

DeConnick: Well, satire is really hard, and ... it's not for me to judge whether we're good at it or not. But, I can see how if you want to talk about contemporary use of satire to address political or social issues, *A Modest Proposal* is better than I'll ever be at anything, ever. You could talk about that, and then say, "See how we can use these same tools to talk about some of our contemporary issues?" So, I mean, I guess that's how I would imagine it being taught. Somebody just informed me that they were teaching [*Bitch Planet*] in a class that had a specific political studies bent, but most of the time it's usually taught in either gender studies or general science fiction.

Blenk: Valentine DeLandro is the artist on that. Are there aspects of his art that you personally think are interesting and worthy of discussion on that level?

DeConnick: Yeah, absolutely. I think it's hard for anybody who works outside of comics to understand this, but everyone's always trying to divide authorship. Like, "Well, Val does the pictures and you write the book." And so it becomes this thing where I'm constantly credited as the author of *Bitch Planet*, and that's not accurate really. That's not how comics authorship really breaks down. So, everything that I just said to you about what I thought the book could be used for in study, that ... applies to the whole of the book, not just the words. The book. And you know, it is a constant conversation, how the story develops between the two of us. So it would be kind of like saying, "We want to talk about the best boys' contributions to this film." Like, you can't take one of us out and give one of us credit for it.

Blenk: Like trying to pick out the individual members of a band to credit with a song?

DeConnick: Yeah. So, I think it's sorta weird, because it's just not for me to make the call as to whether this book is worthy of study. I don't know, if you want to study it I guess it's worthy of study! If you find something in it to talk about or learn from, whether it's something we could have done better or something that you think we did well, then great, I'm super pleased. But, once I make the book, I'm done with it.

Blenk: But you do, it sounds like, stay in the conversation, at cons or over social media. On that note, have you heard of many ... teachers or instructors who have been using the comic in their classroom?

DeConnick: Yeah, somebody sent me a link to a roundtable discussion from a bunch of people who were using it, and ... I can't remember the name of the site that it's on ... But there's a roundtable published online of people who've taught *Bitch Planet* talking about how they've used it and what their experience has been, including someone who was teaching it in prison.

Blenk: So it sounds like not only is there a community that has cropped up around *Bitch Planet* and this idea of noncompliance, but there's also a community building *around the community* of *Bitch Planet*.

DeConnick: Yeah!

Blenk: That's pretty incredible. And, along those lines, I know you kind of hinted earlier that your idea of authorial intent seems to be that once it's out in the world, it's out in the world, and you don't necessarily consider yourself the authority on the text anymore. But have you seen the ideas that you put into the work kind of be misinterpreted or twisted in ways that you found either disagreeable or outright offensive?

DeConnick: I don't know [about] "disagreeable or outright offensive" really. I could say, but people misunderstand and misuse "noncompliant" all the time.

Blenk: In what ways?

DeConnick: Well . . . they'll sometimes use it to mean "nonconforming." And that's different. [With] nonconforming, like you'll get this sort of eighth grade smartass "it's not very punk rock to be punk rock 'cause everybody's punk rock," you know what I mean?

Blenk: [laughs] Yes, yes I do.

DeConnick: Like that thing where it's like, go fuck yourself. Like, I'm so happy you made it to eighth grade, that's fantastic. It's the—ninth grade is your sophomore year, right? It's just, it's a super sophomore understanding. Like oh shit, you think you just put something together. Noncompliant is, for me, a much deeper, much more painful term, and it relates very much to the "bitch" in the title. "Bitch" is used against us constantly, and when we use it in the title, I'm not meaning to be like "I love being called a bitch!" But it's. . . .

Blenk: It's more of a reappropriation of the term, it sounds like?

DeConnick: What I mean to do with . . . the title is an emphasis on the nastiness of it. And, also, a nod to exploitation film. The noncompliant thing, that's—you're noncompliant when the world tells you you're not good enough, you don't fit. . . . I like the double meaning of [when] the world says you're noncompliant. Like, we're going through and we're tossing out all the ones, the parts, that aren't structured properly. That don't fit our impossible standards, by the by. So I have kind of in my head, like, the patriarchy has this assembly line, like this conveyor belt of women coming through like, "Oh, that one's noncompliant, that one's noncompliant, that one's noncompliant." And, the "I won't go along with that" meaning of noncompliant. It's not nonconforming, it's—I'm not sure if I've articulated the difference, but it's very big, there's a wide gap. It's not a subtle difference. And it gets used that way all the time. . . . Like if a woman is conventionally attractive, she can't be noncompliant, because then she's . . . because she can conform.

Blenk: She has the ability, essentially, to pass for compliant.

DeConnick: Right, and she has privilege, but you can't tell somebody's status by looking at them, and the secret is we're all noncompliant because there's an impossible standard. No one can be all of these things at once. Right? That's why all of the compliant women in the book are holograms. It's a fucking joke. So, y'know, it is one of those things where like you never correct anybody, because you can't explain the joke.

Blenk: And if you have to explain it, it becomes less of a joke.

DeConnick: Yeah, and if it means something to you, the way you're interpreting it, if I say that's not the way I meant it, then.... Once I'm done with the book, it's not mine anymore. Once it's out in the world, then it means whatever you want it to mean. I can tell you what my intention was, but that seems... irrelevant in some regard. So anyway, it annoys me when I hear it used in that way sometimes, or when somebody will think like, "Ooh, all these noncompliant women with the tattoos, isn't that compliant?" That's so dumb that you should run for office. Y'know?

Blenk: But it sounds like people are talking about it more, thanks to this comic.

DeConnick: Yes.

Blenk: And... would you like to see it continue to be used in classrooms?

DeConnick: Sure! Yeah! There's no loss in it for me, why wouldn't I? Sure, absolutely. Where's the harm?

Blenk: And, do you see an advantage to continuing to study comics? Or do you foresee a brighter or at least more popular trend toward the use of comics in academics and in schools?

DeConnick: Comics are just another medium and... there are good comics and there are bad comics just like there are good prose novels and bad prose novels and... stories that are worthy of study in any medium. And I've never really understood how if you can have an art class or a music class or a literature class, then you can certainly have a comics class. The popularity of superhero movies doesn't negate the art form. But somehow the popularity of superhero comics . . . makes it easy to pooh-pooh. But I think that's pretty old-fashioned thinking. Well, you're in academia much more than I am . . . but . . . most of the time when I'm interacting with folks from academia I'm interacting with them because they're teaching my book. So, my sample is skewed. But, most of the folks that I've talked to and most of my books, and not just *Bitch Planet* but also *Pretty Deadly*, they're being taught with some regularity now, to the point where, we've had discussions about how do we make materials from the . . . individual issues that we don't republish in the trades available to teachers? Because they're supplemental materials that are important to the context of how that piece was received.

Blenk: That's fabulous.

DeConnick: Yeah, so . . . I don't think we're in danger of going backward, I think. Most of the people you encounter who pooh-pooh comics don't have any idea what they're talking about.

BIBLIOGRAPHY

DeConnick, Kelly Sue, and Jordie Bellaire. *Pretty Deadly*, vol. 1. Image Comics, 2014.
DeConnick, Kelly Sue, and Jordie Bellaire. *Pretty Deadly*, vol. 2, Image Comics, 2016.
DeConnick, Kelly Sue, and Valentine DeLandro. *Bitch Planet*. Image Comics, 2015.
DeConnick, Kelly Sue, and Valentine DeLandro. *Bitch Planet*, vol. 2. Image Comics, 2017.

Conclusion: The Great Responsibility of a Comics Pedagogy

As we close this collection, it seems appropriate to reflect on why we think this assemblage of voices surrounding comics in classrooms is important and what we hope will come next. We edited this volume in a moment in which US public education narrows the kinds of knowledge that are valued, assessed, and measured in classrooms at all stages. Curricular worries about achievement gaps largely ignore the educational "debt" of legacies of inequality that have shaped the experiences of students throughout the country by race, class, and gender (Ladson-Billings). In place of meaningful professional development and teacher training, the education field is seeing an increase in utilizing learning "management" systems and online personalized tools that delegitimize and deprofessionalize the role of teachers. Further, the erosion of teacher unions and the growing number of contingent and nontenure track faculty in higher education highlights that educators, their time, and their expertise, are often casualties in budgetary systems that place education below other neoliberal priorities.

We recognize that a volume on the use of comics may, at first blush, seem like an inconsequential volume within this sociopolitical context we describe above. Why, for example, should comics *matter* in a moment in which #BlackLivesMatter becomes a necessary statement to declare in light of historical, ongoing violence endured by African Americans today? Why should any of the products of culture matter when the current political moment is rife with agita and rage, precluding progress or even respectful discussion? However, we want to emphasize that it is precisely within this context that comics remain an imperative topic of educational equity for teachers, students, and society. Acknowledging the interests and modalities of engagement of youth and adult learners is both a responsive (see Gay) and sustaining (see Paris and Alim) practice in education. In this way, comics reveal and allow learners to question the world around them. The possibilities of the illustrated page invite imagination of what *could be* and provide opportunities for learning, assessment, and healthy relationship-building in ways frequently clouded over by the auspices of high stakes testing. Further, advocating for teachers as experts, designers, and innovators, comics pedagogy emphasizes that teachers make necessary decisions on behalf of and in response to the needs of their students.

These powerful possibilities of comics pedagogy come not without their challenges. As we've noted above, this is a nascent field and our vocabulary, community, and processes for disseminating learning are continuing to be formed. Substantial disciplinary tensions and challenges remain part and parcel with the emergence of comics pedagogy. Not understanding the epistemological grounding of an elementary classroom utilizing Cece Bell's *El Deafo* points to the unique opportunity for enriching the comics pedagogy dialogue. With this in mind, the role of literacy—in particular—is recognizably in flux. Especially in a participatory culture (Jenkins) that blurs the boundaries between consumer and producer (akin to the blurred roles of teacher and learner in a critical perspective of education), what *counts* as reading and writing grows more complicated. Further, comics culture has exploded since the turn of the century; the wave of Hollywood adaptations have turned more attention to an industry that has been producing work for more than a century. Likewise, new digital tools for distribution and production mean that thriving independent comic creators are utilizing new pathways for sharing their work with their audiences. Comic books are more present in the literate lives of more people in society than ever before. More than 20 years ago, the New London Group—a collective of literacy researchers—noted:

> The changing technological and organizational shape of working life provides some with access to lifestyles of unprecedented affluence, while excluding others in ways that are increasingly related to the outcomes of education and training. It may well be that we have to rethink what we are teaching, and, in particular, what new learning needs literacy pedagogy might now address. (61)

The New London Group's emphasis on how pedagogy must shift was intentionally considering the intersection of capitalism, globalization, and technology in the learning practices of young people. Particularly looking at the role of popular culture, Hollywood's lasting emphasis on superhero films, and the growth of a comic readership, comics pedagogy must wrestle both with how literacy practices are shaped within schooling contexts and be cognizant of the global, cultural contexts in which these comics are produced, consumed, and remediated. To this extent, "Teachers will need to continue to consider the literacies practices that happen across spaces, across time, across contexts.

Social movements of resistance and liberation mattered in 1996 [when the New London Group defined multiliteracies], and they matter still today" (Garcia and Seglem 3). Comics culture is changing rapidly, as is the notion of literacy in our increasingly image-based society. Given these challenges and opportunities and frankly, this kairotic moment, what can and should we as educators, scholars, and creators do next?

Into the MultiVerse: New Directions in Comics Pedagogy

If you have ever attended a comic con, you know that they function something like the ancient Greek *agora*, a delightful and diverse meeting place where strangers congregate, converse, and learn from one another. At various comics events we have witnessed a cluster of Spider-people engaged in a spontaneous posing session for delighted onlookers, engaged in a spirited colloquy about feminist theory with a cosplayer dressed as Thor the Goddess of Thunder, and chatted with eager young creators tabling with their newest comics. While we cannot recreate the atmosphere (or the costumes) of a comic con here, we do hope that this volume similarly encourages more conversations amongst educators teaching with comics, inspiring collaboration and innovation. Naturally this book is limited in scope, highlighting the voices of only a few participants, but we know that the discussion in this "unending conversation" surrounding comics pedagogy will continue. To that end, we hope to see even more interaction between various (overlapping) communities—scholars, creators, fans, and teachers.

In fact, we would love to see more exchanges across discourse communities, engaging the "modes of address" outlined by Fischer, and crossing the boundaries between "fan appreciation, essayistic criticism and academic criticism." All of us could benefit from discussions taking place with industry professionals, and furthermore, we see a distinct need to promote discourse around comics in education that moves across grade levels, with theory and scholarship helping to legitimize teaching graphic narratives K-12, and K-12 instructors inspiring academics to explore new areas for research. This may well lead to in-depth qualitative research in classrooms as well as more exchanges of practical teaching ideas, and encourage even more types of research, particularly qualitative and quantitative research methods utilizing ethnography, interviews, and surveys. In the spirit of interdisciplinarity, we also call for additional study and experimentation in teaching comics in STEM classes, using comics not just as content but as means of discovery and expression. We'd also promote more research and conversations with an international focus—given comics history throughout the world, this seems like too good an opportunity to miss, as such work would inevitably shed light on global history, culture and, of course, comics.

As scholars and educators we look with hope to the future and argue for the great responsibility of comics pedagogy. We offer the pieces in the this volume as voices furthering the discourse, seeking to ground the weighty commitments of instructors within the scholarship that helps teachers make empowered instructional choices. As Brian Bendis noted earlier in this volume, as educators we firmly believe in the power and potential of our students, encouraging them to "write what you know, but also what you want." While we recognize the challenges ahead, we find optimism in the passion of comics culture, and we hope to talk shop with everyone soon, perhaps in line at the next comic con.

WORKS CITED

Garcia, Antero, and Robyn Seglem. "This Issue." *Theory into Practice* 57, no. 1 (2018): 1–4.

Gay, Geneva. *Culturally Responsive Teaching: Theory, Research, and Practice*. 2nd ed. New York: Teachers College Press, 2010.

Ladson-Billings, Gloria. "From the Achievement Gap to the Education Debt: Understanding Achievement in US Schools." *Educational Researcher</i>* 35, no. 7 (2006): 3–12.

The New London Group. "A Pedagogy of Multiliteracies: Designing Social Futures." *Harvard Educational Review* 66, no. 1 (1996): 60–93.

Paris, Django, and H. Samy Alim, eds. *Culturally Sustaining Pedagogies: Teaching and Learning for Justice in a Changing World*. New York: Teachers College Press, 2017.

CONTRIBUTORS

Lynda Barry is the renowned comics creator of *Ernie Pook's Comeek, One! Hundred! Demons!, The Good Times Are Killing Me,* and *Syllabus,* just to name a few. She is currently a professor at the University of Wisconsin.

Bart Beaty is a comics scholar and professor at the University of Calgary. His works include *Comics Versus Art* and *Twelve Cent Archie.*

Brian Michael Bendis is an acclaimed comics writer. He co-created *Powers,* and has written for *The Ultimate Spiderman, The Avengers, Guardians of the Galaxy,* and many more. He currently writes *Man of Steel, Superman,* and is curating a custom line of DC comics for later this year. You might know him for co-creating Jessica Jones, or bringing the world Miles Morales and Riri Williams, or for his work on *Scarlet* or *Naomi.*

Jenny Blenk received her MA in English from Portland State University and is an Assistant Editor at Dark Horse Comics. Her current areas of research include disability and mental health in comics, as well as graphic medicine and autobiography.

Ben Bolling is a writer and artist in Durham, North Carolina. He received his BA in English and drama from the University of Virginia and his MA and PhD from the University of North Carolina at Chapel Hill. He coedited *It Happens at Comic-Con: Ethnographic Essays on a Pop Culture Phenomenon.* His creative works can be seen at beaglemans.com

Peter E. Carlson is a literacy curriculum specialist with Green Dot Public Schools, California. In his ten years of classroom teaching, Carlson facilitated high school English-Language Arts courses in South Central Los Angeles. Carlson's research has appeared in the *Oregon English Journal* and in a chapter of the book *Literacy Enrichment and Technology Integration in Pre-Service*

Teacher Education. He earned his masters of urban education from the University of California, Los Angeles.

Kelly Sue DeConnick is an acclaimed comics writer. She co-created *Bitch Planet* and *Pretty Deadly* and has worked on *Captain Marvel*.

Johnathan Flowers is a visiting assistant professor at Worcester State University where his research focuses on affective theories of experience, pragmatist approaches to artificial intelligence and machine learning, and the intersections of phenomenology and popular culture. Flowers has also presented regularly at academic conferences across the country on critical approaches to popular culture and comics, East Asian philosophy, philosophy of race, and feminism.

Antero Garcia is an assistant professor in the Graduate School of Education at Stanford University, where he studies how technology and gaming shape both youth and adult learning, literacy practices, and civic identities. Prior to completing his PhD, Antero was an English teacher at a public high school in South Central Los Angeles. He received his PhD in the Urban Schooling division of the Graduate School of Education and Information Studies at the University of California, Los Angeles.

Dale Jacobs is the author of *Graphic Encounters: Comics and the Sponsorship of Multimodal Literacy* (Bloomsbury Academic, 2013). His essays on comics have appeared in *English Journal, College Composition and Communication, Biography, ImageText, Journal of Comics and Culture, Canadian Review of Comparative Literature, Studies in Comics*, and *Journal of Teaching Writing*. With Jay Dolmage, he has published chapters on comics and disability in *The Future of Text and Image: Collected Essays on Literary and Visual Conjunctures* and *Disability in Comic Books and Graphic Narratives*. He is the editor of *The Myles Horton Reader* (University of Tennessee Press, 2003) and the coeditor (with Laura Micciche) of *A Way to Move: Rhetorics of Emotion and Composition Studies* (Boynton Cook/Heinemann, 2003).

Ebony Flowers Kalir is a cartoonist and an ethnographer. She received her PhD in curriculum and instruction from the University of Wisconsin-Madison and is a recipient of the 2017 Rona Jaffe Foundation Writers' Award. Her book *Hot Comb* will be published by Fantagraphics in Spring 2019.

James Kelley is a middle school teacher at Baker Prairie Middle School and received his MA from Colorado State University.

Susan E. Kirtley is a professor of English, the Director of Rhetoric and Composition, and the Director of Comics Studies at Portland State University. Her research interests include visual rhetoric and graphic narratives, and she has published pieces on comics for the popular press and academic journals. Her book *Lynda Barry: Girlhood through the Looking Glass* was the 2013 Eisner winner for Best Educational/Academic work. She is currently the Secretary for the Comics Studies Society and a member of the Executive Group on Graphic Narratives for the Modern Language Association.

Frederik Byrn Køhlert is lecturer in comics studies and American studies at the University of East Anglia. He is the author of *Serial Selves: Identity and Representation in Autobiographical Comics* (Rutgers University Press, 2019) and *The Chicago Literary Experience: Writing the City, 1893–1953* (University of Copenhagen: Museum Tusculanum Press, 2011). He is also the series editor of Routledge Focus on Gender, Sexuality, and Comics Studies, the editor of *A History of Chicago Literature* (forthcoming from Cambridge University Press), and the course director for the Master of Arts program in Comics Studies at the University of East Anglia.

John A. Lent taught at the college/university level from 1960 to 2011 including stints in the Philippines, Malaysia, Canada, China, and US. Prof. Lent pioneered in the study of mass communication and popular culture in Asia (since 1964) and the Caribbean (since 1968), comic art and animation, and development communication. He has authored or edited eighty-five books, published and edited *International Journal of Comic Art* (which he founded, 1999–), *Asian Cinema* (1994–2012), and *Berita* (1975–2001), chaired Asian Popular Culture (PCA), Asian Cinema Studies Society (1994–2012), Comic Art Working Group (IAMCR, 1984–2016), Asian-Pacific Animation and Comics Association (2008–), Asian Research Center for Animation and Comics Art (2005–) , and Malaysia/Singapore/Brunei Studies Group of the Association for Asian Studies (1976–1983), all of which he founded.

Leah Misemer is a Marion L. Brittain Postdoctoral Fellow at Georgia Tech where, in her first-year writing classroom, she teaches comics as a form of STEM communication. Her blended research and teaching interests include comics, mental health, and community engagement, and you can find her work published in academic journals and edited collections. She is the co-organizer (with Adrienne Resha) of #womenonpanels, an initiative meant to raise the visibility of women and nonbinary scholars in comics studies. She was a student in Lynda Barry's "What It Is" class in Spring 2012, and several of her drawings (and her photograph) appear in Barry's *Syllabus*.

Johnny Parker II is a passionate comics writer and educator. He teaches high school English in South Los Angeles and writes the popular comic series *Broken*, *Teen Horror*, *Black Fist & Brown Hand*, and *Elvish*. His goal in the classroom is to inspire young minds to strive for their dreams and become agents of change in their communities. In comics, his mission is to create engaging stories with diverse characters that all people can see a bit of themselves in.

Nick Sousanis is an Eisner-winning comics author and an assistant professor at San Francisco State University, where he started and runs an interdisciplinary Comics Studies program. He is the author of *Unflattening*, originally his doctoral dissertation, which he wrote and drew entirely in comics form. Published by Harvard University Press in 2015, *Unflattening* received the 2016 American Publishers Association Humanities Award for Scholarly Excellence and the 2016 Lynd Ward Prize for Best Graphic Novel. Sousanis's comics have appeared in *Nature*, the *Boston Globe*, and *Columbia Magazine*.

Aimee Valentine received her PhD from Western Michigan University where she specialized in creative writing and comics studies. Her dissertation, *Good Looking in the Dark: A Narrative across Three Mediums*, weaves prose fiction, playwriting, and comics. She has an MFA from San Francisco State, where her thesis was a collection of graphic narratives. Her comics work has been featured in *Witness*, *No Tokens*, the *Iowa Journal of Cultural Studies*, and *Hot Metal Bridge*. In 2012 she founded inktart.org, an online journal highlighting female comics creators.

Benjamin J. Villarreal is an assistant professor of English at New Mexico Highlands University with an EdD in English education from Teachers College, Columbia University. His teaching and research focus on using games, comics, and film alongside traditional texts in the college English classroom to foster critical media literacies with students. He is also an amateur game designer whose research can be read as interactive narratives.

David Walker is an award-winning journalist, filmmaker, and comic-book writer. Throughout his career, he has written comics for Marvel, DC Comics, Dark Horse Comics, and many more. His comic-book credits include *Power Man & Iron Fist*, *Nighthawk*, *Occupy Avengers*, *Cyborg*, *Shaft*, *Tarzan on the Planet of the Apes*, *The Army of Dr. Moreau*, and *Number 13*.

INDEX

Abel, Jessica, 95, 230
Absalom, Absalom! (Faulkner), 57
Absolutely True Diary of a Part-Time Indian, The (Alexie), 57
Achebe, Chinua, 57
Adobe Creative Cloud, 121–22, 123–24, 132
Adorno, Theodor, 59
"Age-Old Problem: Problematics of Comic Book Historiography, An" (Woo), 64
Ahmed, Sara, 209, 212–15, 216, 217
Alanguilan, Gerry, 200
Alexie, Sherman, 57
Alphona, Adrian, 227
Amanat, Sana, 51
American Born Chinese (Yang), 58, 227
Anderson, Daniel, 120, 129
Andrews, Archie (character), 65
Annotated Christmas Carol, The (Hearn), 137–39
Archie Comics, 31, 65
"Are Comic Books an Effective Way to Engage Nonmajors?" (Hosler and Boomer), 157
Arnold, Matthew, 59
Asterios Polyp (Mazzuchelli), 227, 228, 232, 238
Auschwitz (Levi), 56
Awakening, The (Chopin), 57

Bad Girl Chats, 48
Barry, Lynda, 10, 13, 16, 40, 51, 84, 168–84, 249

Batman, mythos of, 53, 116–33, 135
Batman Chronicles VI, 63
Batman: Noel (Bermejo), 135, 141
Batman: Year One (Miller), 123
"Batman to Beowulf" (Rollin), 145–46
Beaton, Kate, 51
Beaty, Bart, 3, 5, 8, 22, 28, 34, 226, 249
Bechdel, Alison, 40, 44, 51, 58, 227, 228
Beloved (Morrison), 56
Bendis, Brian Michael, 10, 11, 16, 22, 68–81, 155, 248, 249
Bennett, Marek, 7
Bermejo, Lee, 141
Berona, David, 102
Best American Comics, The, 41–42
Bettelheim, Bruno, 140, 141
Billy Ireland Cartoon Library and Museum, 199–200
Bitch Planet (DeConnick), 186, 239–41, 244, 250
Black AF: America's Sweetheart, 222
Blankets (Thompson), 43
Blenk, Jenny, 239–44, 249
Bolling, Ben, 11, 12, 16, 82, 249
Boomer, K. B., 157
Bordwell, David, 58
Bourdieu, Pierre, 60
Brandt, Deborah, 31–32
Brubaker, Ed, 174
Brunetti, Ivan, 13, 172–73, 184
Building Stories (Ware), 103
Burton, Tim, 117
Byrne, David, 7

Campbell, Joseph, 135, 136, 138
Can't We Talk About Something More Pleasant? (Chast), 42
Carlson, Peter E., 122, 249
Carol Corps, The, 79–80
Carter, James B., 24, 30
Cartooning: Philosophy and Practice (Brunetti), 13
Cathy, 49
Chabon, Michael, 54
Charlie Hebdo, 194–95
Chast, Roz, 42
Chopin, Kate, 57
Christmas Carol, A (Dickens), 137–38
Chute, Hillary, 5, 8
Cinderella, 141
cinema studies, 58
Classroom Instruction That Works (Mazano et al.), 13
Closing of the American Mind, The (Bloom), 59
Clowes, Daniel, 58
Cohen, Margaret, 61–62
Cohn, Neil, 207, 219
Comic Arts Conference, vii
Comic Book in America, The (Uslan), 7–8
Comic Book Plus, 61, 66
Comic Book Price Guide (Overstreet), 53
Comic-Con International: San Diego, vii, 68
comics: canon, 5, 22, 28–29, 55, 56; censorship of, 35, 194–95; commercial and cultural transactions in, 31, 33; commodification of, 189–93; female creators of, 15, 22, 38–51, 61, 80; gender biases in, 38–39; history of, 14, 22, 27–28, 29–30, 32, 54, 62, 199–201, 248; horror in, 62, 64, 201; industry, 10–11, 40, 78, 103, 192–93; interdisciplinary studies in, 3, 4–5, 9–10, 11, 22, 24–25, 27–36, 83–84, 149–66, 168, 185, 188, 202, 247; internet publishing of, 44–45, 50; as kitsch, 53–54; labor studies in, 196–98; legal studies in, 193; producing, 12–13, 28, 47, 83, 103, 105, 228; representation in, 22, 23–36, 40–41, 42, 46, 68–70, 74, 76, 79–80; as text, 30–31, 33, 35–36, 83–84
Comics Code Authority, 38, 62, 63, 126
comics pedagogy, 6–7, 30–31, 83, 102, 92–115, 117, 168–84, 230–32, 235–36, 247; challenges in the classroom, 14, 21–22, 177–78, 246–47; collaborative exercises, 105–6, 151; copying, 85, 103, 147, 170–71, 176; co-teaching, 226–27; curriculum building, 155–56, 245; digital tools, 246; early childhood educators, 9–10, 170, 180; emphasis on play, 123–24; exercises, 85, 93–94, 95, 98, 172, 173–74, 228–38; group projects, 64–65; inviting failure, 130; peer groups, 127–28; tandem drawing, 89–90, 91; vocabulary, 11, 121; Western literature and, 59–60, 135, 145, 147, 218
"Comics Studies, the Anti-Discipline" (Hatfield), 24, 36
Comics Studies Society, 4, 251
Comics Versus Art (Ware), 57, 249
commix, 46
Crain, Caleb, 45–46
"Creating the Myth" (Seger), 138

Dark Knight Returns, The (Miller), 57–58, 122–23, 127, 133
Darly, Mary, 201
David Copperfield (Dickens), 135–39, 142–44, 146
Davis, Blair, 23
DC Comics, 63, 67, 190, 196, 249, 252
DeConnick, Kelly Sue, 10, 11, 17, 79–80, 186, 239–44, 250
DeLandro, Valentine, 240
Delaney, Samuel, 12
DeLillo, Don, 58
Detective Comics #27, 53, 121, 127
DiAngelo, Robin, 208–9, 223
Dickens, Charles, 135–48

Dickens and the Invisible World (Stone), 142–43
Dickens Hero, The (Herst), 143–44
Digital Comic Museum, 61
Dimock, Wai Chee, 126
Distinction (Bourdieu), 60
Drawing Words and Writing Pictures (Abel and Madden), 95
Duval, Mary, 201

EC Comics, 63–64
Eco, Umberto, 121
Edwards, Tommy Lee, 128, 129
Egan, Jennifer, 43
Eisner, Will, 30, 74, 75, 76, 207, 217, 251
El Deafo, 246
Elements of Style, The (White), 56
Essential Fantastic Four VI (Kirby), 64
Ethics (Aristotle), 55

Facebook, 48, 75, 122, 128
Faulkner, William, 57
Felkski, Rita, 118–19
Fischer, Craig, 5, 247
Flowers, Johnathan, 11, 16, 185–86, 250
Forum for Comics and Graphic Narratives, 4
Franklin, Noel, 40, 48–50
Franzen, Jonathan, 43
Frasca, Marilyn, 168–69
Freedom (Franzen), 43
Freire, Paulo, 84, 204, 209, 220
Freud, Sigmund, 118
Fun Home (Bechdel), 24, 29, 44, 51, 58, 227, 228, 238

Gaiman, Neil, 5, 105
Gans, Herbert, 59–60
Garcia, Antero, vii, ix, 250
Gardner, Howard, 7
gatekeeper theory, 202
Gebbie, Melinda, 102
Genette, Gerald, 31

Ghost World (Clowes), 58
Gibbons, Dave, 54, 56, 57, 227
Gibson, William, 58
Glasgow Looking Glass (Busch), 201
Gombrich, Ernst, 6
Gone Girl Comics, 49
Good-bye Chunky Rice (Thompson), 43
Graphic Encounters (Jacobs), 7, 26–27, 33, 250
Great Expectations (Dickens), 135–40, 141, 142, 144
Great Gatsby, The (Fitzgerald), 56
Greatest Comic Book of All Time, The (Beaty and Woo), 28, 32, 56
Groensteen, Thierry, 55

Hatfield, Charles, 8, 25, 30, 64, 149
Hawisher, Gail, 21
Hearn, Michael Patrick, 137
Heck, Gary, 198
Here (McGuire), 103
"Hero's Shame, The" (Newsom), 144
Herriman, George, 53
Herst, Beth, 136, 138, 143–44
Hobbes, Thomas, 55
Hollander, Nicole, 40, 47–48, 49–50
Hollywood, 246
Horkheimer, Max, 53–54
Hosler, Jay, 157
Howe, Sean, 7

Ignorant Schoolmaster, The (Rancière), 93
Image and the Eye, The (Gombrich), 6–7
"In the Shadow of Satis House: The Woman's Story in *Great Expectations*" (Schor), 139–40
"Indiscipline, or, the Condition of Comics Studies" (Hatfield), 4
Inks: The Journal of the Comics Studies Society, 23
inkt|art (inktart.org), 46–48, 252
Interdisciplinary Curriculum Design and Implementation (Jacobs), 150, 155

International Comic Arts Forum, 4
International Journal of Comic Art, 127
"Is There a Comic Book Industry?" (Woo), 191
It Ain't Me, Babe Comix, 40

Jacobs, Dale, 7, 15, 22, 250
Jacobs, Heidi, 150–51
Jimmy Corrigan: The Smartest Kid on Earth (Ware), 57

Kalir, Ebony Flowers, ix, 11, 16, 83, 85–91, 179, 180–81, 250
Kant, Immanuel, 55
Karaganis, Joe, 54
Kartalopoulos, Bill, 42
Kelley, James, 16, 83, 149–66, 250
Kickstarter, 48
Kidder, Tracy, 56
Kirby, Jack, 64
Kirtley, Susan, ix, 251
Køhlert, Frederik Byrn, 251
Konopacki, Mike, 198
Krazy Kat, 53
Kress, Gunther, 26
Kuper, Peter, 102

Landis, Max, 131
language of drawing, 170–71
League of Extraordinary Gentlemen, The (Moore), 146, 147
Lent, John, 16, 185, 251
Lethem, Jonathan, 42
Levi, Steve, 56
Limits of Critique, The (Felski), 120
Lord of the Rings, The (Tolkien), 58

Macbeth (Shakespeare), 55, 136
Madden, Matt, 95, 101
manga, 73–74, 153, 191, 201, 207, 217, 218–19
Marvel Comics: The Untold Story (Howe), 196

Maus (Spiegelman), 5, 24, 29, 54, 56–58, 59–60, 79
Mazzucchelli, David, 123, 227, 228
McCloud, Scott, 26, 28, 30, 40, 41, 42, 43, 44–45, 55, 57, 102, 185–86, 207–25, 230, 234. See also *Understanding Comics: The Invisible Art* (McCloud)
McCullers, Carson, 57
Mill, John Stuart, 55
Mill on the Floss, The (Eliot), 57
Miller, Frank, 57, 58, 122, 123, 127
minicomics, 103
Misemer, Leah, 16, 168–84, 251
Moore, Alan, 5, 54, 102, 105, 146, 147. See also *Watchmen*
Morrison, Toni, 56
Ms. Marvel (Amanat and Wilson), 51, 227
"Multigenre, Multiple Intelligences, and Transcendentalism" (Ruggieri), 7
multimodal thinking, 5, 6, 13, 23–24, 26, 30, 32–33, 35, 92, 117–33, 219, 236, 251
"Multiple Intelligences and Comics" (Bennett), 7
My Black Friend (Sitomer), 73

Neuromancer (Gibson), 58
New London Group, 26
Newsom, Robert, 144
Nietzsche, Friedrich, 118
Night (Wiesel), 56
99 Ways to Tell a Story (Madden), 101
Nolan, Christopher, 117
Noori, Margaret, 223

One! Hundred! Demons! (Barry), 169, 179, 249
Open Syllabus Project, 54–55
Ortega y Gasset, José, 59
Overstreet, Robert, 53

Palestine (Sacco), 51
Parker, Johnny, II, 252
Pedagogy of the Oppressed (Freire), 6, 84

Pep Comics #22, 65
Persepolis (Satrapi), 24, 51, 56–57, 58, 79, 120
Pichelli, Sara, 155
Porcellino, John, 95
Portland State University, 68
Pretty Deadly (DeConnick), 244
Pride and Prejudice (Austen), 55

Rancière, Jacques, 93
Reader, the Text, the Poem, The (Rosenblatt), 145
Reading for Understanding (Schoenbach et al.), 13
Reisman, Abraham, 41
Ricouer, Paul, 118
Robbins, Trina, 39, 46
Rohde, Mike, 98
"Roundtable: Comics and Methodology" (Davis and Woo), 23
Ruggieri, Colleen, 7

Sacco, Joe, 51
San Diego Comic Con, vii, 68
San Francisco State University, 94
Sandman (Gaiman), 58
Satrapi, Marjane, 51, 56–57, 120
Save the Cat (Snyder), 128
Schor, Hilary, 136, 139–40, 141–42
Schutz, Diana, 103
Seger, Linda, 138
Seldes, Gilbert, 53
Semiotics and the Philosophy of Language (Eco), 121
Sketchnote Handbook, The (Rohde), 13, 98–99
Skim (Tamaki), 43
Snyder, Blake, 128–29
Soul of a New Machine, The (Kidder), 55–56
Sousanis, Nick, 10, 11, 177, 186, 252
Spider-Man (character), 77, 135, 136, 137, 138, 143, 146, 149
Spiegelman, Art, 5, 56–57. See also *Maus*
Steirer, Gregory, 3, 4, 5, 187

Stone, Harry, 142–43
Strange Case of Dr. Jekyll and Mr. Hyde, The (Stevenson), 146
Stuck Rubber Baby (Cruse), 120
Superman (character), 63, 76, 77, 132, 135, 196, 221–22
Surowiecki, James, 56
Syllabus: Notes from an Accidental Professor (Barry), 51, 101
System, The (Kuper), 102
System of Comics, The (Groensteen), 55

Tamaki, Jillian, 43, 227
Tamaki, Mariko, 43
Taylor, Todd, 120
Text Mapping Plus (Lapp et al.), 13
"Theory of Resonance, A" (Dimock), 126
Things Fall Apart (Achebe), 57
"This Is Information" (Moore and Gebbie), 102
This One Summer (Tamaki), 227
Thompson, Craig, 43–44
Tolkien, J. R. R., 58
Troutman, Philip, 4
Tumblr, 119, 122, 124, 128
"22 Panels That Always Work" (Wood), 103–5
Twisted Sister, 40

Ultimate Comics All-New Spider Man (Bendis and Pichelli), 155
Uncanny X-Men, The, 65–66
Understanding Comics: The Invisible Art (McCloud), 8, 11, 16, 25, 55–56, 66, 79, 101, 123, 173, 207–25
University of North Carolina at Chapel Hill, 119
Uses of Enchantment, The (Bettelheim), 140
Uslan, Michael, 5–6

Valentine, Aimee, 15, 252
Villarreal, Benjamin, 16, 83, 135–48, 252

visual literacy, 5–6, 13, 21, 27, 51
visual note taking, 99–100

Walker, David, 10, 11, 16, 22, 68–81, 252
Ware, Chris, 5, 57
Watchmen (Moore and Gibbons), 54, 57–58, 227
Wertsch, James, 151, 152, 156–57, 159, 161, 162, 164
West, Adam, 123, 127
White Noise (DeLillo), 58
Williams, J. H., 95
Wilson, G. Willow, 51
Wimmin's Comix, 40
Wisdom of Crowds, The (Surowiecki), 56
women in comics, 38–51
WonderCon, vii
Woo, Benjamin, 28–29, 32, 56, 64, 66, 191
Wood, Wally, 103

Yancy, George, 208, 210, 212, 213, 214, 215, 217, 218
Yang, Gene Luen, 58, 227

www.ingramcontent.com/pod-product-compliance
Lightning Source LLC
Chambersburg PA
CBHW070303240426
43661CB00057B/2632